Camden the nourice of Antiquitie,
And lanterne unto late succeeding Age,
To see the light of simple veritie,
Buried in ruines, through the great outrage
Of her owne people, led with warlike rage,
Camden, though time all monuments obscure,
Yet thy just Labours ever shall endure.

Spencers Ruine. of Time.

Understanding
Book-Collecting

Grant Uden

Antique Collectors' Club

© 1982 Antique Collectors' Club
World copyright reserved
Reprinted 1983, 1992, 1995

ISBN 0 907462 13 8

While every care has been exercised in the compilation of the information contained in this book, neither the author nor the Antique Collectors' Club accept any liability for loss, damage or expense incurred by reliance placed on the information contained in this book.

British Cataloguing-in-Publication Data:
A catalogue record for this book is available from the British Library

Printed in England on Consort Royal Satin from
Donside Mills, Aberdeen, by the
Antique Collectors' Club Ltd., Woodbridge, Suffolk IP12 1DS

Frontispiece: "No other woman has that sweet speaking smile, with which she nods to Jonathan Lamb, the old parish clerk." Original drawing by Hugh Thomson for George Eliot's Scenes from Clerical Life.

The Antique Collectors' Club

The Antique Collectors' Club was formed in 1966 and quickly grew to a five figure membership spread throughout the world. It publishes the only independently run monthly antiques magazine, *Antique Collecting*, which caters for those collectors who are interested in widening their knowledge of antiques, both by greater awareness of quality and by discussion of the factors which influence the price that is likely to be asked. The Antique Collectors' Club pioneered the provision of information on prices for collectors and the magazine still leads in the provision of detailed articles on a variety of subjects.

It was in response to the enormous demand for information on 'what to pay' that the price guide series was introduced in 1968 with the first edition of *The Price Guide to Antique Furniture* (completely revised 1978 and 1989), a book which broke new ground by illustrating the more common types of antique furniture, the sort that collectors could buy in shops and at auctions rather than the rare museum pieces which had previously been used (and still to a large extent are used) to make up the limited amount of illustrations in books published by commercial publishers. Many other price guides have followed, all copiously illustrated, and greatly appreciated by collectors for the valuable information they contain, quite apart from prices. The Price Guide Series heralded the publication of many standard works of reference on art and antiques. *The Dictionary of British Art* (now in six volumes), *The Pictorial Dictionary of British 19th Century Furniture Design*, *Oak Furniture* and *Early English Clocks* were followed by many deeply researched reference works such as *The Directory of Gold and Silversmiths*, providing new information. Many of these books are now accepted as the standard work of reference on their subject.

The Antique Collectors' Club has widened its list to include books on gardens and architecture. All the Club's publications are available through bookshops world wide and a full catalogue of all these titles is available free of charge from the addresses below.

Club membership, open to all collectors, costs little. Members receive free of charge *Antique Collecting*, the Club's magazine (published ten times a year), which contains well-illustrated articles dealing with the practical aspects of collecting not normally dealt with by magazines. Prices, features of value, investment potential, fakes and forgeries are all given prominence in the magazine.

Among other facilities available to members are private buying and selling facilities, the longest list of 'For Sales' of any antiques magazine, an annual ceramics conference and the opportunity to meet other collectors at their local antique collectors' clubs. There are over eighty in Britain and more than a dozen overseas. Members may also buy the Club's publications at special pre-publication prices.

As its motto implies, the Club is an organisation designed to help collectors get the most out of their hobby: it is informal and friendly and gives enormous enjoyment to all concerned.

For Collectors — By Collectors — About Collecting

ANTIQUE COLLECTORS' CLUB
5 Church Street, Woodbridge Suffolk IP12 1DS, UK
Tel: 01394 385501 Fax: 01394 384434
or
Market Street Industrial Park, Wappingers' Falls, NY 12590, USA
Tel: 914 297 0003 Fax: 914 297 0068

By the same author

The prices in this book are pre-1981 or 1981

The prices in this book are pre-1981 or 1981. In order to give readers some idea of the movement of these prices from year to year the author has agreed to write two articles a year for the Antique Collectors' Club Magazine *Antique Collecting,* giving an indication of price fluctuations throughout the year for similar, if not identical, books/documents priced in the book.

To
MARK HAYMON
Bibliophile
President of a Bibliographical Society
whose membership has always been limited to two
from
THE SECRETARY

'Pardone me where I have erryd or made fawte, whyche yf ony be is of ygnoraunce and ageyn my wylle.'
(William Caxton)

Contents

Of course, there are book 'buyers' and book 'collectors'. Since collectors are born & not made, all the wealth in the world will not make one...

Never go out in decent clothes, thus you are ready at all times to crawl around dirty floors, investigate attics, garages, out-houses and cellars. Turn over every book in the bargain box, every dusty pile in the corner.

Keep your strength up, so that you are fit enough to shift heavy pieces of furniture, mangles, bookcases, etc. Who knows...somewhere behind there may be a large unexplored cupboard bursting with books, untouched by hand for twenty odd years..well, you can dream, can't you?

In a crowded bookshop, you can always recognise the collectors. That's us with the grubby knees, the untidy hair, the jumble sale clothes, worn elbows, and a sort of glazed contented look.

Juanita J. Rigden, in the *Antiquarian Book Monthly Review*

The Bibliomania, or the collecting an enormous heap of books without intelligent curiosity, has, since libraries have existed, infected weak minds, who imagine that they themselves acquire knowledge when they keep it on their shelves.

Isaac D'Israeli, *Curiosities of Literature*

Acknowledgements

I gratefully acknowledge the generous co-operation of a number of publishers, editors and auctioneers for permission to reproduce photographs; especially Lord John Kerr and Sotheby Parke Bernet & Co., Lawrence Fine Art of Somerset (many of whose photographs were by Colin Jeffrey of Crewkerne), the Longman Group and Faber & Faber Ltd. Many photographs were especially taken by Raymond Clements of West Wittering, Chichester.

For the loan of books and other valuable material I am particularly indebted to Sarah Badel, Francis Baxendale, Mark Haymon, Clifford Pearce, Mrs. Grant-Uden and Alec L. Zaiger.

For permission to quote from books and periodicals, my sincere thanks to the Editor of the *Antiquarian Book Monthly Review* and his contributors Juanita J. Rigden, Gaby Goldscheider and W.O.G. Lofts; Frank Hardie (Martin Hardie, *English Coloured Books*, 1906, new edition 1973); Joseph Connolly (*Collecting Modern First Editions*, 1977); Messrs. Cassell Ltd. (Simon Nowell-Smith, 'The Language of Book-Collecting', in *Talks on Book-Collecting*, 1952); Charles J. Sawyer (Charles J. Sawyer and F.J. Harvey Darton, *English Books 1475-1900*, 1927) and Alan G. Thomas (*Great Books and Book Collectors*, 1975).

The Antiquarian Booksellers' Association have been most obliging in allowing me to reproduce their current list of members and addresses.

In one or two cases I have been unable to secure answers to letters or have not traced the copyright owner. In any such instance I hope my good intention will be accepted.

Finally, to Simon Houfe, watchful from the collector's corner, my thanks for his discerning and constructive scrutiny.

Foreword

For the rest, why read or collect books unless you have a mind to it? I do not advocate either. Most people have neither read nor owned books, yet they go on living. Go, then, choose your book and your time. There is no compulsion.

Holbrook Jackson, *The Anatomy of Bibliomania*

If someone asks me 'What shall I collect?' I am tempted to reply 'If you have to ask the question — nothing'; for this vague approach seems to me to be prompted by unsound motives. The instinct and wish to collect books, and the area of interest and knowledge involved, should be a matter of the heart, not the head; not any affair of detached intellectual option, but an inward, and sometimes almost emotional, urge. Sometimes it will be immediately obvious; sometimes overlaid and hidden, needing some accident or experience to trigger it off.

Many of us have deep-seated interests which, for one reason or another, have never been able to surface properly; objects of significance and curiosity to us that we have never been given eyes to see. Life's stern preoccupations and responsibilities can see to that. Book-collecting, in my experience, is a great means to open magic casements. Kipling lamented 'I've never reached the Amazon, I've never reached Brazil.' I don't know if eventually he went from Southampton in one of those 'great steamers white and gold' and found his jaguar and armadillo; if not, he could have done the next best thing and collected books about the Amazon and Brazil.

Many people who will never attempt to scale Everest or journey heroically to the South or North Pole make fine collections on mountaineering and polar exploration. They do not, I suspect, make a cold, unimpassioned decision to do so; rather, within them, there is some kinship, in imagination if not in reality, with those dedicated figures going on resolutely to disaster or triumph. The father of English poetry, when he could not sleep, bade one fetch him a book 'to rede and dryve the night away'; Leigh Hunt could stand at a second-hand bookstall for hours, so transported 'in worldly forgetfulness' by some old book that on one occasion the stall-holder, 'in a satirically polite way', offered him a chair, saying that he must be tired. James Payn, in Chambers's Journal, 1864, put the case very well:

> A congenial book can be taken up by any lover of books, with the certainty of its transporting the reader within a few minutes to a region immeasurably removed from that which

he desires to quit. The shape or pattern of the magic carpet whereon he flies through space and time, is of no consequence. The son of science is rapt by a problem; the philosopher by an abstruse speculation; the antiquary is carried centuries back into the chivalric past; the lover of poetry is borne upon glittering wings into the future. The charm works well for all. Books are the blessed chloroform of the mind.

We have great exemplars in every walk of life, King and commoner, monk and merchant, peer and 'prentice-boy. Richard Aungerville or de Bury, Bishop of Durham, told us six and a half centuries ago that all the glory of the world would be buried in oblivion unless God had provided mortals with the remedy of books. Nearly seven hundred years before that, Biscop Benedict, a thegn of the King of Northumbria, brought together a fine library at Wearmouth. Henry, Prince of Wales, gifted son of the less worthy James I, was already a book-collector, doubtless inspired by Raleigh, when typhoid struck him down at the age of eighteen. George III, adjudged mad by the ignorance of his age, assembled a library that is the pride of the British Museum.

Thomas Frognall Dibdin, who began life as a curate and was certainly as mad as makes no difference on the subject of books, was fortunate in a schoolmaster in whose study 'he caught or fancied he caught, the electric spark of the Bibliomania' and came in the fulness of time to spend most of his waking hours in the Earl Spencer's matchless library at Althorp, and to giving us such delights as his *Bibliomania* and *Bibliographical, Antiquarian, and Picturesque Tour.* Andrew Carnegie, bobbin-boy in a cotton factory and telegraph operator, became one of the greatest book-men of them all, not so much as a collector as an inspirer of them, building and equipping over 2,500 public libraries. How many of us did he thus nourish?

Speaking from personal experience, when I was about seven years old an old lady whose father had been governor of several prisons gave me the signatures of William IV and Queen Victoria which, to amuse her as a young girl, he had cut from old remissions of sentence. As she came to tea one afternoon, she passed behind my chair and placed them by my plate. It was one of the most important moments of my life, opening up a whole and unsuspected new world for me, initiating innumerable future actions and decisions, giving me a dominating interest, ever enduring and expanding.

I was fortunate in that inspired moment of generosity. But I am convinced that in very many of us there is an enthusiasm, a hunger if you like, waiting to be satisfied, to find adequate expression; and that, again, for many of us, the answer can be found in books and their natural allies, letters and documents.

There is a music at the heart of me
Waiting the tongue to utter it, the hand to play;
There are still wings that bide their liberty
And the warm splendour of the waking day.

Some day the castle lord, contemptuous-kind,
Will turn in mercy as he passes by,
Will toss the long-sought key from careless hand,
And you shall fly at last, and you shall fly.

All this, perhaps, explains why I cannot answer the question 'What shall I collect?' I hope I can help with the next logical question. '*How* shall I collect?'; but the first is a matter for your own mind and heart, and who am I to decide for you your whims and fancies, your unpredictable likings and loves? I should probably get it wrong every time. I know a distinguished scholar whose greatest pride is not the row of literary texts to which he has himself contributed, but his rather battered collection of P.G. Wodehouse; a country clergyman's wife who, when she can escape parochial duties, ferrets out early girls' school stories; a professional soldier who has devoted his leisure to heraldry; a stockbroker whose life-long quest has been coloured aquatint books; a distinguished actor's wife who, though her ancestors marched with Cadwaladr and Owain ab Gruffyd (Owen Glendower to the likes of you and me) has transferred her allegiance to Richard III and Napoleon. Who can account for, diagnose, prescribe for, these preoccupations?

Walter de la Mare wrote somewhere:

> Books there may be upon this shelf
> Wherein lies hidden your very self;
> But none can be of lasting gain
> If that same self you should refrain.

In the end, that is the answer, which you alone can supply. Ask your very heart.

Chapter 1

The Language of
Book-Collecting (i)

> But is there a language of book-collecting? I know of no
> dictionary or grammar or primer of the syntax of the language
> of book-collecting...This bond of language, of a language
> spoken not only in collectors' clubs but in all the
> best...bookshops, is closer than any bond linking mere
> readers of books as such.
>
> Simon Nowell-Smith in *Talks on Book-Collecting* (1952)

I had considered beginning this book with a short definition of what a
book is, then recalled that one way of disrupting an otherwise amiable
weekend is to ask the company to do this in a single sentence. Of the many
attempts, perhaps the most blatantly practical was that of the book trade
which, before the introduction of decimal coinage, assumed that a book
was any publication that cost sixpence or more.

Thirty years ago a solemn UNESCO conference announced to the
waiting world that a book is a non-periodical publication containing forty-
nine pages or more, not counting the covers. The mystical nature of forty-
nine as compared with, say, fifty was not explained; and no one,
apparently, ventured to disturb the comity of nations by suggesting that
the definition, as offered, embraced railway time tables, nurserymen's
seed lists and cricket score books. It also covered many auctioneers' and
booksellers' catalogues; and, on reflection, it seemed to me that these
particular publications, always interesting in one way or another, would
provide a suitable starting point to the task of understanding book-
collecting. Certainly a considerable section of the collector's shelves
should be reserved for them, as an indispensable source of information
and stimulus.

Book catalogues range, of course, from the laudable to the laughable.
Some have obviously been drafted by the office boy *en route* for a tea break;
many have been compiled by business men of integrity and long
experience; and, sometimes, they have been lovingly written by scholars
for scholars, or at least for booksellers who have scholars as customers.
The best are text books in themselves and in a few years become expensive
items in the saleroom.

A CATALOGUE and true Note of the *Names* of such *Persons*, which (vpon good liking they haue to the *Worke*, being a great helpe to *Memorie*) haue receiued the *Etymologicall* DICTIONARIE of X[superscript] *Languages*, viz. *English, British or Welch, French, Italian, Spanish, Portuguese, High-Dutch, Law-Latin, Latine, Greeke, Hebrew:* with the *Reasons* and *Deriuations of Words* in all these *Tongues*, with the *exposition* of the *Termes* of the *Lawes* of this *Land*, and the *description* of *Offices*, and *Titles* of *Dignities:* And a most copious *Spanish Dictionarie* at the end thereof all in one volume, from the hands of Mr. MINSHEV the *Author* and *Publisher* of the same in *Print*; In consideration they finde that by computing and printing the same at his owne charge, for the publike good, and the aduancement of *Learning* and *Knowledge*, hee hath not onely exhausted and spent therein all his Stocke and Substance, but also run himselfe into many and great *Debts*, vnpossible for him euer to pay, without assistance of the like *Receiuers* of the said *Bookes* from his hands. In regard the *Company of Stationers* of *London*, vtterly refusing to buy them from him; hee is forced to tender them himselfe to such like worthy *Persons* as are here in this *Catalogue* truly set downe. The *Trueth* whereof if any question or doubt be, they may enquire of any whose *Names* bee here presumes to publish to witnesse the same; offering himselfe to any *censure*, if hee shall set downe any *name* or *thing* herein, that agrees not with the approued *verity*. All which, as himselfe, hee referres to all mens worthy *Natures* and *Generous Interpretations*, re-mayning hopefull of them, as to their alreadie much in dutie bound. It they may be pleased vpon the sight & reading of so many *Names* of *Noblenesse & worth*, to follow their example in their *fauour* to good *letters*, in helpe to take off the rest of his *Bookes*, In doing whereof, their *Names* are likewise to be inserted into this *Catalogue* with the former, & the *Author* to remain in like maner equally to diem as to the rest for euer *obliged & bound* to do them *honor & seruice*.

If in setting these *Names* there hath not beene obserued the *respect* due to the *rankes* and *qualities* of *Persons*, Hee intreats the *Reader* to vnderstand that hee hath not done it out of *neglect* of the regard hee owes to them, but onely to follow the order be vsed in the deliuery of the *Bookes* to them, which was not according to their *Degrees*, but *promiscuously* as they tooke them.

The KING.	Master of the Ordinance of	set Herald and Surueyor	Mr. *James* Pursley Gen. Kee-	Doctor Hunt, Chaplaine to
The QVEENE.	*England, & of his Maiesties*	of his *Maiesties* woods.	per of his *M:* Records of	the Kings Maiestly.
The PRINCE.	most Hon. priuy Councell.	Mr. *Brooke*, Yorke Herald.	House-hold at Court.	*Theophilus* Field, Doctor of
	Sir *Thomas Edmonds*, Con-	Sir *Daniell Dunne*.	Mr. *Walker* Batcheler of Di-	Diuinity, and Chaplaine to
The Lord Arch-B. of *Cant*.	*troler of his Ma: house*,	The La. *Margueris Wotton*.	uinity & Prea:st *Chyswick*.	the Kings Maiestly.
The L. Bishop of *London*.	*and of his Maiesties most*	The La: *Fra:ca Baseley*.	Mr. *Le Metaur*, Deputy to	Doct. Dunne Chaplaine to
The L. Bish. of *Winchester*,	*Honorable priuy Councell.*	The La: *Gasford*.	the first Fruits Office.	Kings Maiestly.
Deane of his Maiesties	Sir *Lewis Tresham*, Knight	Mrs. *Elizabeth Trye*.	Captaine *Tompson* of Kent.	Doctor *Hakewell* Chaplaine
Royall Chappell, and Pre-	and Baronet.	Sir *John Benet* M:r. of the	Mr. *William Redman* Esq.	to the *Prince* his Highnes.
late of the Garter.	Sir *Robert Ayton*, Secretary	*Prerogatiue Office*.	Mr. *Deane Dewry* Esq.	Doctor *Day* Chaplaine to
The L. Bish. of *Ely his Ma-*	to the *Que: Maiestly*, and	Sir *Edward Rauleygh* Knit	Mr. *Walter* of *Wa:els*. Esqu.	the Prince his Highnesse.
iesties high Almoner, and	one of her *Maiesties Councel*.	D. *Edo. Chamberlin* of Lon-	Mr. Doctor *Menerell* Doct.	Doct. *Walkington* Chapl: to
of his Maiesties most Ho-	Sir *Robert Flood*, Admirall	sit *Charles Somerset* one of	of Phisicke.	the L. *Treasurer* of Engl.
nourable priuy Councell.	to the *Qu: Maiestly* & one	the Sonnes of the L. *Priuy*	Mr. *Topsell* Prea:her at S.t	Mr. *Middliston* Chaplain &
The L. Bishop of *Durham*.	of her *Maiesties Councell*.	seale the Earl. of *Worcester*.	*Buttolphs*.	Confessor to the Prince.
The L. Bishop of *Lincolne*.	Sir *William Twisseden* Knight	Sir *Hen: Holmes*, one of the	Mr. *Lockey* a Counceller at	
The L. Bishop of *Salisbury*.	and Baronet, Gent: *Vsher*	gent: Pensioners to his *M.*	Law.	Mr. *May* Chaplaine to the
The L. Bishop of *Hereford*	of the priuy Chamber to	Sir *Edw. Bassoll* Knight.	Mr. *Ascough* a Counceller	Honourable Society of
The L. Bishop of *Rochester*.	the Kings Maiestly	Mr *Brent* Esquire.	at Law.	Lincolnes Inne.
The L. Bishop of *Norwich*.	Sir *Ias. Fullerton* one of the	Mr. *Francis Standish* Gent.	Mr. *Eras: Earle*, Student of	Mr. *Tho: Spencer*
The Deane of *Westminster*.	Prince his Highnesse Coun.	Mr. *Thomas Cockain* Gent.	Lincolnes Inne.	Esq. Chss. Broke.
	Sir *Marmaduke Darrell*, Co-	Mr. *William Hakewell* Soli-	Mr. *Dauenant* of Oxford.	Mr. *Amb:a Irbye*. Benchers
The L. *Chancellor*, Baron of	ferer to the Kings Maiestly.	citor generall to the *Q: M*.	Mr. *Barkham* Secretary to	Mr. *Tho: Hutch-* of LIN-
Verulam, his Ma:	Sir *Richard Coxe* one of the	Sir *Clement Edmonds* Clerke	the Company of March-	*cocky*. COLNS
The L. *Chiefe Iust:* Montag.	Clerkes of the Greene-cloth.	of the Councell.	ants of Hanborow.	Mr. *Wil: Dauys* INNE.
The Master of the Rolles, Sir		Sir *Gyo: Caluert* Knit and	Mr. *Ioseph Siluester* Secretary	Mr. *William Ra-*
Iulius Caesar & of his Ma-	The L. *Rosse* late his Maie-	one of the Principal Secre-	to the Company of Mar-	*uenscrofe*.
iesties most Hon priuy Coun.	sties Ambassador in Spaine.	taries to his Ma: and of his	chants of *Middleborow*.	Mr. *Christ: Brooke*.
The L. *Hobart*, L. *Chiefe Iu-*	The Earle of *Warwick*.	Ma: most Hon: Priuy C.	Mr. *Edw. Cryek*, Citizen	
stice of the Common Pleas,	The L. *Rich*, Bar. of *Leez*.	Mr. *Lemuns Munkey* Clerke	and Marchant-tayler of L.	Sir *Iob: Dacombe*, Chancel:l
Sir *Lawrence Tanfield* Lord	his Sonne and heyre.	of the Signet to his Ma:	Mr. *Le: Cryek* his eld. Son,	of the Dutchy of Lancast.
Chiefe Bar: of the Exchequ.	Sir *Henry Rich* his Bro: and	Mr. *Leeck*, Secretary to the	*Henry Person*, the Sonne of	Mr. *Charles Chibborne*, Ser-
Iudge *Dodderidge*.	Capt. of the Guard to his	Earle of *Pemb.* L. *Chamb.*	Mr. *Rich: Person*, Citizen	geant at Law.
Sir *William Sidney* Knight &	*Maiesty*.	Mr. *Wil: Robinson*.	and Marchantaylor of Lo.	Mr. *Iohn West* Esq; Groome
Baronet.	Sir *Nathan Rich* Knight.	Sir *Edw. Waldiaur* Knight, Cl:		of the Kings Maiesties Pri-
Sir *Henry Yeluerton* his Ma-	The Lord *Russell*.	of the Pelles.	Mr. *Cappell* a Preacher of	uy Chamber and Deputy
iesties Attorney Generall.	The Lord *Windsore*.	Mr. *Winn*, Cl.of the petty Bag	the French Chutch in Lo.	Remembrancer to his Ma-
Sir *Iames: Ley* his Maiesties	The Lord *Ridgeway*, Baron	Mr. *Ioh: Castle*, Deputy Cler,	Mr. *Aurelium* another.	iesty in the Exchequer.
Attourney Generall in the	of *Galen-Ridgeway*.	of the priuy Seale.	Mr. *Roting* one of the Prea-	Mr. *Parker* Esquire Deputy
Court of Wards, &c.	The L. *Digby Vice-Cham-*	Mr. *Patrick Young*, keeper	chers of the Duch Church	Clerke to the Most Hon:
Sir *Charles Caesar* one of the	berlaine to the K. and of the priuy	of the Kings Librarie	in London.	Priuy Councell in his Ma:
Masters of Chancery.	*Councell*, & his *Maiesties*	Mr. *Brown* Esquire, Clerke of	Mr. *King* another.	High Court of Star-cham-
Mr. *Clapham* one of the 6. Cl.	Ambassador in Spaine.	the Spicery.	Mr. *Snidowns* a Duchman,	ber.
Mr. *George: Euelin* another.	Sir *Christo: Hatton* Knight	Mr. *Pey* Esquire Cler of the	& Doct. of the 2 ciuil Law.	Mr. *Gyles Van de Put* Dutch
	of the Bath.	Kitchin to the K. *M:*	Mr. *Dierick Host*, Dut Mar.	Marchant.
The Duke of *Lenox*. L.s	Sir *Edward Conaway*	Mr. *Will: Trouse* Esq. Clerk.	Mr. *Gill* of Pauls Schoole,	Mr. *Abra: Neck* Dutch Mar.
High Steward of his Ma-	Sir *Iohn Booke* Cobham.	of the Kitch: to the *Q.M*.	Schoole-master.	Doctor *Burges*, Doctor of
iesties house.	Sir *Fran: Lee*, Kn: of the Ba:	Mr. *Browne* Gent:	Mr. *Wase* of *Wesfm*. Sch.	Phisicke and a Preacher.
Lo *Tho: Howard*, E. of *Suff*.	Sir *William Slingely*,	Mr. *Caldwell*, Esq: Seryeant	Mr. *Hopers* of Marchant-	Mr. *Osfeild* Preacher at *Tho-*
The Earle of *Pembrooke*, L.	Sir *Thomas Bromley*.	of his Ma: Bake-house	taylors Scho: Schoole-ma.	*ffleworth*.
Chamberl. to his Maiesty,	Sir *Allen Apsley* Lieutenant	Mr. *Guiliam* one of the Cler.	Mr. *Haynes* of *Christs Hos-*	Mr *Wase* School-m.st *Thst*.
and Chancelor of the V-	of the Tower.	of his Maiesties Cofferet.	*pitall Schoo*: School-maist.	Mr. *Palmer* Batcheler of Di-
niuersity of *Oxford*.	Mr. *Arthure Ingram*.	Mr. *Walthew* Seryeant of the	Mr. *Gray* of *Suttons Hospi-*	uinity, Preacher & Vica
The Earle of *Arundel* one	Mr. *Philip Burlemachi* Ita-	Confectionary.	*tall Scho*: Scool-maist et.	at S.t *Brides* in London.
of his *Maiesties most Ho-*	lian Marchant in London.	Sir *Iohn Laurence*, the first	Mr. *Best*, Scholl-M.	Sir *Henry Robinson* Knight
priuy Councell.	Mr. *Tho: Warmicke* Esq. one	vndertaker of this worke	Mr. *Reynolds*, in London.	Dauid Stamers of London
The Earle of *Bedford*.	of the Gent: *Vshers* or	when it lay dead at the	Mr. *Weathersby*, School-M.	Marchant.
The E. of *Dorsets* Reward.	Presence wayters to the	Presse for wast of mony.	of *Chichester* an 1. Mathem.	Mr. *Andrewes* Preacher
The Marquesse of *Bucking-*	Queenes Maiestly.	Mr. Doctor *Ashworth* of	Mr. *Harding* Visher of *Wes-*	S.t *Iames Clerkenwell* and
ham, Master of the Horse.	Mr. *Tho: Wilbraham* Esq.	great *Milton* another.	*minster* Schoole.	Chapl: to the L. *Chancel*
The Earle of *Southampton*,	Mr. *Rooch:* of *Allen*.	Mr. *Paule Peart* and Mr.		Sir *Io: Frankline* Knight.
Captaine of the Isle of *Wight*.	Sir *William Seager*, Garter	*Brigges Geom*: Reader of	The French Church Library	Mr. *Mines* Counc. at La.
Viscount *Lisle* L. Chamber-	K. at Armes.	*Gresham* Col: 3 & 4.	in London.	Sir *Iohn Bingey* of the El
laine to the *Qu: Maiestly*.	Mr. *Camden Clarentieux* K.	Sir *Henry Spilman*,& Mr.		che quer.
L. *Carew Vice-Chamberlaine*	at Armes.	*Henderson* & the two vndet-	The Dutch-Church Libra-	Sir *Giles Mount-Person* Kt
to the Queenes Maiestly, &	Mr. *Robert Treswel*, Somer-	takers for great summes.	ty in London.	Mr *Treeman* Esq, of the 1
				ner Temple Counc, at La

At M.r *Brownes* a Booke-binder in little Britaine without Aldersgate.   *Verte Folium.*

Not long ago an auction house somewhere in the south-west of England was confronted by two volumes (of four) of *A History of Florence* by Thomas Adolphus Trollope, elder brother of the more celebrated Anthony. The catalogue entry emerged as: 'A Trollop's History of Florence, volumes 1 and 2 only', leaving readers to surmise that volumes 3 and 4 were too scurrilous to include.

By way of contrast, consider a catalogue entry for one of the greatest feats of scholarship of our early literary history, John Minsheu's polyglot dictionary giving equivalents in eleven different languages:

> MINSHEU, JOHN: Hegemon eis tas glossus; id est, Ductor in Linguas, the Guide into Tongues. With their agreement and consent one with another, as also their Etymology, that is, the Reasons and Derivations of all or the most part of wordes in...eleven Languages. Two parts in one volume, *large folio modern brown morocco, new endpapers,* First Edition, 1617. Title in woodcut borders, the second title with printer and place left blank. Some browning, two leaves professionally re-margined, not affecting text, a few other minor repairs, slightly cropped. Original price written on title and contemporary signature of Richard Wynne; later signature of Edward Mompesson; list of Subscribers, including 'Mr. Winn, Cl. of the petty Bag' (underlined), Sir Francis Bacon, William Camden, Sir Christopher Hatton, John Donne etc.; early woodcut bookplate of the Honble Edward Monckton of Somerford Hall, Stafford. An interesting copy of THE FIRST BOOK PUBLISHED BY SUBSCRIPTION IN ENGLAND, with the evidence that it is an original subscriber's copy, i.e. that of Richard Wynn or Win (d.1649), groom of the bedchamber to Charles I when Prince of Wales, accompanying him to Spain in 1623 and becoming Treasurer to Queen Henrietta Maria. The subscriber's list is probably the most illustrious ever compiled, including as it does many of the Court, high officials and scholars of England.   STC 17944.

Here are some other examples:

> CHATTERTON, E. KEBLE: Old Sea Paintings. *4to white buckram gilt, t.e.g., rest uncut,* First Edition 1928. 15 tissued coloured plates and 15 in black and white, with the three extra

Left: Page from John Minsheu's Ductor in Linguas *(1617), the first book published in England by subscription; showing part of the list of subscribers. Note the heavy cropping by the binder, which has thrown the page out of alignment and cut into the printer's ornaments at the head.*

The copy of Marryat's Mr. Midshipman Easy *described in the text. Note the original grey boards, the paper spine labels and the uncut top and fore-edges.*

The early nineteenth century boxed travelling library — Bibliotheque Portative du Voyageur — described in the text. The case measures 8½ ins. by 5ins. and is of a rare type popular with coach travellers.

illustrations hand-printed in colour. Out-of-series copy of an edition of only 100 copies on specially made rag paper.

MARRYAT, CAPTAIN FREDERICK: Mr. Midshipman Easy. 3 vols., *8vo orig. boards and paper spine labels, uncut, almost imperceptibly rebacked,* First Edition 1836. All half-titles (with advertisements on versos) and advertisement leaf at end of Vols. II and III...Fine copies, rare in this state, solander cased...Sadleir described a second issue with 'second edition' on the labels. These labels do not carry the words.

VALERIUS MAXIMUS, GAIUS: His Collections of the Memorable Acts and Sayings of Orators, Philosophers, Statesmen...together with a Life of that Famous Historian. *8vo 19th century half morocco,* 1684. The twelve-portrait frontispiece laid down, some slight browning to early leaves...WING V33A (listing only Library of Congress in America and none in the U.K.).

TROLLOPE (A): The Duke's Children. 3 vol., FIRST EDITION, half-titles, lacks advertisements, original cloth, slightly rubbed. Sadleir 57.

BYRON, GEORGE GORDON NOEL, Lord: Childe Harold's Pilgrimage, A Romaunt: and Other Poems. *8vo grained red morocco gilt* by Taylor and Hessey, *wide gilt borders of running foliage, corner fleurons, a.e.g.,* fifth edition 1812. Fine contemporary FORE-EDGE PAINTING of a romantic landscape, with arched bridge over wide river, a ruined circular tower, etc.

BIBLIOTHEQUE PORTATIVE DU VOYAGEUR. A box, calf gilt, containing the works of Corneille, Racine, and Le Sage's Gil Blas, 12 vols., all calf gilt, Paris c.1800. A curious and nice copy of a traveller's library in its case.

REID, W.H. and WALLIS, JAMES: The Panorama: or Traveller's Instructive Guide; through England and Wales...Accompanied by a Description of each county. *8vo...orig. half leather, printed boards (very worn, spine defective)* n.d. (c.1820). Hand-coloured engraved map of England and Wales and 49 (of 52) hand-coloured engraved county maps. CHUBB CCCLXXII. Chubb had seen only one copy.

Here we have come hard up against some of the language of book-collecting described by Simon Nowell-Smith in the quotation at the head of this chapter. For anyone setting out along its delectable paths (and perhaps for some who have already travelled part of the way) there are probably thirty or forty terms, expressions, abbreviations and references that require some explanation.

What, for example, is meant by folio, 4to and 8vo? What are original boards, half morocco and calf gilt? What is the significance of cropped, browning, laid down? What is the difference between an edition and an issue? When is a book uncut or out-of-series? How does one interpret such enigmas as STC 17944 and Wing V33A?; who are the mysterious Chubb and Sadleir?

Most, if not all, of these and other questions, will be dealt with in the course of the following pages, but we will begin with the 'format' (earlier pronounced formah, but now almost universally rhyming with doormat), that is, the shape and size of a book.

There are at least three ways of tackling this, one precise, one complex (inevitably, the collector's method) and one rough-and-ready. Here are the standard sizes of octavo (8vo) British books (as distinct from American):

Name	Abbreviation	Size in ins.	Vertical metric height in cms
Pott Octavo	Pott.8	6¼ x 4	15.8
Foolscap Octavo	F'cap.8	6¾ x 4¼	17.1
Crown Octavo	Cr.8	7½ x 5	19.0
Large Post Octavo	L.Post.8	8¼ x 5¼	20.9
Demy Octavo	Dy.8	8¾ x 5	22.2
Medium Octavo	Med.8	9 x 5¾	22.8
Royal Octavo	Roy.8	10 x 6¼	25.4
Super Royal Octavo	SuR.8	10 x 6¾	25.4
Imperial Octavo	Imp.8	11 x 7½	27.9

This sort of finicky scale will rarely be encountered in everyday life, though some cataloguers use a few of the more common terms, such as royal octavo. The custom is spreading of giving actual dimensions, with metric equivalents. This is particularly important with early and rare books, where a difference in height or width of margin can make a substantial difference to the value. A 'tall copy', i.e. one whose 'head' and 'tail' (top and bottom) margins have been trimmed only lightly by the binder, will cost more than less generously treated copies from the same printing. One should regard with caution anything described as 'cropped', which indicates varying degrees of ruthlessness, some serious. The cataloguer may temper the blow by saying 'cropped, not affecting text' or 'cropped, touching only a few headlines', but let the buyer beware.

There are sometimes things even more important than text. I was once offered a seventeenth century book whose printed surface was immaculate; but the diarist John Evelyn had written manuscript notes down the outer margins, and these had been mercilessly sliced through by a later binder. On the strength of the association, the price was still £600 — very much too high for Evelyn hung, drawn and quartered.

Sometimes the binder has been so gently minded, or so strictly instructed, that the edges are left pleasantly rough and unshaved. In such a case the book is uncut, often considered a desirable feature, especially in private press books. Frequently the fore and tail edges are left uncut, while the top is trimmed and gilded or 'gilt'. In such a case the book will often be described as t.e.g. — top edge(s) gilt. If all edges are treated in this way, the abbreviation is a.e.g. An admonitory note is necessary here about the difference between 'uncut' and 'unopened' — a distinction not always appreciated by would-be collectors and, more reprehensibly, by some cataloguers and embryonic booksellers. Uncut means, as already indicated, with the book's edges untrimmed. Unopened means that it has so escaped the guillotine that the folds of the sections of the paper are still intact at the top and fore-edge, and the owner will have to resort to the paper knife, or the nearest weapon to hand. The purist may say that a metal blade will leave a deposit on the paper that will eventually turn

A tall folio copy of Camden's Britain *(1637). The margins are so wide that an illustrator has been able to use them for drawings of over two thousand coats of arms.*

brown, and opt for a wooden or bone knife. I have found that the edge of a stiff postcard is effective. The least pardonable implement is the forefinger, though its use is apparent on some bookshelves. James Thomson, author of *The Seasons,* sometimes employed a candle snuffer on his books, and Wordsworth was not above using a greasy butter knife.

Returning to the question of format, the purist bibliographer has his special mysteries, related to the number of times the original sheet of paper was folded. In the sixteenth century two sizes were particularly common — 15ins. x 20ins., and 12ins. x 16ins.[1] If we take the larger size and fold it once down the middle, it is clear that we shall have two 'leaves' (or four 'pages'), each 10ins. x 15ins. A book of such dimensions would properly be termed a 'folio'. (Folio can also have the special meaning of a leaf of parchment or paper numbered only on the front, as happens in some early manuscripts and books.)

If the sheet is folded a second time, we shall arrive at something smaller and squarer, consisting of four leaves or eight pages in each section. When these sections or 'gatherings' have been collected together, this will give a quarto (4to) book. Fold again and the result is eight leaves (sixteen pages) and an octavo. Theoretically, this folding can go on into a Lilliputian world with a terrifying terminology, but the following table will suffice for most practical purposes:

No. of folds	Name	Abbreviations
1	Folio	Fo. or 1
2	Quarto	Qto., 4to or 4
3	Octavo	Oct., 8vo or 8
4	Sextodecimo	16mo
5	Tricesimo-secundo	32mo

There are also ways of folding a sheet to give a duodecimo (12mo) vicesimo-quarto (24mo) etc., but these can lead to bibliographical complications that need not be discussed here.

Our purist, if he wishes to determine the true format of a book, will take account of these various foldings and will resort to the study of the 'chain lines', 'wire lines', and the position of the 'watermark'.

Until the end of the eighteenth century all paper was made by hand in a framed mould with a wire bed. In one direction were five or six wires crossing the mould horizontally with, vertically, many more wires placed closer together. The widely spaced lines are called chain lines, the

---

1 The double leaf of the largest copy yet discovered of the First Folio of Shakespeare's Plays (1616) has been recorded as 13ins. x 17ins.

narrowly spaced lines running across them are wire lines. (The general terms wire lines or wire marks are sometimes used indiscriminately for both, but it is safer to preserve the distinction.) If we hold almost any early book up to the light, the lines will be immediately visible, left on the sheet of paper when the liquid has been shaken from the mould. This is 'laid' paper as distinct from 'wove' paper, which shows a fine mesh pattern instead of chain and wire lines.

Recalling now the various foldings of the original sheet we have discussed, it will be clear that, as the number of folds alters, so will the direction of the chain and wire lines. A simple experiment with these lines drawn on a small sheet of paper will demonstrate that, whereas the chain lines run vertically on a folio folding, they will run horizontally if a second

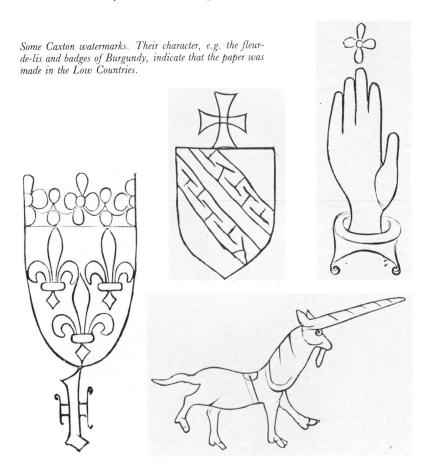

Some Caxton watermarks. Their character, e.g. the fleur-de-lis and badges of Burgundy, indicate that the paper was made in the Low Countries.

fold is made (for a quarto) and revert to the vertical for an octavo.

There is another important matter. Paper manufacturers from a very early period introduced another piece of wire into the network, to provide some sort of trade device or distinguishing mark. These took a great variety of forms — stars, crosses, crowns, jugs, bugles, shields, initials, etc. The most exhaustive work on them is C.M. Briquet's *Les Filigranes* (1906), which reproduces some 16,000 watermarks used from 1282-1600. It is to be hoped that you can consult a library copy, otherwise the four volumes may relieve you of £200-£300.

Going back to our paper-folding exercise, it will become apparent that, if there is a watermark of an upright ewer or jug approximately in the centre of a right hand double folio leaf, a second fold will dramatically alter its position and show it sprawled on its side across the centre fold; and that the next fold will reveal the watermark mysteriously truncated somewhere up at the top of the page.

William Blades (1824-90), the great printer-typographer and authority on Caxton, tried to reduce all this to a simple and rigid formula. He concluded:

> In any old book, if the chain lines run down, and the watermark is found about the centre of the page, that book must be a folio.
>
> If the chain lines run across and the watermark appears in the middle of the last leaf of a section, that book is quarto.
>
> If the chain lines run down, and the watermark is found at the top edge of a leaf, tnat book must be octavo.

This is a very good rule-of-thumb guide. Unfortunately, papermakers were not always so considerate as to dispose their watermarks so conveniently, with the result that eccentricities may be found.

There is another, very reliable, method of deciding whether a book is quarto, octavo, etc. But we have already got into fairly deep bibliographical water, and I propose to leave this till I have something to say about 'signatures' and 'registers' in Chapter 10, when we shall be examining ways of checking the completeness of books. Otherwise, the zestful student is referred to Ronald M. McKerrow's *An Introduction to Bibliography for Literary Students* (1st edition 1927, later impressions with corrections), which will give him all, and probably more than, he wants and should be on every serious collector's shelves.

For the comfort of those who may have found some of the foregoing explanations either tedious or exasperating, I turn briefly to my third method of determining the format of a book, which I described as rough-

Above and left: Typical groups of octavos in calf and morocco gilt; right: folios and quartos similarly bound. The centre volume is in quarter vellum.

and-ready. It is also simple and practical. Most people, even collectors, get through life without bothering overmuch about sizes. A dealer I knew many years ago in Leicestershire had reduced the system to its stark basic requirements. His 'mark-up' was 'a bob for the big 'uns, a tanner the little 'uns'. (For the benefit of a younger generation, I should perhaps take the precaution of saying that a bob was the equivalent of 5p and a tanner was half that.) It always unnerved me to think that, some lucky day, I might find a distinguished 'little 'un', such as the first edition of *Paradise Lost* or *A Pilgrim's Progress* for less than a *Chatterbox Annual* or *With the Flag to Pretoria.*

He had something of the rights of the matter, though he was guilty of over-simplification. His system involved only the use of the eye and required some refinement to make it more generally acceptable. A tall volume considerably higher than its width, is a folio, which can be small or large. An average upright-shaped volume, the size of an ordinary novel, is an octavo, small or large. Between the two, and squarish in shape, is a quarto which, again, if it is not average can be small or large. A book like a folio lying on its side is an oblong folio. Presumably there could be an oblong quarto or octavo, though I think I have only once met such a description.

This somewhat rudimentary nomenclature, which will dismay all true bibliographers, will probably cover about ninety-five per cent of books. I must confess that only rarely do I feel constrained to crick my neck carefully checking chain lines and wire lines and following the gymnastics of watermarks. David Holloway, in his delightful *A London Childhood,* recalled his father helping him put a toy model together and not following the detailed instructions on the box. By way of defence he said: 'There's a right way and a best way'. My concluding advice is: Learn the right way, then you are at liberty to choose the best way.

Already in this chapter I have mentioned two important and much-quoted reference books, and it may be convenient at this point to return to our catalogue excerpts and clear up such obscurities as STC 17944, Wing V33A, and the frustrated Mr. Chubb, who had seen only one copy of a book.

Cataloguers, whether booksellers or auctioneers, dearly (and understandably) love to add lustre to their productions by citing unimpeachable sources. To begin with, it gives the impression that they have done their homework. Secondly, they may, quite altruistically, wish to direct the student's attention to the best work on the subject, so that the accuracy of the description can be checked and, sometimes, one copy set against another for purposes of comparison. Most of all, they delight in scoring a point in the battle for rarity. If they can say confidently 'Not known to X' or 'Not in Y', their day is made. To be able to write 'No copy recorded' calls for a special celebration.

There are, however, a number of cautions to be observed before such findings are accepted uncritically. First, if a book has gone unnoticed and unrecorded for centuries, it is likely to be very unimportant. Secondly, if a work does not appear under one heading, for instance in the *Short-Title Catalogue* (see STC below), it may well be listed somewhere else in the book under a name or heading the searcher has not checked. Thirdly, if a work is not mentioned in one source book, which may be less than exhaustive, it is likely to be in a later, and better, one. And, perhaps most important of all, one must not misinterpret a work of reference, however scholarly and authoritative it may be, and expect it to do more than it sets out, or claims, to perform (see below, under WING).

To give a full list of standard source and reference works, covering every subject, would need a complete volume. There is, in fact, one in existence called, appropriately, *A Bibliography of Bibliographies;* but I add a short list of some commonly cited, especially by major auction houses and the higher echelons of booksellers. References tend to become prolific where incunabula and other very early books are concerned, when, instead of one, six or eight authorities may be cited, British and Continental.

ABBEY — The catalogues of bindings and illustrated books, mainly in aquatint and lithography from 1770-1860, collected by one of this century's greatest bibliophiles, Major John Roland Abbey, and now largely dispersed through a series of major auction sales.

References are usually given in the form of: Abbey Scenery *(Scenery of Great Britain and Ireland in Aquatint and Lithography, 1770-1860)*, Abbey Life *(Life in England in Aquatint and Lithography, 1770-1860)* and Abbey Travel *(Travel in Aquatint and Lithography, 1770-1860).*

The catalogues themselves in limited editions of four hundred copies, were formerly expensive items, but later reprints have brought down the price.

ABC — *American Book-Prices Current,* which has been published annually since 1895 and which has recently been the subject of a considerable advertising drive in Britain, somewhat to the detriment of this country's *Book Auction Records* (see BAR below), which has sometimes tended to lag behind in publication dates and is in some respects not so complete, e.g., it includes no Autograph and Manuscript prices as its American counterpart does.

ADAMS — H.M. Adams, *Catalogue of Books printed on the Continent of Europe, 1501-1600, in Cambridge Libraries* (1967).

BAR — *Book Auction Records,* first published as a quarterly, dating from

1903, now annually, with periodic General Indexes covering several years. While considerable recent efforts have been made to improve editorial performance and punctuality of issue, some of John Carter's criticisms of thirty years ago still stand: "so much has to be read between the lines that the novice should be wary in drawing inferences from these records. In particular, bibliographical details and points attached to the entries should not be uncritically accepted."

Nevertheless, it is the only major publication of its kind in this country and most booksellers and collectors rely on it as a good general guide to values. Copies are available for consulation in most large public libraries. Long runs of back volumes often appear in sales. Unless they are wanted for historical and research purposes, they are not worth buying, since prices tend to be wildly out of date.

BISHOP — William W. Bishop, *Checklist of American Copies of 'Short-Title Catalogue' Books* (see STC below).

BMC — *British Museum Catalogue of Books Printed in the Fifteenth Century.* The Library has its vast general catalogue (available in microscopic and sight-destroying form in many public reference libraries) and a number of special catalogues; but BMC normally means the volumes listing incunabula (books printed before 1500)[2] which, beginning in 1908, are indispensable for the serious student of the period, splendidly illustrated and with scholarly introductions. The catalogues, especially the earlier volumes, are likely to be more expensive than some of the incunabula they list.

BRUNET — Jacques-Charles Brunet, *Manuel du Libraire et de l'Amateur de Livres.* First published in three volumes in 1810, the best known edition is the fifth, 1860-80, six volumes and two supplements, recently reprinted. 40,000 rare and valuable books are listed, with particular strengths in Latin and French.

CHUBB — Thomas Chubb, *The Printed Maps in the Atlases of Great Britain & Ireland... 1579-1870.* First published in 1927, it climbed to the £50-£70 bracket but has now been reprinted.

DNB — The Oxford University Press *Dictionary of National Biography,* one of the most-used works on the collector's shelves. It was founded by George Smith (1824-1901) in 1882, and by 1901 had reached a massive total of sixty-six volumes. Mercifully, this has now been reduced. There is even a modern two-volume edition (which ought to be outlawed by the Health Service), reducing the vast work to tiny type painful to read and unlovely to behold. For the average collector the best buy is the *Concise*

---

2 See footnote to p.36.

Dictionary of National Biography, a two-volume epitome of the main work, from the beginning to 1950. If more extensive information is required, a walk to any self-respecting public reference library should suffice.

DUFF — E. Gordon Duff, *Fifteenth Century English Books* (1917).

HAIN — The *Repertorium Bibliographicum ad Annum 1500,* an alphabetically arranged list by author of some 17,000 incunabula, originally embarked on by Ludwig F.T. Hain (1781-1836) and based on what was to emerge as the Bavarian State Library. The English bibliographer W.A. Copinger (1847-1910) published a supplementary three volumes 1895-1902 and various appendices have been added to the total. Copinger's supplement is cited as Hain-Copinger or just Hain-Cop. Dietrich Reichling added nearly two thousand additional incunabula 1905-14 in a series of appendices, and Reichling may also be cited. There was a reprint of the work in 1948.

HALKETT AND LAING — The invaluable *Dictionary of Anonymous and Pseudonymous English Literature,* which first appeared from the pens of the industrious Samuel Halkett (1814-71) and John Laing (1809-90) in four volumes 1882-88. By 1956 subsequent editors and researchers had raised the total to eight volumes and the work continues.

LOWNDES — William Thomas Lowndes, *The Bibliographer's Manual of English Literature,* four volumes, 1834, revised 1858-64 and reprinted several times. The 'New Edition, revised, corrected and enlarged' was by the publisher and bookseller Henry G. Bohn (1796-1884) who, in Lowndes's later years, employed him as a cataloguer after, in Bohn's words, "his long course of Bibliographical drudgery had reduced him, both in body and mind, to a mere wreck of his former self...always conscious that Bibliography has no recognised status in England." Bohn's edition has a very valuable supplement of nearly 350 pp. listing literary clubs, societies and private presses, with their publications. Imperfect (and occasionally inaccurate) though the work is, it sometimes yields information not readily obtainable elsewhere. The 1834 edition claimed upwards of 50,000 notices of separate books published in, or relating to, Great Britain and Ireland.

McKERROW — Ronald B. McKerrow, *An Introduction to Bibliography for Literary Students* (first published 1927), a classic basic manual.

PHILLIPPS — Such expressions as 'the Phillipps copy' and 'Middle Hill boards' refer to Sir Thomas Phillipps (1792-1872) and his method of binding his manuscripts in rough protective covers. Phillipps's avowed ambition was 'to have one copy of every book in the world'. If he did not obtain that objective, he succeeded in amassing some 60,000 manuscripts — the largest private collection in Europe — with the aim of preserving for posterity every unpublished work he could lay hands on. The dispersal of this vast collection began in 1886, a substantial mountain being acquired by the booksellers Lionel and Philip Robinson in 1945. They later invested the ownership in the hands of the Trustees of the Robinson Trust who, in 1965, inaugurated an important series of sales which still continue. Unknown and unsuspected treasures have emerged from this argosy, the most dramatic being the manuscript of part of the translation of Ovid's *Metamorphoses* published by Caxton. Half of this priceless manuscript was in the hands of the Pepysian Library at Magdalene College, Cambridge, and the two were happily reunited. Another find was the commonplace book of the poet Robert Herrick (1591-1674).

Those interested in reading more of this eccentric book-maniac can do no better than study A.N.L. Munby's five-volume *Phillipps Studies* or, at another level, his *Portrait of an Obsession* (1967).

PROCTOR — Robert George Collier Proctor (1868-1903), of the British Museum, whose four-volume *Index to the early printed books in the British Museum. . . to 1500, with notes of those in the Bodleian Library* (1898-1903) lists some 10,000 books with details of country of origin, town and printer, with assigned numbers that are still quoted in catalogues. His work became the basis of the *British Museum Catalogue of Books Printed in the Fifteenth Century* (see BMC above).

One of the greatest incunabulists despite his short life, Proctor was also interested in Icelandic literature and designed a new Greek type. He disappeared while on a walking tour in the Tyrol. His *Bibliographical Essays* were published in 1905.

SABIN — The most comprehensive reference work for books on America — *Bibliotheca Americana, a Dictionary of Books relating to America from its Discovery to the Present Time,* begun by Joseph Sabin (1821-81), who saw the first thirteen volumes appear, and continued by Wilberforce Eames and R.W.G. Vail to reach a total of twenty-nine volumes, 1868-1936.

STC — *A Short-Title Catalogue of Books printed in England, Scotland and Ireland and of English Books printed abroad, 1475-1640.* A bibliographical landmark and probably the most cited of all English reference books. Compiled by A.W. Pollard and G.R. Redgrave, with the assistance of other dedicated bibliophiles, the first (1926) edition listed over 26,000 works and editions in alphabetical order and numbered serially. Thus, Caxton's advertisement *If it plese ony man to bye ony pyes*[3] will be cited as STC 4890, and James I's *A counter blaste to tobacco* as STC 14363. A substantial (and

---

3 'Pye' = pye-book or pica, a book showing what lessons or prayers should be read on various Saints' Days. 'Pica' and 'small pica' survive as names of type sizes.

expensive) revision has begun to appear and is being cited as 'new STC', with some alteration of the old numbers.

WING — Donald Wing of Yale University, *Short-Title Catalogue of Books printed in England, Scotland, Ireland, Wales and British America, and of some English Books printed in other Countries 1641-1700.* Virtually the continuation, with some territorial expansion, of the preceding work, the three volumes being published 1945-51. The work is often misinterpreted, or miscited, to give a false impression of rarity; thus, 'only five copies according to Wing' is a stupid statement, since the compiler deliberately limits himself to locating five copies in American libraries and there may well be twenty others. The same sort of caution must be exercised in STC citations. The compilers of that work warn that it is a 'dangerous work for anyone to handle lazily.' Like its companion Wing, it is not a census of copies and "it is only when less than three copies are recorded from English sources, and less than two from libraries in the United States, that any deduction can be drawn that the copies mentioned are all of which the compilers had notes."

It must again be emphasised that this list is only to give examples of commonly quoted reference books. Almost every important author (and many unimportant ones) and every field of collecting can boast a standard authority. If you are a Swift collector you will certainly want Herman Teerink's bibliography on your shelves. Devotees of Robert Louis Stevenson will need Colonel W.F. Prideaux's *A Bibliography of the Works of Robert Louis Stevenson.* Specialists in English drama will turn to Sir W.W. Greg's *Bibliography of English Printed Drama.* Michael Sadleir may well be cited for Anthony Trollope, W. Blunt for botanical illustrations, Garrison and Morton for medical books, Darlow and Moule for bibles, Padwick for cricket, Arber for herbals, Fulton for the scientific works of the Hon. Robert Boyle.

How shall we know (a) if a bibliography exists and (b) to what book a catalogue reference such as 'Darlow and Moule' refers? The answer to (a) is, ask your librarian and consult the *Bibliography of Bibliographies;* to (b), look up the name or names in *Book Auction Records,* kept in most public libraries, where you will almost certainly find, for example: Darlow, T.H. & Moule, H.F., *Printed Editions of Holy Scripture;* the point being that source books of this nature are coveted by collectors, so that, given an author, titles are almost always to be found in auction records.

Chapter 2
The Language of Book-Collecting (ii)

> The language of book-collecting, if there is such a thing, is a hotch-potch in which the chief ingredients are borrowed from the language of bibliography, borrowed, that is to say, at second-hand from the various book-productive and book-distributive trades. It is inevitably so. For every book-collector, and every bookseller, is in greater or less degree a bibliographer.
>
> Simon Nowell-Smith in *Talks on Book-Collecting* (1952)

It is time that we turned to the inside of our book and began to explore its mysteries and terminology.

The normal book, when it is opened, will display two pages or 'papers' empty of print, though they may be decorated. On the left is the 'paste-down' or 'paste-down endpaper', on the right the 'free endpaper'. Though these may be plain, use is often made of paper of a different texture, and even of colour, from that of the main text. Such comparatively unimportant details can sometimes help to determine priority of issue. For example, the first issue of the first edition of Dickens's *A Christmas Carol,* according to some of the pundits, has green endpapers, while the second issue has yellow. If the publisher wishes to make his book more attractive, he may decide to have 'marbled' endpapers. Marbling was practised in the east well over a thousand years ago, but it was late in arriving in Europe. Francis Bacon, writing in 1627, said ''The Turks have a pretty art of chambletting paper which is not in use with us'', though, in fact, it did reach this country at about that date. A manual describing the art was written in Holland in 1674, and at that time it was the Dutch who produced the best work. In recent years British papers have been widely used all over the world.

The process is complicated, but produces some beautiful effects. It consists, basically, of transferring floating colours, combed or twisted into delicate patterns, from the surface of a gum solution. The best results are obtained from watercolours, oils being less clean and controllable. It should not be difficult to distinguish between the genuine work and the more shoddy effects produced by lithographic reproduction.

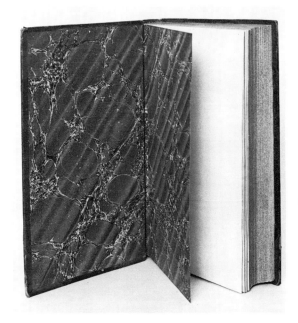

One volume of an 1847 edition of Walpole's Memoirs of the Reign of George II, *illustrating the marbled paste-down (left) and the free endpaper (right).*

In some elaborately produced books you will meet a stiffer type of endpaper with a wavy pattern like rich fabric. This is 'watered silk'. Another elaboration is the use of leather, often decorated, for the paste-down. Such inside linings, more common in Continental books than English, are known as 'doublures' (from the French *doubler,* to line), there being no English equivalent. If the binder has gone to town with his gilt on the outside, he may well have been tempted to spill over onto the inside edges, giving pleasant lacy-patterned borders to the paste-down, usually termed 'inside dentelles'. On the outside they would be 'dentelle borders', wide or narrow. Again, we borrow from the French, this time for lace or tracery.

Turning over the free endpaper to the next double page, we shall usually arrive at the first appearance of print, unless the publisher has been very free with his endpapers and given us some blanks. On the right will be found a simple version of the book's title, without author's name or publisher's imprint. This is the 'half-title'. It is sometimes (especially in America, where, unfeelingly, they have often adopted their own bibliographical terminology) called the 'fly' or 'bastard' title.

This insignificant looking page is of much more importance than might appear. Rebinders often discard it and thereby do the collector a serious

*and kept them out by a zealous contesting and publike bearing wit-
nesse against them by word and writing, and that therefore such as
have with too much tendernesse and complyance tolerated Errours, Er-
rour will one day grow up to that head that it will not tolerate or suffer them to speak truth; We have a Proverb here, That the Devill is
not so soon risen, but Christ is up before him; and if any of his precious
servants have slept and lien longer a bed then their Master hath done, and
have not spoken or printed soone enough for Jesus Christ in other matters, yet oh that in this matter of the Sabbath God would betimes a-
waken; and that these weaknesses might stir up their strength : for I
much fear and foresee that if it be not done, there is an houre and a
nick of temptation in such a juncture of times approaching, wherein the
enemy will come in like a flood, and rise up from all quarters against the
Doctrine of the Sabbath, and then farewell all the good dayes of the
Sonne of man, if this be lost, which then men shall desire to see and shall
not see them. I have therefore been the more willing to let my own
shame and weaknesse appear to the world (if so it be found) if this might
be any means of doing the least good for keeping up the price of Gods
Sabbaths in the hearts of any; I have therefore spent the more time about
the Morality of the Sabbath, because the clearing up of this, gives light
to all the rest.*

Tho. Shepard.

Imprimatur,

Joseph Caryl.

A Commonwealth imprimatur in Thomas Shepard's Theses Sabbaticae. Or, the Doctrine of the Sabbath *(1649); the licence in this case granted by Joseph Caryl, a divine who frequently preached before the Long Parliament.*

disservice. The purist bookman wants his book complete with the half-titles, if they were there in the first place, and it is an appreciable demerit mark if the cataloguer has to confess 'lacking half-titles' or 'volume III without half-title', even though they are present in the other two. Some of the greatest sufferers in this respect are such prized works as Jane Austen's, where it can make a surprising difference to the price.

The half-title often carries on the 'verso' (back) the printer's imprint, as distinct from the publisher's, and perhaps a list of other works by the same author. In early books, especially those of the sixteenth and seventeenth centuries, this page may well display an 'imprimatur' (Latin for 'let it be printed'), a licence from some official, religious or secular, authorising the publication. Normally, this is reserved nowadays for works approved by the Roman Catholic Church. Other phrases with more or less the same

THE SEA-MANS
DICTIONARY:

OR,

An EXPOSITION and DEMONSTRATION
of all the Parts and Things belonging to a

SHIP.

TOGETHER WITH

An EXPLANATIOS of all the Terms
and Phrases used in the Practick of

NAVIGATION.

Composed by that Able and Experienced Sea-man
Sir HENRY MANWAYRING Knight,
And by him presented to the late Duke of BUCKINGHAM,
the then Lord High Admiral of ENGLAND.

I Have perused this Book, and find it so universally necessary for all
sorts of Men, that I conceive it very fit to be at this time Imprinted
for the Good of the Republick.
Septemb. 20. 1644.

London, Printed by W. Godbid for Benjamin Hurlock, and are to be
sold at his Shop over against St. Magnus Church on London-
Bridge near Thames-street. Anno Dom. 1670.

*Right: Another
seventeenth century
licence, this time
incorporated in the title-
page; below: a modern
licence granted by the
Archbishop of Milan.*

Imprimatur

† THOMAS,

Episcopus Medioburgensis
Die 19 Martii 1947.

meaning are *nihil obstat* ('nothing hinders') and *cum licentia* ('with licence'
or 'with permission'). If the formula appears on a separate leaf, this is
often referred to as the 'licence leaf' or 'privilege leaf'.

This oppressive measure on the part of the authority aroused much anger among writers. In 1693, Charles Blount wrote:

> Learning hath of late years met with an obstruction in many places which suppresses it from flourishing or increasing...and that is the inquisition upon the press, which prohibits any book from coming forth without an imprimature.

And earlier, in the noblest of all defences of the freedom of the press, Milton had protested:

> What advantage is it to be a man, over it is to be a boy at school, if we have only 'scaped the ferule [cane] to come under the fescue [rod] of an Imprimatur?

We arrive at what, from the collector's point of view, is one of the most important parts of the book — the title-page. If you are fortunate enough to own, or to find, an incunabulum[1] or book printed before 1500, do not be too alarmed if it has no title, since many books of the period had none, at least in the sense that we understand, the publisher/printer contenting himself with a curt statement of the title and author's name, known as a 'label title', or else a small introductory paragraph (sometimes using a different coloured ink) known as the 'incipit', from the Latin 'it begins'. The term 'initia' is sometimes used, but much more rarely.

The label title to Caxton's The Chastysing of goddes chyldern, *c.1471.*

In a later chapter, on the cult of the first edition, I shall have more to say on what a vital part the title-page can play. On it we normally get the full title and sub-title, the author's name or pseudonym, his qualifications and, sometimes, the titles of other important or popular books he has written with, at the foot, the publisher's imprint and, more often than not, the date.

---

1 A book printed before 1500, the word deriving from the Latin for 'in the cradle' or 'belonging to the cradle', i.e. of printing. This specialised meaning of the word is of some antiquity. The plural is incunabula. The Englished forms 'incunable' and 'incunables', though a century old, are to be spat at.

RIME
DEL COMMENDATORE
A N N I B A L C A R O.

Col Priuilegio di N. S. PP. PIO V.
Et dell'Illuftrifsima Signoria
di VENETIA.

IN VENETIA.
Appreſſo ALDO MANVTIO.
M D LXIX.

One of the most famous publisher's imprints and devices, that of Aldus Manutius (1450-1515), founder of the Aldine Press in Venice and introducer of italic type. At the date of this book, 1569, the press had been taken over by Aldus's youngest son, Paulus. The celebrated dolphin and anchor device (the dolphin for swiftness and grace, the anchor for strength and reliability) was adopted by the English printer William Pickering.

37

A fine seventeenth century copper-engraved title-page.

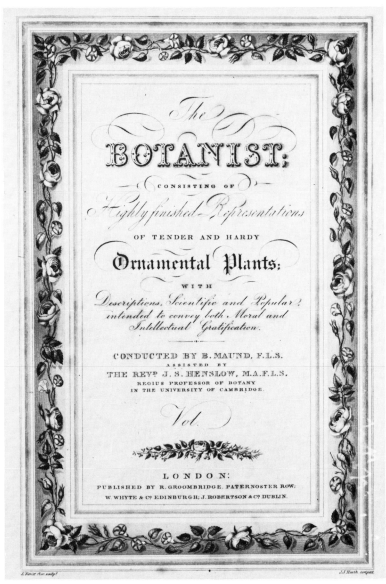

The attractive engraved title of a famous botanical work, printed in five volumes, 1836-42. It is sometimes known as a factotum title, since it was designed for general use, leaving the volume number to be filled in.

PICTURESQUE TOUR

OF

THE RIVER THAMES;

ILLUSTRATED BY

TWENTY-FOUR COLOURED VIEWS, A MAP, AND VIGNETTES,

FROM ORIGINAL DRAWINGS TAKEN ON THE SPOT

BY

WILLIAM WESTALL AND SAMUEL OWEN.

A vignette title-page, 1828. A vignette is an illustration without border or frame, the picture shading off into the surrounding paper.

To quote, at this stage, only one or two examples of the significance all this can assume, the first appearance (first edition, first issue) of Lamb's famous *Elia* (1823) has the imprint:

LONDON:
PRINTED FOR TAYLOR AND HESSEY,
FLEET STREET.
1823.

The second issue gives the address as 93 Fleet Street and 13 Waterloo Place. Incidentally, just to show how difficult life can be, the true first issue has no half-title — one of the rare instances when its absence is a point in its favour.

There are four variants of the title-page of Dickens's *Battle of Life;* two have dates, two do not; in two the title is on a scroll with a cupid, on one the scroll has no cupid, in one there is no scroll at all. A mad world, my masters.

The bibliographer Lowndes, over a hundred years ago, categorically listed eight different title-pages for the first edition of Milton's *Paradise Lost,* pointing out such differences as large or small italic capitals for the poet's name; in one case the use of his initials only; groups of stars between words, or none; with or without fleur-de-lis ornaments, etc. It took the industrious Lowndes nearly a hundred lines to explain it all. Then, in 1927, Sawyer and Darton wrote that his fifth and sixth titles could not be traced. Never having cornered Milton, I am content to take their word for it.

While we are dealing with titles, it will be convenient to mention the 'drop title' or 'dropped-head title'. These refer to a title set lower than the first line of a page of ordinary text. In a publication such as a pamphlet, which may well have no separate title-page, the title often appears as a dropped head on the opening page of the text. Chapter headings are almost always 'dropped' to a standard height throughout a book. There is also the 'running head' or 'running title', which is the line of type, consisting of the title of the book or of a section of it, above the text.

Facing the title-page is often to be found the 'frontispiece', devoted to a portrait or some interesting part of the subject matter. When illustrations are numbered, the frontispiece is not usually included, and a catalogue description should always make it clear whether or not the stated number of plates has taken account of it, e.g. '12 plates including frontispiece' or 'frontispiece and 20 plates'.

The frontispiece can sometimes provide another piece of valuable evidence in determing the edition or issue of a book. In *Gulliver's Travels (Travels into Several Remote Nations of the World),* 2 vols., 1726-27, the true first edition has a frontispiece oval portrait with an inscription set in two

member of an important household, accustomed to entertain and receive other influential fellow-merchants and customers, both from home and abroad.

A year after William Caxton's arrival, knowledge of what was accounted good conduct became even more important; for Robert Large was elected Lord Mayor and rode in procession to Westminster, with all the mercers in new robes and sixteen trumpeters blowing silver trumpets before him.

This year marked the climax of Large's career and he did not live much longer. In the spring of 1441 he died, leaving a long list of bequests in his will. Among them was one of 20 marks to his apprentice William Caxton.

The youngster was not released from his apprenticeship by the death of his master. The set term of years must still be worked out. If no other master was nominated in Large's will, it was the responsibility of the executors to find the apprentice a new home. This might be at home or abroad, for there were plenty of opportunities for young men in the great centres of the wool trade overseas.

Who made the arrangements we do not know but, according to Caxton's own statement, in 1441, the same year in which he lost his first master and had to leave the house in Old Jewry, he took ship for the Low Countries.

The Kentish lad was already far afield and it would be many years before he came home again.

90

I 2

The Governor of the English Nation

When William Caxton arrived in Bruges, towards the middle of the fifteenth century, the city had long been established as one of the most important in Europe.

Merchants from every neighbouring country and state were gathered there, and from it the long tentacles of trade stretched out to the far corners of the world. The trade-routes twisted through Lyons and Marseilles to Alexandria and the Red Sea; through Milan and Venice to the Sea of Azov and the banks of the Volga; eastward through Antioch and Baghdad to Samarkand and China; north-east to Danzig and Riga and Novgorod.

The river quays were filled with the thousand noises and smells of shipping and merchandise—the whine of rigging, the rattle of anchor chains, the creak of pulleys, the slap of water, the hooves of horses on the cobbles and the rumble of wheels as the hand-carts and wains hauled their loads to the shops and warehouses; the scent of Eastern spices, of resinous timber, of warm wool with the oil still in it, of ripening fruit, of tarred cordage and hemp.

Before he had finished, William Caxton knew those quays like the back of his hand, knew them far better than the lanes and wharves of London; just as the Hall in the

91

A typical 'opening'. On the left is the verso (back, reverse) of one leaf, on the right the recto (front, obverse) of another. Note that the verso always carries the even page number and the recto the odd number. Note also the running title (top left) and the drop-head title (right).

lines beneath the oval, not round it. On such slender threads hang small fortunes and great acquisitions.

We can now turn right to the other end of the book, where there should be another paste-down and free endpaper, though in earlier books the latter will often be missing, having been appropriated by some seventeenth or eighteenth century housewife as a shopping list or for copying a cooking recipe. Shelley was known to use endpapers for making paper boats.

Since the first printers often did not use a front title-page, or did not include on it all the important information we are accustomed to see there today, they employed instead the device known as the *colophon*[2] (from a Greek word variously translated as 'summit', 'top' and 'finishing stroke') right at the end of the main text and, normally, before the index. Such printer's inscriptions form a study in themselves, varying greatly in length

---

2 As with a number of bibliographical words, the origin is interesting. The ancient city of Colophon, north of Ephesus, was ruled by wealthy citizens who, for its defence, contributed a famous troop of cavalry. Any charge by these élite horsemen was reckoned to be the 'finishing stroke' of a battle, hence its application to books.

and detail and often being attractively arranged in the shape of a diamond, a wine or hour-glass, etc., and accompanied by a majestic printer's device or coat of arms.

The colophon of Caxton's *The Game and Play of the Chess Moralised* reads:

> And send yow thaccomplisshement of your hy noble Joyous
> and vertuous desirs Amen: Fynsshid the last day of merche the
> yer of our lord god. a. thousand foure hondred and lxxiiii.

In *The Dictes and Sayengis of the philosophres* (1477) he gives rather more information:

> Here endeth the book named the dictes or syengis of the
> philosophres enprynted by me william Caxton at Westmestre
> the yere of our lord MCCCC Lxxvii.

Since complete title pages, in the modern sense, appear in most books from about 1520, the colophon thereafter declined in use and, where found, gives only cursory information in extension or confirmation of what was stated at the outset. There has, however, been some revival of the device, especially with modern private presses affecting a fondness for the past and for the great days of the colophon, beginning with the great Mainz Psalter of Fust and Schoeffer in 1457.

Another very early feature was the use of advertisements. I have already quoted one used by Caxton, and by the seventeenth century the booksellers and publishers were in full cry. It may be noted in passing that the advertisement supplement, far from being a modern development, first appeared in 1666 in this country. The *London Gazette* in June of that year declared that "a Paper of Advertisements will be forthwith printed apart, and recommended to the Publick by another hand."

Advertisements may be found at either end of a book, but occur much more often at the back. They are of two sorts — those which are an integral part of the book, printed on the same paper and gathered up for binding with the rest of the sections (though they will usually be paged separately); and leaves or sections printed separately, sometimes on different paper altogether, which may even be of a different size. As might be expected, most advertisements incorporated in books proclaim the publishers' own wares; but with books issued in parts, such as those of Dickens, they can be a joyous medley covering everything from top hats to mouse traps, pills to perambulators and hair oils to phrenology. Such extraneous matter as a sample of cork or a piece of heather may swell the fun.

To the ordinary reader advertisements may count for nothing; but to the bookseller and book-collector they can make the difference between £50 and £500. Leaving aside publications in parts, which are a special

Advertisement leaf from the fourth volume of Doctor Johnson's Lives *of the most eminent English Poets (1781). The value would be affected adversely without it.*

problem, books which should contain advertisements cannot be reckoned complete without them, so that, if they have been removed or discarded in a rebinding, the value suffers considerably, even though the text is perfect. Moreover, they can furnish valuable bibliographical evidence. The following examples from *Book Auction Records* illustrate the importance attached to their presence:

AUSTEN, JANE — Emma. 1816. 1st Edn 3 vols, hf title for vol 1 bnd at end, no hf titles to vol 2 & 3, publrs advt at end of vol 3.

STEVENSON, ROBERT LOUIS — Kidnapped. 1st Edn. With advt for Treasure Island on p-312, 16pp of advts dtd 7-86.

KINGSLEY, REV. CHARLES — Westward Ho. 1855. 1st

44

Edn. 3 vol. hf titles, adt lf bnd at front, & 16p publ cat dated Feb. 1855 bnd at end of vol I, front free end papers torn away, origin.cl.

EVANS, MARIAN or MARY-ANN 'George Eliot' — Silas Marner. 1861. 1st Edn. Hf title 811 of advts at end.

If you can readily interpret all this laconic shorthand you are either a well-tried collector or an extraordinarily apt pupil. As well as the references to advertisements, you will, I hope, have noticed the importance attached to half-titles.

Since advertisements are often dated, they can be useful in establishing priority of issues; but they can also be misleading and should always be interpreted with caution. It is not unknown for an advertisement section to be switched from one book to another, to convert an ordinary work to a more coveted one.

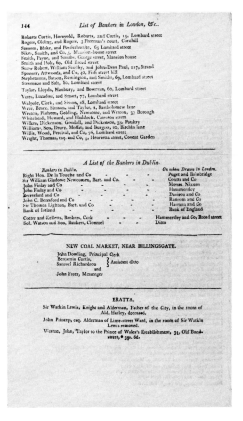

A curious errata notice from Holden's Triennial Directory of London, *1805, with the printer misspelling errata.*

45

Other apparently trivial features are the 'errata' (sometimes 'corrigenda') and 'addenda', which are the mistakes and omissions discovered after the book has been printed or during the final stages. If the work has not gone too far, there is often some blank page, or part of one, where these can be noted; otherwise they will normally be printed on a special slip or leaf which can be 'tipped-in' (lightly attached by glue or paste at the inner edge). Johnson's *Journey to the Western Isles of Scotland* (1775) has eleven errata on twelve lines, the second issue having only six. The true book-collector must accept this sort of eccentricity along with all the other criteria. Obviously, a lifetime of experience is needed to recognise or remember such minutiae, and most of us will need to fly to our bibliographies.

Printers began the errata business very early, for a 1478 edition of Juvenal lists mistakes on two leaves, the printer attributing them to the carelessness of a workman. I am fond of a notice which appears on a rare advertisement leaf in some copies of Robert Boyle's *Experiments and Notes about the Producibleness of Chymicall Principles* (1680):

> The Reader is desired to
> take notice, that as, the
> Date of the License witnesses,
> this Booke, should have been
> Printed long agoe, and there
> has been a mistake in the bot-
> tome of the Title Page, where
> the Year 1680 has been put in-
> stead of the Year 1679. in which
> it was really Printed off, though
> not publickly expos's to Sale, til
> the beginning of this Month
> of January. $16\frac{79}{80}$ [3]

3 For an explanation of this method of dating, see Appendix II.

Chapter 3

'The Art, Mystery and Manual Occupation' of Bookbinding

(Elizabethan Statute of Apprentices)

Nevertheless, Sir, there are some things more fit to be looked at than others; for instance, there is nothing more fit to be looked at than the outside of a book...It is, as I may say from repeated experience, a pure and unmixed pleasure to have a goodly volume lying before you, and to know that you...need not open it unless you please...There is no place, in which a man can move or sit, in which the outside of a book can be otherwise than an innocent and becoming spectacle.

Thomas Love Peacock, *Crochet Castle*

While we are dealing with format it will be appropriate to consider the binding. The Greeks, as ever, had a word for it — two words, in fact, literally meaning 'to fix a book', which, as a rough definition, is as good as any to describe the process of putting a protective cover round the printed sections. *Biblion* and *pegnunai* give us 'bibliopegy', which is the art of binding books, and 'bibliopegist', the student and lover of bindings.

The aspirant to such a designation, if he wishes to collect, has a number of courses open to him. If he is an oil sheik he can concentrate on books which have been bedizened with gold and silver, with diamonds, rubies, pearls and the whole galaxy of precious and semi-precious stones; with rich brocades, velvets, silks and laces, along with skins from ostriches, peacocks, reindeer, elephants and other denizens of field and forest.

There is the world of the bibliopegically curious which, full of charming conceits, can be expensive to journey in. The eighteenth century book-collector Clayton Mordaunt Cracherode had a father who travelled round the world in buckskin breeches. The dutiful son had a book bound in what one writer has called his 'circumnavigating unmentionables'. The third Duke of Roxburghe (1704-1804), a collector on the grand scale after whom the exclusive bibliophilic Roxburghe Club was named, had a number of tracts concerning Mary Tofts, who perturbed the

A typical Stuart embroidered binding, covering a copy of a 1628 Bible bound with a Book of Psalms, showing roses, cornflowers and strawberries, worked with silk and silver thread.

gynaecologists of her day by claiming to have given birth to a litter of rabbits. The Duke, with a grave sense of the appropriate, had the tracts bound in rabbit skin. Surviving adherents of the House of Stuart would doubtless like to acquire one of the books bound in Charles I's waistcoats. More of us would covet a Wordsworth volume bound in a piece of Dorothy's gown, green with white sprays on it. Students of our naval past may treasure those small books bound in wood salvaged from the *Mary Rose,* which heeled over and sank off Portsmouth in 1545; or brought up from the *Royal George* which, a tarnished monument to the neglect of the Admiralty, went down at Spithead in 1772 with nearly a thousand souls.

Such examples could be multiplied. But most of us would probably eschew the ostentatious and eccentric, and settle for an honest and straightforward run of bindings that have a plain tale to tell of their place and time.

The collector is at once confronted with a choice: shall he assemble his collection with only the binding in mind, or shall he pay regard to the contents of the book as well?

There is no doubt that, given patience and pertinacity, he can follow the first course at relatively small cost. It is, for example, some sort of commentary on our times that, if one is content to stick to theology, with some Greek and Latin texts thrown in, it is possible to assemble a representative collection from the sixteenth century onwards. The folios and quartos laboured on so industriously by forgotten clerics and divines, the erudite editions of minor classical writers, have long been gathering dust in countless book shops.

Even completeness is not essential to the dedicated bibliopegist. An odd volume, acquired for a few shillings, tells its story as adequately as a complete text. A copy with its title missing and lacking a plate or two is as eloquent, binding-wise, as its more perfect brother. It is significant that auction houses often sell an interesting example with the caveat 'as a binding, not subject to return', meaning that they do not guarantee the contents of the book which, in such cases, are of secondary importance.

In many imposing antique shops you will see stately bookcases full of attractive calf and vellum. Look closely and you will often find that this splendour is composed of odd volumes and unwanted subjects; but, as an enhancement to the bookcase, they are an invaluable aid to selling it. More shamefully, some owners of newly acquired imposing homes delight in 'libraries' which, seen in the gloom or at a distance, bestow a pretty glow of opulence and erudition but which, at close quarters, disintegrate into a heterogeneous muddle of worthless books, sometimes bought in bulk. I once saw a cellarful of pleasant bindings, all cleaned and polished, waiting shipment to America. It was binding as mere furniture that Burns had in mind when he wrote:

> Through and through the inspired leaves
> Ye maggots make your windings;
> But, oh! respect his lordship's taste,
> And spare his golden bindings.

We cannot escape some simple technicalities. When you take a book from the shelf, you probably lay your forefinger along the top edge or 'head', and either pull it straight out or tilt it down. Your finger is crooked over the 'headband' and your palm is cradling the 'spine', at the foot of which is the 'tailband'. Since about 1750, except in the most expensive and exclusive type of work, most head and tailbands have been purely decorative and functionally useless, used to give a respectable air of antiquity and good craftsmanship. Originally these bands were made of silk or cotton worked over cord, leather or vellum and fastened inside the spine. You will frequently see old headbands cracked or torn where ruthless fingers have hooked over them to wrench books from shelves. If you catch a guest doing this, do not invite him any more, unless it be to allow him to apologise.

Broadly speaking, there are two ways of putting a cover round a book.

The stitched sections can be held together by strips of muslin or canvas called 'mull' or sometimes 'scrim', with overlaps each side. The 'boards' or stiff covers,with the selected covering material, are made up separately. The printed book is then inserted into the case by machinery and attached to the boards by gluing down the mull overlaps, after which the endpapers are pasted down to hide them. If you glance inside the average modern book you will clearly see the mull or tape strips under this paste-down (as compared with the free endpaper). This is a 'cased' binding, which serves for the majority of modern editions. 'Case' can be used in other senses, e.g. in 'solander case', from its inventor Daniel Charles Solander (1736-82). When used in connection with books, the solander is a protective box with fall-down sides, often itself shaped like a book.

Experiments have been made with other ways of attaching the printed pages to the external case. One of the least fortunate was the 'gutta-percha' or 'caoutchouc' method, popular from about 1840-70, especially for illustrated table books. i.e. elaborately produced editions for display in the drawing room rather than reading. A rubber solution was substituted for sewing to hold the leaves together. Satisfactory for a time, this afterwards perished, with the result that it is now almost impossible to find an example where most, if not all, of the leaves are not loose in the binding. An early specimen was Lear's *Book of Nonsense* (1846).

A clever and decorative composition often mistaken for wood (especially ebony) was the rock-hard papier mâché used with great effect by publishers such as Longman in the 1840-60 period to give an impressive Gothic appearance. Good examples are *The Parables of Our Lord* (1847) and *The Miracles of Our Lord* (1848), both illustrated by Noel Humphreys, and the particularly fine *Record of the Black Prince* (1849), with its 6mm-thick carved covers, pierced to show a regal red lining beneath. Such books, usually splendidly 'illuminated' within, in the spirit and tradition of early handwritten manuscripts, cost about 21s. (105p) in their day. Thirty or forty times that would be a fair price today and they will undoubtedly continue to rise in the market. Owen Jones's *The Preacher* (1849) shows another experiment, the designs being burnt into wood covers.

Setting these and other tricks and experiments aside, we must turn to the second of the two chief methods of covering a book which, oddly enough, is by binding it. The reader may well ask what I have been talking about hitherto. The answer is that, properly speaking, the honourable word 'bound' should not be applied to a cased book, though it is admittedly in general use. Satisfactory though casing may be for books which a careless age does not expect to be long-lived, it cannot compare in craftsmanship and durability with the old method properly practised.

In a 'bound' book, the printed gatherings are sewn onto four or five

The Sentiments and Similies of William Shakespeare, *designed by H. Noel Humphreys (first edition 1851, second edition 1857). A papier mâché binding with terra cotta portrait medallion and crimson backing.*

horizontal cords, the ends of which pass through holes in the covering boards and are firmly glued. Here is the vital distinction: binding and printing are structurally one, not separate as in a cased book. All that remains is to wrap the covering material round and glue it down to the boards. It will follow that, unless they have been sunk into prepared grooves, the horizontal cords will stand out on the spine as pronounced ridges, and the leather or other covering will have to be moulded or 'nipped' over them. The result is the distinctive 'raised bands' of early books, the spaces between the bands often being referred to as compartments. One must add the necessary, and perhaps confusing, word of caution that many cased books appear to have raised bands. This is an amiable trick intended to deceive. They are phoney devices built up of strips of card or other material to give an appearance of genuine binding. Incidentally, if you see a catalogue description of 'antique' applied to a binding, it usually means exactly the opposite. The collector will know that it is faked up in the style of an earlier period.

I have already used the term 'boards' several times, and much will be seen and heard of them in book-collecting. In the fifteenth and sixteenth centuries covers were often boards in the true Anglo-Saxon sense, being of oak or beech covered with leather. If the paste-down is missing or adrift, you will experience the pleasant sight of wood looking clean and fresh from the plane that smoothed it four hundred years or more ago. Nowadays boards can means pasteboard, cardboard, strawboard or any other stiff material used in hard-covered books. I shall have something to say about original boards a little later.

In the sixteenth century and later there was much covering in limp parchment or vellum, the difference between the two being almost impossible to define accurately. That was the case in 1519 when William Horman, vice-provost of Eton, described the material as "that stouffe that we wryth upon: and is made of beestis skynnes; is somtyme called parchement, somtyme velem." It is fairly safe to say that 'vellum' is now usually reserved for the finer types. To make life difficult, 'Japanese' or 'Japon' vellum — beloved of producers of editions de luxe — is not vellum at all, but a smooth, glossy-surfaced paper with a yellowish tint. Another common early covering material was forel, an inferior off-white parchment. It has been described as roughly dressed deerskin, as used by certain monastic binders.

Early publishers often sent out books simply sewn, with no proper covers at all, or in a temporary binding, in the expectation that many of their customers would wish to have volumes bound in their individual preferred styles, perhaps to match the rest of their libraries. Examples of this exclusiveness are naturally highly prized and expensive. Mary Queen of Scots chose black morocco emblazoned with the royal lion of Scotland; the French statesman Jean Baptiste Colbert had his 50,000 books bound in a morocco specially imported by treaty with the Sultan of Morocco; one of the d'Urfe family opted for green velvet for his library of four thousand; Madame du Deffand, friend of Voltaire and Horace Walpole (to whom she left the care of her dog Tonton), endeavoured to immortalise her cat by using a gold stamp of it on the spines of her books; the three daughters of Louis V each had her own colour with the fleur-de-lis in the centre of each cover — Adelaide red, Victoire olive green and Sophie citron. A hundred other examples could be found.

A 'Grolier' binding is one of the greatest treasures a collector could wish for. Jean Grolier, Vicomte d'Aiguisy (1479-1565) was one of the greatest patrons of fine bindings the world has known. His library of three thousand volumes was dispersed in 1675 and the whereabouts of some 350 are known. His chief binder was Claude de Picques, who worked under Grolier's close supervision so that, amidst the intricate variety of decoration, a number of common features can be found. In particular, Grolier's books are famous for gilt stamps on the upper covers: sometimes

'Grolierii Lugdunensis et Amicorum' ('for Grolier of Lyons and his friends', Lugdunum being the Latin name, appearing in many publishers' imprints, for Lyons); sometimes just 'Io Grolierii et Amicorum' (for Grolier and his friends); and, almost always on the lower cover, a text from the Vulgate, Psalm cxli. 6, 'Portio mea Domine sit in Terra Viventium' (My portion, Lord, be in the land of the living). Even the munificient patronage of binders by Grolier was outclassed by that of his sovereign Henry II (1519-59). Described as 'cold, haughty, melancholy and dull', he at least came to life in the splendour of his books, some eight hundred of which are in the Bibliothèque Nationale in Paris.

Some of the most distinguished English binders in the seventeenth and eighteenth centuries were Samuel Mearne (working c.1660-83), in whose shop much work was done for Charles II; several unidentified craftsmen working for the two Queens — Catherine of Braganza and Mary of Modena — (known as Queens' Binder A, B, and C) and William Nott (who may have been Binder A), of whom Pepys wrote in 1669:

> W. Hewer and myself towards Westminster; and there he carried me to Nott's, the famous bookbinder, that bound for my Lord Chancellor's library: and there I did take occasion for curiosity to bespeak a book to be bound, only that I might have one of his binding.

The finest of them all was probably Roger Payne (1739-97), paradoxically an uneducated, hard-drinking workman, content to live in squalor, yet, over the years 1770-97, producing for such patrons as Lord Spencer work that influenced the craft not only in England but in France, whose binding had for so long been supreme. Payne cut his own tools from honeysuckle, acorns, vines and leaves and worked in a restrained manner on a red-brown calf impregnated with birch bark oil — a leather often known as 'russia'.

Contemporary with Payne was a famous Yorkshire family of father and sons who achieved fame in three fields. 'Edwards of Halifax' covers William (1723-1808) who founded the firm, c.1755, and his sons James, William, Thomas and Richard. Of the five, probably only William Snr. and Thomas were practical binders, the rest migrating to London and proving themselves good businessmen as booksellers, travelling widely and selling fine books, including the Halifax products. The particular bindings associated with Edwards are known as 'Etruscan', usually of calfskin and decorated with classical motifs from vases and other ornaments. Edwards produced his effects by burning the patterns into the leather with acid. The second specialisation was fore-edge paintings, the technique of which is described later in this chapter. The third, and perhaps the most celebrated, was the use of vellum, made transparent, so that delicate paintings could be placed underneath and remain protected. It has often been said that the family kept the process secret, but this seems unlikely, since it is known that pearl ash was used to secure the transparency. Though father William probably invented the technique, it was his son James who, in 1785, took out a patent for his ''new invention of Embellishing books bound in vellum, by making drawings on the vellum which are not liable to be defaced but by destroying the vellum itself.''

By the eighteenth century the older and rougher leathers had largely given way to finer products, often polished and patterned in a variety of ways, e.g. calf could be 'sprinkled' (speckled by acid in a regular pattern), 'mottled' (having an irregular all-over pattern, also produced by acid) or 'diced' (having a pattern of diamond squares). 'Half-calf' or 'half-bound' means that the spine and overlap of about an inch, together with the outer corners, are covered with calf, leaving the rest of the sides in cloth or paper, often attractively marbled. A book with only the spine covered is termed 'quarter calf', 'quarter morocco', etc. If the leather or vellum portions are unusually wide, the term 'three-quarters' may be used. One popular nineteenth century patterning was 'tree calf', a delicate arboreal effect being produced by the interaction of chemicals. Less lovable was 'divinity calf', which John Carter, with restrained distaste, called ''an unpleasant kind of smooth calf, usually of a colour between lavender and cocoa''; but, with its bevelled boards and red edges, it should have its place in a collection.

A case of appropriate bindings — marbled boards and a handwritten label for the Rough Minutes, polished calf and a morocco label for the finished Trustees Accounts.

Right: A handsome array in calf, morocco and vellum. The Iliad *and* Odyssey *are in niger morocco, a soft locally tanned skin from West Africa.* Eros and Psyche *is in pigskin.*

An elegant morocco binding, with the royal arms. The typical morocco patterning is clear.

A fine nineteenth century calf gilt binding. Such work was often 'signed' with the binder's ticket or, after about 1830, with the name stamped in very small letters on the inside edge of the front or back cover.

More esteemed than calf is 'morocco', always fashioned from goatskin. Whereas calf is smooth, without perceptible grain, morocco can vary considerably in texture. Devotees can explore the mysteries of 'hard grain', 'straight grain', 'levant', 'crushed', 'turkey', etc., but there is no space to elucidate them here (the glossary at the end of the book will help with many terms). A combination of calf and morocco is not uncommon, through 'inlaying' one with the other or by the use of morocco title and author labels on the spines of calf-bound books.

In the eighteenth and early nineteenth centuries it became the custom to bind a number of small books and, especially, pamphlets up together in calf or morocco, often suitably labelled on the spine. Sometimes time has decreed that certain books or pamphlets are of much greater importance that the others and some booksellers have an objectionable habit of dismembering the volumes and pricing the 'disbound' portions separately, to their financial advantage. In my opinion it is a practice to be resisted. If the binding is pleasant, what matters if there be curious friends and bedfellows within? Most of us are happy in mixed company. Then, too, the question of rebinding the extracted portion arises, when it emerges with its pathetic trails of thread and dabs of glue.

With leathers becoming increasingly expensive and the demand for books ever increasing, publishers looked for cheaper methods of production, especially for large editions. The answer came with 'cloth', introduced in the 1820s. The vital date was long held to be 1825, on a work published by Pickering; but other claims are being advanced, and some inexpensive fun may be had by searching booksellers' shelves in the endeavour to push the date back a little. A similar quest can be pursued for the first book with gilt lettering on the spine — generally accepted as being the third volume of a set of Byron published by Murray in 1832. The firm of Longman claims the first dust jacket, on Heath's *Keepsake* for 1835.[1] None of these dates or examples is sacrosanct.

Decorated and pictorial paper covers or 'wrappers' are another noteworthy feature of the nineteenth century, especially for popular authors. Much of Dickens was first published in monthly parts — often '20 in 19', the last number being a double one. Distinctive colours were used, green for Dickens, yellow for Thackeray. Cloth-bound editions were issued almost simultaneously and others in calf and morocco soon appeared. Fashion being what it is, with rarity the overriding factor, the position arises that the collector will have to pay very much more for the ephemeral, roughly produced parts, with their many inaccuracies and

---

1 The discovery of an example of this jacket would be a fine prize. Only one was known and that, in the words of a note from John Carter to Richard Cooper, former archivist to Longman, "was lost in Oxford years ago en route to the Bodleian with my publishers' cloth collection."

jumble of advertisements, than for the vastly more elegant and durable leather. It should be noted that, properly speaking, wrappers are quite different from jackets or dust wrappers, which are not part of the binding but simply an extraneous protection.

This fanatical regard for esteemed works as they were first given to the public leads to intimidating variations in price. A fine copy of *Pride and Prejudice* in original boards, uncut, and with paper labels, can take the buyer into four figures; a beautiful set in calf or morocco costing perhaps a tenth of that, and one in cloth considerably less still. The board-and-label copy of Marryat's *Mr. Midshipman Easy* illustrated earlier — admittedly with the added attraction of being Admiral Sir Thomas

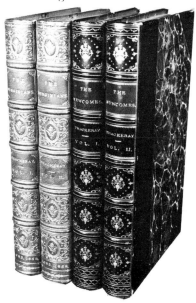

Thackeray's The Virginians *and* The Newcomes *handsomely bound in three-quarter morocco gilt and in half-calf gilt, in each case with marbled sides; impressive, but not worth nearly as much as the humble original parts in paper wrappers.*

A representative nineteenth century collection, with Thackeray in original wrappers at either end; Charles Reade, George MacDonald and John Stuart Mill in original cloth; and Tales of my Landlord *and* Walks in Oxford *in boards with paper labels.*

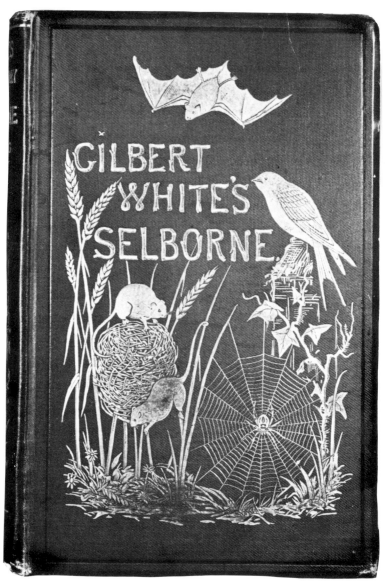

Gilbert White's Natural History and Antiquities of Selborne *(first edition 1789) in* elaborate cloth gilt, 1887.

Masterman Hardy's copy — cost the buyer some £165 recently. He could have found a much more durable and attractive later edition for £20-£30. First editions of Byron, Shelley, Keats, Hazlitt, Wordsworth, Carlyle, Tennyson, Lamb, the Brontës, Scott, George Eliot, Trollope, Jane Austen, Wilkie Collins, De Quincey, Coleridge, the Brownings, Meredith — all the nineteenth century novelists, essayists and poets, show, within different scales of popular esteem, the same sort of comparative values in their bindings. These criteria, sensible or not, apply almost exclusively to literary works.

Frightened off by such high figures, many collectors renounce the attempt to assemble a complete range of bindings over the centuries and, sensibly, turn to more limited fields; for example, to books stamped with the coats of arms or crests of early owners in gilt or 'blind' (without gold or colour). Often the bookseller or cataloguer has not bothered to identify the arms, so that a good deal of pleasure can be obtained from rectifying their indolence or ignorance. Schools and colleges, cathedrals and learned institutions, may all be found represented in this group. The lavish decoration of cloth with gilt and coloured pictures by the Victorians is receiving increasing attention. On Marryat's *The Pacha of Many Tales* (1835) you will find a splendid full-rigged ship of the line stamped in blind on dark blue; Septimus Piesse's holiday book for children *Chymical, Natural, and Physical Magic* (1865) has a white cloth cover printed in six colours and gold; an 1887 edition of *The Natural History and Antiquities of Selborne* has, in bright gilt on blue cloth, an owl, two bats, a snail, two mice, a swallow, a spider in its web and a variety of foliage, including ivy, fields grasses and cornstalks. A volume by Noel Humphreys on the art of illumination can boast at least ten colours on white leather blocked in gold. Colour-printed cover pictures of pets, harvest fields and American Indians vie with beefeaters, pious children and exotic birds. On one Jules Verne edition I have counted nearly forty different objects including a submarine, a balloon, a camera, an elephant, a variety of telescopes and other navigational instruments, a ship's wheel, enough spears to equip a Zulu regiment and sufficient chains to furnish a galleyful of slaves. If you want the whole rumbustious, arrogant, self-satisfied, smug, righteous, courageous, opinionated, dedicated, class-ridden, adventure-seeking, patriotic life of an era in full technicolour, you can do no better than collect Victorian bindings.

One mark of pride in this 'art, mystery and manual occupation' is the 'signed binding', i.e. one on which the binder has left his recognisable mark. In early books this often occurs in the form of a cipher, initials incorporated in the decoration, or even a name stamped in blind. It is sometimes obscure and the writer confesses with some shame that he possessed for some forty years a Tudor binding with the cunningly

vertical

A signed Tudor binding of blind-stamped leather over beech boards, showing heads in medallions. It is one of a group from an unidentified binder who incorporated his initials, R.B., in his cover decorations and has twice interwoven them here.

interwoven intials 'R.B.' — those of an unidentified London binder working c.1550-81. I discovered them almost by accident through the researches of J.B. Oldham,[2] who had traced over 160 examples of bindings from this workshop, which used various 'rolls' (tools having a continuous or repeated design round the edge of a wheel), including Tudor emblems, the falcon and the golden fleece, as well as the signed one — 'R.B.' with heads in medallions. It is curious that a much-employed binder, as he obviously was, should have left no trace in the records. Mrs. Mirjam Foot of the British Library (and currently Editor of the *British Library Journal*) who kindly looked into the problem for me, pointed out that while there were some stationers whose initials and dates fitted, such as Richard Baldwyn, who worked in London till 1590, there is no evidence of any one of them having been a bookbinder.

From about 1780-1820, binders' tickets were fairly widely used, i.e. printed or engraved slips pasted in the front of the book. A third method is for the binder to stamp his name (usually in minute letters) on the inside edge of a front or back cover, or sometimes on a fly leaf.

A collection of signed bindings can be a fine sight, but the collector must not expect to get away with it lightly. The most famous names (in addition to those already mentioned), Hering, Bedford (1799-1883), Rivière (1808-82) whose work included the binding of *Domesday Book,* Zaehnsdorf (1816-86) who specialised in restoration work, Sangorski and Sutcliffe founded in 1901 and binders of Elizabeth II's Coronation Bible, Douglas Cockerell (1870-1945) who served his apprenticeship with the Doves Press, and his master Cobden-Sanderson (1840-1922), will sometimes cost him dear. He must also be forewarned against misguided optimism (or calculated misrepresentation) on the part of the seller. Signed bindings by superb craftsmen deservedly command a higher figure than those less certainly identifiable, and some booksellers and auctioneers yield to the temptation of ascribing a binding on very slender evidence. It has even been known for an esteemed binder's ticket to be transferred from a battered volume to a more handsome specimen with which he had no demonstrable connection.

The moral is, deal with an expert who will lay his reputation on the line and back his opinion with a receipt. Never buy without close examination of the evidence, and treat with caution the auctioneer's 'sold as a binding, not subject to return', since in any case there is probably something unsatisfactory about the book and the doubt may extend to the attribution.

Of course, even a famous binder can have an off-day. There is on record a confession of Cobden-Sanderson's, who said of a failure to bind a

---

2 James Basil Oldham, *Blind Panels of English Binders* (1958), *English Blind-Stamped Bindings* (1952), and *Shrewsbury School Library Bindings* (1943).

copy of Tennyson's *In Memoriam* to his satisfaction: "I could spit upon the book, throw it out of the window, into the fire, upon the ground and grind it with my heel."

While we are dealing with the externals of the book it will be appropriate to finish with a note on the fore-edge, which is sometimes the object of special attention.

Interesting, though scarcely decorative, was an early custom of writing the author's name and title in ink on the fore-edge — a reminder of times

A watercolour of Cartmell Church (Co. Palatine of Lancaster) on the fore-edge of a 1660 Bible in a later dark blue morocco binding.

A romantic landscape on the fore-edge of an edition of Byron's Childe Harold's Pilgrimage, *18*

when spines carried no information and books were often put on shelves in a way we would consider back-to-front, with the fore-edge outwards.

Sometimes the fore-edge will be found 'gauffered' (gauffred or goffered), i.e. decorated by the impression of heated tools into the gilt. Our grandmothers used a goffering-iron for plaiting and crimping parts of their garments and aprons. On some early gauffered edges traces of colour will be discernible.

But by far the most attractive and skilful decoration of the fore-edge is in the form of 'fore-edge painting'. Though other, and earlier, examples are known, the term is normally employed for a typically English technique first evolved in the seventeenth century but not fully developed till the eighteenth and early nineteenth centuries. This special art involves slightly fanning out and cramping the fore-edge to give a firm surface, and then painting on it, in very dry watercolours, a landscape or conversation piece. The picture accomplished, the pages are restored to their normal position and the edge gilded. The fascinating result is that the painting is now completely invisible till the pages are fanned again. In the most intricate examples, the fore-edge is fanned both ways and a double picture is secured.

At their best, these exercises are remarkably skilful and attractive, and the collector must expect to pay appropriately, especially for authentic early examples. It must be said that, if the artist knew his, or her, job, it will be a bold man who can unhesitatingly distinguish between a fore-edge painting of 1780, 1880 or 1980, with their delicate muted effects. A number of nineteenth and early twentieth century publishers, in response to public demand, employed special artists in this field and made no pretence that they were anything but modern. Less honestly, there are some booksellers who have a little man round the corner who will always oblige with a 'contemporary' painting on the fore-edge of an 18th or early 19th century book. The writer was once with a small London bookseller who unblushingly pointed out a volume of Arctic travel which he was just about to despatch for the full treatment of glaciers, polar bears and seals.

It is a popular field of collecting, pleasant to behold and with a spice of magic about it. Remember, the paintings are invisible; and there is always the chance that one has remained undetected on the fore-edge of some travel book, bible, prayer book or collection of verse. The book is unlikely to be very valuable in itself, for owners are understandably chary of submitting precious items to such manoeuvres as splaying and clamping. It is always worth gently riffling the pages of a gilt-edged book when the bookseller is not looking; though the devious fellow has probably done it already.

❊❊❊❊❊❊❊❊❊❊❊❊❊❊❊❊❊

Chapter 4

The Illustrated Book

> While the plodding votary of meaning is anxiously inquiring
> out the sense...his fellow-worshipper, remembering that our
> eyes were not given us for nothing...roves, in gazing ecstasy
> from page to page, till here and there arrested by the choice
> vignette or richly tinctured plate.
>
> James Beresford, *Bibliosophia*

Illustrated books have a special appeal for many collectors, who are
fortunate in having a very wide field and a range of prices to suit almost
everyone.

The earliest form of printed book illustration was the woodcut, and the
art, with varying fortunes, has survived to the present day, so that the
collector has more than five centuries to survey and a range of skill, from
the superb work of Albrecht Dürer (1481-1504) to the charming
absurdities of the chapbook printers, who inserted the same cuts in
different publications with a reckless disregard for subject and
appropriateness. The early popularity of the woodcut may be judged by
the fact that, as early as 1493, the *Nuremberg Chronicle,* a history of the
world to 1492, contained 1,809 cuts — 645 different and 1,164 repeats.

Though the distinction is rarely noted (or perhaps known) there is a
difference between the woodcut and the wood-engraving. The first is cut
with a knife along the grain, the second on the cross-section with a burin.
Many illustrations described as woodcuts are not, strictly speaking,
woodcuts at all since, from about 1830, it became common to make
stereotypes and electrotypes from the original wood blocks, which would
stand up to only comparatively small editions. In such works as Bewick's,
it is possible to see the deterioration that has occurred from the use of
badly worn blocks. It takes a considerable expert to distinguish
impressions from good wood blocks and the metal blocks made from
them.

Great names along the trail include Albrecht Dürer, Hans Holbein,
Hans Lutzelburger, Jean Cousin, Bernard Salamon, Jean Michel
Papillon (who wrote a famous treatise on the art in 1766), Thomas
Bewick, William Blake, Thomas Stothard, the Dalziel Brothers and
Gustave Doré. Among the many modern practitioners are John Nash,

The fourth chapitre of the second book treteth of the ordre of chevalrye and knyghthode and of her offyces and maners capitulo   quarto

He knyght ought to be maad al armed upon an
t hors in suche wise that he haue an helme on his heed
and a spere in his right hond / & couerd with his shelde, a
swerd & a mace on his lyft syde ·clad with an hawberk &
plates tofore his breste ·legge harnoys on his legges· spo
res on his heelis ,on hys handes hys gauntelettes ·hys
hors wel broken & taught and apte to bataylle & coueryd
with his armes · whan the knyghtes ben maad they ben
bayned or bathed · That is the signe that they sholde lede

A woodcut illustration from Caxton's The Game and Play of the Chess Moralised,
c.1475.

65

de oceano adiecit. Qui tamé tanto nomine q̃ ſit paruus uides .
Nã licet apud nos athlãticum mare licet magnũ uocetur: de cæ
lo tamen diſpicientibus nõ poteſt magnũ uideri: cũ ad cælũ ter
ra ſignũ ſit & pũctũ: q̃d diuidi non poſſit í ptes. Ideo aũt terræ
breuitas tam diligéter aſſerit: ut paruipendédum ambitũ famæ

Woodcut zone map from Ambrosius Theodosius Macrobius's Somnium Scipionis ex
Ciceronis Libro de Republica Exerptum *(1483), the first printed map of the world on
which ocean currents are shown.*

red deer of Wolmer ever known to haunt the thickets or
glades of The Holt.[1]

At present the deer of The Holt are much thinned and

FALLOW DEER.

reduced by the night-hunters, who perpetually harass them
in spite of the efforts of numerous keepers, and the severe
penalties that have been put in force against them as often

---

[1] Mr. Bennett has pointed out that there could scarcely be two situations more dissimilar than The Holt and Wólmer Forest. The Holt is on the gault, and has all the richness of meadow and nobleness of oak wood that distinguish that formation. It consequently offered to the fallow deer, while they remained in it, plentiful grazing, abundance of browzing, and open and sheltered glades; advantages suited to the habits of that half domesticated race, introduced into this country by man, and still requiring at his hands care and protection. Wolmer Forest, on the lean and hungry sand, scarcely affords any grass, and has no high covert; and the red deer attached to it would have been limited for their provender almost exclusively to the lichens, the heath tops, and the twigs of the very few stunted bushes that occur here and there on its surface: retirement could only have been obtained for them by plunging into the unfrequented hollows interposed between its ridges. The more tender and exotic deer was placed, and it might have seemed almost naturally, in the richer and more sheltered forest of The Holt; the hardier and native race subsisted on the coarse fare of the dreary and cheerless waste of Wolmer.—ED.

A wood-engraved illustration 'in text'.

AND BEHOLD, THERE WAS A MAN NAMED JOSEPH, A COUNSELLOR;

A wood engraving by Eric Gill from The Four Gospels of Jesus Christ, *Golden Cockerel Press (1931).*

A double-page copper-plate engraving (much reduced) from one of the most famous books on horsemanship, the Duke of Newcastle's Methode et Invention nouvelle de dresser les Chevaux *(1658), translated as* A General System of Horsemanship *(1743).*

Paul Nash, Eric Gill, Stephen Gooden, Eric Ravilious, Reynolds Stone, Agnes Miller Parker, Blair Hughes-Stanton, Cecil Buller and John J.A. Murphy. These and many others have worked for private presses and in limited editions where fine illustrations are especially prized.

As ever, fashion and altered taste can be irrational, if not unfair. Despite all his brilliance as illustrator of Fielding, Milton, Richardson, Shakespeare, Spenser, Pope and the rest, there is now little demand for Stothard. Edward (1817-1905), George (1815-1902) and Thomas (1823-1906) Dalziel (there were in all seven brothers Dalziel), who were in the forefront of the revival of the woodcut after the temporary predominance of the steel engraving, may be bought cheaply in a profusion of books (if rather more expensively in Lear's *Book of Nonsense* and some of Lewis Carroll's classics). Gustave Doré (1882-83) has paid the penalty of producing too many books too large for modern taste. His Milton and Dante fetch pathetically small sums in comparison with the labour and skill they cost. The one book in constant demand is his *London. A Pilgrimage* (1872) which, with its vivid pictures of the life and people of the period, will make about £100.

Copper-plate engravings were first used for book illustration in England in 1540, when Richard Jonas published a translation of a

Wisdom and Activity collecting the various Treasures of the Vegetable Kingdom.

Published by Henry Fisher, Caxton, London 1822.

Fine engraved frontispiece by Sydenham Edwards to Green's Universal Herbal, *1823.*

German work on childbirth, and the first copper-plate title-page came five years later, with Thomas Gemini's *Compendiosa totius anatomie delineato.* The next two centuries saw an extensive use of this method of book illustration, but it was too costly and delicate for large editions. It proved a splendid medium for the copy books of the writing masters, such as George Bickham, whose best known book, *The Universal Penman,* is an expensive item. Occasionally whole books were copper-engraved, the most notable example, probably, being an edition of Horace by John Pine (1690-1756), which gave an effect of fine precision but was ruinously expensive, since the text was first typeset, then an impression on paper was transferred to copper, on which the engraver exercised his skill. Early music is often engraved throughout, the rectangular plate-marks being clearly visible.

Steel engraving followed the copper-plate in the 1820-30 period, an innovation which gave plates less susceptible to wear, but too often involved a loss of artistic merit. A plethora of books of topographical views at home and abroad used steel engravings, many of them of poor quality. They have enjoyed a vogue in recent years which they do not always merit and they now seem to be losing some of their popularity. Commenting on a considerable drop in sales at a book fair, one experienced bookman wrote about these travel books: "That such a range of books which I find boring beyond belief — I prefer to call them non-books — was due for a shake-out, appeared inevitable to me."

Collectors are naturally anxious to secure, if they can, the first examples of the various media used for illustration. While they are unlikely to be successful with the woodcut and the copper-plate, they may well achieve their ambition with some other processes. The first 'lithographed' book in England was Philip Andre's *Specimens of Polyautography* (1803), a collection of prints by Thomas Stothard (1755-1834) and others. The first 'relief half-tone' appeared in 1854 with a print by Paul Pretsch (who took out the patent in London) and de la Rue of 'The Scene in Gaeta after the Explosion.' The beginnings of 'photogravure' came in 1826 with the reproduction of a portrait of Cardinal D'Amboise by a photo-mechanical method.

The first published book using photographic illustrations was William Henry Fox Talbot's *The Pencil of Nature,* which appeared in six parts, 1844-46 and is an important landmark in that it was the first book in the world illustrated without the aid of an artist in pen, pencil or paint. Richard M. Cooper, former archivist of the house of Longman, who published the book, makes the point, however, that a small 'privately printed' pamphlet published a month or two before *The Pencil of Nature* contains a single photographic frontispiece "and therefore can perhaps take prior claim to be the first book in the world illustrated by

PLATE I

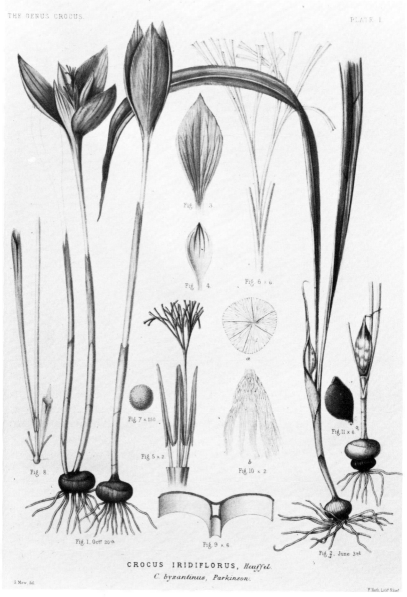

CROCUS IRIDIFLORUS, *Heuffel.*
C. byzantinus, Parkinson.

Lithographed plate from George Maw's A Monograph of the Genus Crocus *(1886), the drawings for which Ruskin described as 'most exquisite. . . and beyond criticism.' Lithography (stone printing, often using smooth limestone), was first used in England in 1803.*

photography, but it did not play the significantly influential part of *The Pencil of Nature* in establishing photographic illustration.'' In 1977 a single part of the work (Part 2, of six) made £3,400 at auction.

All these inventions and processes involve technical processes whose details have no place in a book of this compass. Those who wish to pursue the matter further can readily turn to specialist books or to such admirable general works as Geoffrey Ashall Glaisher's *Glossary of the Book* (first published 1960 and recently reissued).

Any account of English book illustration would be inadequate without a tribute to Edmund Evans (1826-1905) who brought to a wonderful peak of success the revival of the art of colour printing from wood blocks and gave us the delightful colour plate books of Kate Greenaway,[1] Richard E. Doyle, Randolph Caldecott and Walter Crane. Kate Greenaway has long been a firm favourite among collectors who will pay £2,000-£3,000 for a collection of her *Almanacks* and £30-£50 for most single specimens. Doyle's most popular book is *Fairyland* (1870) which, with its sixteen coloured plates — almost always loose — is likely to cost the collector about £50. Caldecott and Crane continue to rise steadily.

Sometimes in this chapter we have been talking about processes, sometimes about artists. They are separable; but in the end it is only when process and artists come together that the most memorable work is achieved: when Dürer and woodcut, Daniell and aquatint, Greenaway and colour printing meet in immortal partnership. Another unforgettable alliance is that between artist and author. Who can think of *Alice* without Tenniel, of Dickens without 'Phiz' (Hablot K. Browne), of A.A. Milne and Pooh without Ernest Shepard? Hugh Thompson and H.M. Brock are two others whose names are becoming increasingly linked with the authors they have illustrated so admirably, and their work will make a sound investment. Book illustration is a field marked by sharp increases in price over the last two decades. Arthur Rackham's *Peter Pan in Kensington Gardens* in the limited signed edition could be bought in 1960 for around £40-£50 and the *Peter Pan Portfolio* for about the same amount. Either is likely to cost £200-£300 now. Edmund Dulac (rising rapidly) now fetches £60-£100 for a good copy. In the 1960s £2-£3 would have been enough. Kay Nielson's *East of the Sun and West of the Moon* in the limited signed

---

1 Strangely enough, although a good deal of Kate Greenaway's success was due to Edmund Evans, whom she first met at his country home in 1877 with a number of illustrations she had made for her own verses, she apparently did not always think highly of his work. In an unpublished letter to Locker-Lampson in 1887, referring to the 1888 *Almanack,* she wrote: ''Mr. Evans has just sent the almanacks — so I send you one on — isn't it badly done. I really do think it's a shame.'' As a result of the 1877 visit, Evans printed 20,000 copies of *Under the Window* at 6s. (30p) and had the satisfaction of seeing the whole edition quickly sold out, despite the apprehensions of the publishers. Evans records that he found it so difficult to keep up supplies that booksellers were charging 10s. (50p) each for copies.

Calligraphic (from the Greek words for 'beauty' and 'writing') title-page of a famous work by Thomas Malton, illustrated by one hundred aquatint plates.

'Entry to Ramsgate Harbour.' Aquatint plate from Philip James Loutherbourg's Romantic and Picturesque Scenery of England and Wales *(1805).*

edition will take £300-£400 from your bank balance today. Twenty years ago, with your wits about you, you might have bought it for £5 or less. The unsigned edition fetched over £200 recently in a provincial sale. It goes without saying that any original drawing for an illustration by an esteemed artist (see frontispiece) is likely to fetch a large sum. A Heath Robinson drawing was recently offered for about £800.

Original watercolour by W. Heath Robinson (1872-1944), book illustrator whose work is rising rapidly in value.

'Falco Peregrinus.' Hand-coloured lithograph plate from John Gould's Birds of Great
Britain *(five volumes 1862-73). Generally considered the greatest of British bird illustrators,
Gould produced in all forty-one folio volumes illustrated by 2,999 plates.*

Some people find it difficult to distinguish between a 'plate' and other types of illustration. If engraving has been involved this is normally simple since, unless the book has been heavily cropped, the rectangular plate mark is visible as a slight indentation. But, as used generally, a plate is a whole page illustration, coloured or otherwise, printed separately from the text and usually on a different type of paper which lends itself to glossy reproduction. Other illustrations may be incorporated in the text and are often called 'cuts' or 'figures'. Catalogues will say, for example '40 coloured plates, other illus. in text', sufficiently distinguishing between the two types. Unless the 'cuts' are by a famous wood engraver such as Bewick, not much attention is paid to illustrations in the text; but there is enormous demand for certain types of 'plates'.

At the top of the list are botanical, ornithological and topographical books from the late eighteenth and early nineteenth centuries; and if you can find any important book from that era, especially if the plates are hand-coloured, for less than double figures, you have done very well. Some invariably go well into four figures. Even parts of series, e.g. Sir William Jardine's *Natural History of Humming Birds,* in two small volumes from the long series of The Naturalists' Library in forty volumes, can fetch £100 or over. The full set has over 1,300 hand-coloured plates and is now worth upwards of £1,000 in good condition.

John Gould's *Birds of Great Britain* in five large volumes, 1862-73, with every tiny iridescent feather almost as meticulously coloured as its Maker fashioned it, has reached some £14,000 and regularly fluctuates, according to condition, in the £6,000-£10,000 bracket. John Prideaux Selby's *Illustrations of British Ornithology* (two volumes 'elephant' folio, 1821-34) will now cost £3,000 or more. Of the most famous of all bird books, John James Audubon's *Birds of America* (1827-38), I will only say that you will need to sell some fifteen or sixteen of your collection of Shakespeare First Folios in order to buy it.

Of the topographical and travel works there is none finer or ranking higher than William Daniell and Richard Ayton's *A Voyage Round Great Britain,* eight volumes, 1814-15, with over three hundred superb coloured aquatint plates. Martin Hardie wrote: "Where all the plates are so excellent, it seems unfair to make distinctions, but where Daniell especially excels is in suggesting the warm haze that hangs over a summer sea, or sunlight playing on the roofs of a fishing village and the walls of its harbour." Anyone who has had the privilege of handling the book, even though he may never possess it, will not dispute the wisdom of the £13,000 it has fetched. It is often offered ('often' being something of an exaggeration) as '8 vols. in 4' instead of the original eight separate volumes.

The word 'aquatint' has begun to obtrude itself, and it is worth taking space and time for this particular form of illustration, because of its particular beauty and because fashion, in this case probably rightly, has elected it to the aristocracy, if not the crown royal, of the illustrated book world.

The aquatint, as a book illustration, was predominant in the period 1790-1830. A French scapegrace painter named Jean Baptiste Le Prince has been credited with its invention or at least its perfecting. The secret came, via the Hon. Charles Greville, into the hands of Paul Sandby (1725-1809) who, in 1775, published *Twelve Views in Aquatinta* and thus began a vogue that reached its artistic peak with such artists as Thomas Malton (1748-1804) and William Daniell (1769-1837), mentioned above.

A

VOYAGE

ROUND GREAT BRITAIN,

UNDERTAKEN IN THE SUMMER OF THE YEAR 1813,

AND COMMENCING FROM THE LAND'S-END, CORNWALL,

BY RICHARD AYTON.

WITH

A SERIES OF VIEWS,

Illustrative of the Character and Prominent Features of the Coast,

DRAWN AND ENGRAVED

BY WILLIAM DANIELL, A.R.A.

VOL. II.

LONDON:

PRINTED FOR LONGMAN, HURST, REES, ORME, AND BROWN, PATERNOSTER-ROW;
AND WILLIAM DANIELL, NO. 9, CLEVELAND-STREET, FITZROY-SQUARE.

1815.

Title-page of 'the greatest colour-plate book of all time' — Daniell and Ayton's A Voyage round Great Britain (1815).

'*Westerham Mill, Kent.' Aquatint plate from John Hassell's* Aqua Pictura *(1813).*

An aqua 'tint' is produced by acid biting into a copper plate. If the finished illustration is examined under a magnifying glass, the surface will appear as a mass of tiny rings, all linked but of varying size. Various methods have been tried for producing this 'ground'. Sandby seems to have covered the plate with a fluid consisting of resin dissolved in spirits of wine, a solution which, when dried out, leaves a granulated surface. A more common method was to use a whirling fan to cover the copper plate with fine resin dust. When the plate was heated and the resin brought to melting point, myriads of dust particles adhered, touching each other but with minute spaces between. When acid was applied these interstices, which were unprotected, were bitten into. If ink was then rolled on and the plate washed, the ink remained only in the tiny 'bitten' spaces, giving the finely granulated appearance of the finished aquatint already referred to.

The colouring of the prints throws up some great names, for it was an apprenticeship training undergone by artists of the calibre of Girtin and Turner. After two or three fairly neutral coloured inks had been used for the printing — say, brown for the foreground and blue for the sky and more distant scenery — the finishing was by hand, and washes of great subtlety and precision were laid on to give the desired effects. It could be monotonous work for an aspiring and impatient young painter and Thomas Girtin (1775-1802) for one rebelled against the repetitive work, with the result that his master Edward Dayes had him put in prison for breaking the terms of his indentures. Publishers such as Ackermann had to employ a considerable body of engravers and watercolourists to keep the work moving smoothly.

Rudolph Ackermann issued some fifty books with coloured plates, including the well-known *Repository of Arts, Literature, Commerce, Manufacture, and Politics,* which appeared monthly over a period of nearly twenty years. Even broken sets can fetch large sums, and a complete bound run is likely to cost the buyer anything up to £4,000, which would have gone a long way to paying Ackermann's army of workmen. Martin Hardie, in *English Coloured Books* (1906) has pointed out that Ackermann's *Microcosm of London* (1810) contains 104 plates and that a thousand copies were printed, thus involving, for this work alone, the meticulous hand-colouring of 104,000 separate plates. Ackermann was no soft taskmaster. It is worth quoting in full Hardie's graphic account of a typical day's work by one of the artists:

> Let us consider for a moment how one of Rowlandson's plates for this work would be produced. The artist was summoned to the Repository from his lodgings in James Street, in the Adelphi, and supplied with paper, reed pen, Indian ink, and some china saucers of watercolour. Thus equipped, he could

dash off two caricatures for publication within the day: but in the case of the coloured books he worked with greater care. With his rare certainty of style, he made a sketch, rapid but inimitable. This he etched in outline on a copper plate, and a print was immediately prepared for him on a piece of drawing-paper. Taking his Indian ink, he added to this outline the delicate tints that expressed the modelling of the figures, and the shadowing of interiors, architecture, or landscape. The copper plate was then handed to one of Ackermann's numerous staff of engravers — Bluck, Stadler, Havell, and the rest. When Rowlandson returned in the afternoon he would find the shadows all dexterously transferred to the plate by means of the aquatint. Taking a proof of this or his own shaded drawing, the artist completed it in those light washes of colour that are so peculiarly his own; and this tinted impression was handed as a copy to the trained staff of colourists, who, with years of practice under Ackermann's personal supervision, had attained superlative skill.

There were a number of special difficulties in the successful accomplishment of what was very delicate work and, all in all, the collector of aquatint books is getting full value for money, high though the price may be. Among the most prized of Ackermann's books are his histories of the Universities of Oxford and Cambridge and of various famous public schools, his *Picturesque Tours* in England and many foreign countries, and his illustrations of costume and architecture.

Staying, for the moment, with coloured illustrations, an interesting collection could be made of so-called 'nature printing', which had a short life in the nineteenth century. The technique was used to obtain exact representations of botanical and natural history specimens (and even of textiles) from the objects and materials themselves. These were subjected to such heavy pressure on a soft metal plate such as lead, that an image was left with the delicate detail of the original. Colours were then applied and copies taken off. This is to describe the process in the most rudimentary way. The details were such that Austria and England were nearly involved in war over the matter. Alois Auer, Director of the Government Printing Office in Vienna, had published a pamphlet, *The Discovery of the Natural Printing Process,* in 1853, and this was immediately translated into a number of different languages. Commercial rivalry was involved and the wish to better the lithographed lace sample books circulated by the trade in England. Auer did, in fact, produce such fine raised patterns that Austrian government representatives found the resemblance so close "that they took them to be real lace, until, by touching and closely examining them, they convinced themselves that they were the production of the printing press''. Auer went on to produce other types of impressions, including some remarkable oak leaves and, in 1852, took out a patent for his *Naturselbstdruck* or natural self-acting printing method.

At this point an Englishman, Henry Bradbury (1831-60) put a cat among the pigeons. He had himself studied nature printing in Vienna and was intent on proving that Austria had no claim to exclusive rights. He pointed to experiments in the process two and a half centuries before (and could, in fact, have gone back to the fifteenth century). Bradbury delivered a lecture to the Royal Institution of Great Britain on *Nature-Printing: its Origin and Objects* and published it in 1856. Before that, in 1854, Bradbury and Evans had published a series of twenty-one plates with the title *A few leaves from the Newly-Invented Process of Nature-Printing.* The in-fighting was considerable and not all the fault was on Auer's side. When Bradbury died before the age of thirty, most of the interest in the process seems to have perished with him. He accomplished fifty-one large folio plates for Moore and Lindley's *The Ferns of Great Britain and Ireland* (1855), the first English book so illustrated, and two hundred plates for the four-volume *Nature-printed British Sea-Weeds* (1859). As with Auer's lace, the verisimilitude was striking and *The Times* reported that touch alone could convince the beholder that the minutely detailed weeds with their infinitely varied tints were not actual specimens from the sea shore.[2]

Nature printing is a very good example of a field of collecting in which the serious student can come to command a knowledge and expertise that the general bookseller is unlikely to match. Nevertheless, the well-known examples will probably be costly. The *Sea-Weeds* (text by William Gorstart Johnstone and Alexander Croall) is likely to make £200-£300; and a copy of the *Ferns,* with one of the original copper plates showing the plants in high relief, made £450 in 1978.

A special category of illustrated book is the 'extra-illustrated' or, 'grangerised' work, so called after James Granger (1723-76) who, in 1769-74, published a five volume *Biographical History of England* with blank leaves for the purchaser to add additional illustrative material — portraits, facsimiles, plans, topographical scenes, even original letters and documents. Sometimes such material is simply tipped-in or stuck down on a blank; the professional may prefer to inlay it on paper to match the size of the volume, which will often be fairly large. If the extra illustrations are copious enough, the whole will need rebinding. The description 'extended' can be used to describe a two- or three-volume work which has

---

2 There were, in fact, such publications. *Treasures of the Deep: or, Specimens of Scottish Sea-Weeds* (Glasgow, 1847) contained forty-six beautifully mounted 'actual specimens', mainly from the Ayrshire coast.

been enlarged to eight or ten volumes by the accumulation of extra illustration.

Biographies are frequent subjects for this type of exercise, a period of history or a topographical work. A famous example is housed in the Bodleian: Clarendon's *History of the Rebellion* and Burnet's *History of his Own Time* expanded to fifty-seven volumes, with four additional volumes of outsize plates. A copy of Dibdin's *Bibliographical Decameron* (1817) is recorded with 1,500 extra illustrations. Some sixty years ago a copy of Lady Dilke's *French Illustrated Books,* extended to fifty-eight volumes, with nearly 10,000 additional illustrations, was offered for sale at £2,000. A bookseller named James Gibb extended his Bible to more than sixty folio volumes, each so heavy that it could be lifted only with difficulty.

Well done, extra-illustration can be a valuable achievement and a source of enjoyment to the collector for many years. Discredit occurs only when an otherwise amiable pastime is perverted by the destruction of many books to glorify one. Unhappily, too, extended works which have taken much love and toil to compile can be a quarry for the despoiler, who will ruthlessly remove for separate sale topographical prints, autograph letters, etc., which have much increased in value since the extra-illustration was carried out. When buying extended works, the collector should make sure that they have not been the subject of depredations of this nature.

"Pretty things," wrote Sawyer and Darton of illustrated books in general, "pleasant to fondle, more ready to display to a bibliophile those tiny points of an exquisite technique over which it is legitimate to gloat...the spot of ink adjusted on a Corinthian's cheek to a thousandth of an inch, or a black line so thin and firm that you can almost see the metal caressing it on to the honest untimbered white paper."

Chapter 5

Private Press
and Press Books

> I hope it will not seem chauvinistic to claim that the modern
> movement for the betterment of printing was, in its inception,
> an English one. The best books of today do not look in the
> least like Kelmscotts, but without Morris they might never
> have been created at all.
>
> Alan G. Thomas, *Great Books and Book Collectors*

Among the many different groups of collectors is a fastidious band who
are content only with the finer, more exclusive (and in some cases, more
quirky) examples of the printer's art in the shape of so-called 'press
books'. Though the term is commonly used as an umbrella to cover all
types, we should properly attempt a distinction. To be accurate, 'private
press' should be applied only to a press where the owner's or operator's
chief objective is to print a fine book, without being at the mercy of a
publisher's instructions and a first necessity to show a profit, even though
he may sell his wares through commercial channels.

In other words, and in this case Eric Gill's, "a private press prints
solely what it chooses to print." It was Gill's opinion, not shared by
everybody, that "the distinction has nothing to do with the use of
machinery or with questions of the artistic quality of the product". John
Carter, on the other hand, concluded that "as generally understood, the
term private press would be applied only to a shop where the work was
hand-set and hand-printed". In either case, though not invariably,
editions are limited to modest, and sometimes very small, numbers.

There have been a number of attempts at detailed classification, some
very involved and certainly not avoiding a great deal of overlapping of the
categories. There are presses which are strictly private in the Carter sense,
operating in anything from a back kitchen to a fully equipped shop,
perhaps content simply to joy in the smell of printer's ink and the magic of
creation, without aiming to sell a single book; publishing firms calling
themselves presses who rightly pride themselves on the high quality of
their output; commercial printers who are equally jealous of the standard
of their press work; teaching establishments attached to universities,
colleges and schools for experimental and training purposes; official

presses, controlled by governmental or other agencies; fugitive and clandestine presses, often short-lived and hazardously operated, because of an adverse political or religious climate, or because their owners are dodging copyright laws; and there is a hotch-potch of firms who pretentiously arrogate to themselves the word 'press', to which they have little or no right in terms of either fine printing or independence.

Though there are many earlier examples,[1] both in this country and abroad, the private press movement in England is very largely a feature of the late nineteenth and twentieth centuries, with William Morris as its

---

1 For a particularly useful list see Bohn's four-volume edition of Lowndes's *Bibliographer's Manual,* which devotes over fifty pages to them at the end of Vol. IV.

THE

UNIVERSAL HERBAL;

OR,

BOTANICAL, MEDICAL, AND AGRICULTURAL

DICTIONARY.

CONTAINING AN ACCOUNT OF

All the known Plants in the World,

ARRANGED ACCORDING TO THE LINNEAN SYSTEM.

SPECIFYING THE

USES TO WHICH THEY ARE OR MAY BE APPLIED, WHETHER AS FOOD, AS MEDICINE, OR IN THE ARTS AND MANUFACTURES.

WITH THE BEST

METHODS OF PROPAGATION,

AND THE

MOST RECENT AGRICULTURAL IMPROVEMENTS.

Collected from indisputable Authorities.

ADAPTED TO THE USE OF

THE FARMER—THE GARDENER—THE HUSBANDMAN—THE BOTANIST—THE FLORIST— AND COUNTRY HOUSEKEEPERS IN GENERAL.

BY THOMAS GREEN.

THE SECOND EDITION, REVISED AND IMPROVED.

VOL. II.

LONDON:

PRINTED AT THE CAXTON PRESS, BY HENRY FISHER,
Printer in Ordinary to His Majesty.
PUBLISHED AT 38, NEWGATE-STREET; AND SOLD BY ALL BOOKSELLERS.

A Caxton Press title-page of 1823, from the printer-in-ordinary to George IV.

most magnificent pioneer at the Kelmscott Press. Through all his work as artist, printer, writer and craftsman comes the breath of another age, a quality felt by all who knew him. The portrait painter William Richmond wrote:

> He was the manliest fellow that ever tried to pull an effete society together. He had the roughness and strength of a Norseman together with the tenderness, nay, even shyness, of a woman; a great, big, generous character...

and the poet W.B. Yeats recalled:

> The broad vigorous body suggests a mind that has no need of the intellect to remain sane, though it gives itself to every fantasy...A never idle man of great physical strength and extremely irascible — did he not fling a badly-baked plum pudding through a window upon Christmas Day? — a man more joyous than any intellectual man of our world...

Though his press lasted only eight years, it gave an impetus to later fine work which it is difficult to overestimate. With Emery Walker he turned back to the Roman types of four hundred years before and to the beauty of woodcut title-pages. Much of the work was based, not on the single, but on the double page as the right unit for design.

Of the more than fifty books to come from the press, there is no doubt that the finest was his Chaucer of 1896, reckoned by many to be the greatest book printed in England since Caxton, of which he printed 425 copies with an additional thirteen on vellum. It contained eighty-seven woodcut illustrations after Edward Burne-Jones and woodcut borders and initials by Morris himself. For a great book by a great man, in the original holland-backed boards, collectors do not begrudge £3,000-£4,000, according to condition. A vellum copy will necessitate consultation with a bank manager.

While we are with the greatest works of the period, mention must be made of a work of comparable distinction, the Doves Press edition of the Bible (five volumes, 1903-5), described by Colin Clair as "in its magnificent simplicity one of the noblest books ever produced in this country". This miraculous work was achieved on one hand press by a single compositor, J.H. Mason, who went on to become head of the London School of Printing. Despite its beauty, many would think superior to Morris in its majesty, it may well cost the collector less than a third of the price of the Kelmscott Chaucer.

But not many will be able to move in this rarefied atmosphere and, mercifully, there are lower strata in which to breathe and have one's being. The press and private press world is a wide, and sometimes wild, one showing a great diversity of taste, standard and price. Products range from the truly estimable and inspired to the merely pretty and, sometimes, meretricious. The ordinary collector should not, I feel,

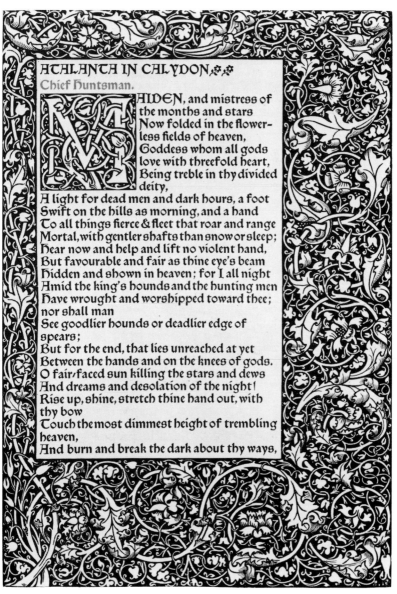

ATALANTA IN CALYDON.❧❧
Chief Huntsman.

MAIDEN, and mistress of
the months and stars
Now folded in the flower-
less fields of heaven,
Goddess whom all gods
love with threefold heart,
Being treble in thy divided
deity,
A light for dead men and dark hours, a foot
Swift on the hills as morning, and a hand
To all things fierce & fleet that roar and range
Mortal, with gentler shafts than snow or sleep;
Hear now and help and lift no violent hand,
But favourable and fair as thine eye's beam
Hidden and shown in heaven; for I all night
Amid the king's hounds and the hunting men
Have wrought and worshipped toward thee;
nor shall man
See goodlier hounds or deadlier edge of
spears;
But for the end, that lies unreached at yet
Between the hands and on the knees of gods.
O fair-faced sun killing the stars and dews
And dreams and desolation of the night!
Rise up, shine, stretch thine hand out, with
thy bow
Touch the most dimmest height of trembling
heaven,
And burn and break the dark about thy ways,

A typical Kelmscott Press page from William Morris's edition of Swinburne's Atalanta in Calydon *(1894). The type is Morris's Chaucer, as used in the masterpiece.*

concern himself overmuch with subtle distinctions between altruism and commercialism, teaching and doing, hand and machine setting, very limited and less limited editions. Exclusiveness can be pretentiousness; amateur status can sometimes be an excuse for shoddiness and inefficiency; addiction to antiquity can result in obscurity and a tedious nostalgia.

Whatever their character, there is one curious feature shared by most private press books, which is that they are very rarely read — a fact testified to by the fact that an extraordinary number are found unopened, as though their charm and beauty may not be defiled even by the gentlest slitting of the sacred sections at the top and fore-edges. I think I have read somewhere a bookseller's comment that it would be fair to describe an 'opened' private press book as 'rare in this state'. Be that as it may, these books are certainly easier to find in fine condition than almost any other kind, even after fifty or sixty years.

There is, however, one category to which this does not apply. I refer to the type of work produced by the fugitive and clandestine presses which, in their nature, usually had a ready and eager public not too scrupulous in its handling of reading matter. Rather, if found at all, such work is likely to be roughly handled and very much read.

The story of some of these presses is a fascinating one to follow, as the printers surreptitiously pull off their pamphlets and broadsides in some kitchen or remote country house, load up and press on to the next location, with an eye ever over their shoulder for the pursuers. None is more famous than the so-called Marprelate Press which, in the hands of a group of bigoted Puritans, launched a series of scurrilous attacks, from about 1580-90, on Archbishop Whitgift and the bench of bishops. Izaac Walton said "these were grown into high esteem with the common people" who, as always, dearly loved anyone and anything tilting at their lords and masters, spiritual or secular.

The prime mover was Robert Waldegrave, son of a Worcestershire yeoman, who, having served an eight-year apprenticeship, set up his own press and was soon in trouble. In 1588 his press was seized and much of his type defaced. With the remnants he escaped to East Molesey and began again. He reappeared at Fawsley, near Daventry, at Coventry and at Wolston Priory, after which he fled to La Rochelle, leaving others to carry on. His career had an extraordinary culmination when he eventually turned up in Scotland and was appointed Royal Printer to James VI, afterwards James I of England.

But, apart from such celebrated examples, the private press movement really belongs to the late nineteenth and twentieth centuries, as the following selection of some of the best-known will show. I have not attempted to distinguish between 'presses' and 'private presses'.

Name	Founder	Dates	Output and notable books	Special features, etc.
MARPRELATE East Molesey, Fawsley, Coventry, etc.	Robert Waldegrave (till 1590), then others	c.1580 onwards	*Marprelate Tracts* (clandestine Puritan tracts)	Waldegrave twice imprisoned. Later Royal Printer to James VI
STRAWBERRY HILL Twickenham	Horace Walpole	1757-1797	First book, *Odes by Mr. Gray* (1757)	Type from Thos. Caslon
CHISWICK High House and College House, Chiswick Mall	Charles Wittingham senior, then junior (from 1840)	1810-1962	Series of Aldine Poets. Books of Common Prayer, *Diary of Lady Willoughby* (1844)	Fine typography and press work. Whittingham junior printed for William Pickering
LEE PRIORY Ickham, nr. Canterbury	Sir Samuel Egerton Brydges	1813-1822	Over fifty texts and small publications in 'leaves'	Limited editions of rare Elizabethan texts, copy supplied by Brydges
DANIEL Frome and Oxford	Rev. C.H.O. Daniel (with help of family)	1845 (Frome) 1876 onwards at Oxford	Some fifty-eight books, mainly for private distribution	Revived Fell type, first cut c.1672. Press still used for instruction at Bodleian Library
KELMSCOTT Hammersmith Upper Mall	William Morris and Emery Walker	1891-1899	Masterpiece Chaucer (1896) 425 copies plus thirteen on vellum	Revived old methods on hand-presses. Designed Golden, Troy and Chaucer types

continued

Name	Founder	Dates	Output and notable books	Special features, etc.
ASHENDENE Ashendene, Herts., and Chelsea	C.H. St. John Hornby	1894-1935	Editions of Dante (1902-5), Don Quixote (1928)	Types close to incunabula, bold with wide margins, initials in gold, red and blue
VALE Warwick St. and Craven St., London	Charles de Sousy Ricketts	1898-1904	Produced eighty-three books	Fine editions of English classics. Many wood-engravings by Ricketts. Light and graceful productions
ERAGNY Hammersmith	Lucien Pissaro (with wife Esther)	1894-1914	Issued thirty-two books. First book *Queen of the Fishes* (1894)	Coloured wood-engraved illustrations. Designed Brook type and others
ESSEX HOUSE Mile End Rd., London, and Chipping Camden	Charles Robert Ashbee	1898-1910 1899 from Chipping Camden	Issued some ninety books	Endeavoured to carry on Kelmscott traditions and bought some of its presses. Coloured titles and initials. Bindery attached to premises
DOVES Hammersmith	Thomas James Cobden-Sanderson and Emery Walker	1900-1916	Masterpiece five-volume Bible (1903-5)	Redrew 1476 Jansen type. Hand-painted initials, etc., by famous artists, including Edward Johnston and Graily Hewitt. Had own bindery

Name	Founder	Dates	Output and notable books	Special features, etc.
CUALA (until 1908 known as Dun Emer)	Elizabeth C. Yeats, sister of W.B. Yeats	1902-	Irish literature	According to W.B. Yeats, products were like an old family magazine. "A few hundred people buy them all."
SHAKESPEARE HEAD Stratford-on-Avon, and Oxford	Arthur Henry Bullen	1904 (1929 from Oxford)	Ten-volume series of *Stratford Town Shakespeare*	Aimed to print Shakespeare in his own town, with other works of period. Taken over by Blackwell of Oxford in 1929
RICCARDI	Herbert P. Horne	1909-	Publications of Medici Society	Printing done by Chiswick Press. Designed Riccardi and Florence types
ST. DOMINIC'S (afterwards DITCHLING), Ditchling	Hilary D.C. Pepler and Eric Gill	1915-1937	*Book of Hours* (1923), illustrated by Eric Gill	Centre of experimental printing. Notable wood-engraving
GOLDEN COCKEREL Waltham St. Lawrence, Berks.	Harold Midgely Taylor, Robert Gibbings (from 1924)	1920-	Books illustrations by Gill, Gibbings, Nash Bros., etc.	Fine books at modest prices. Press acquired 1933 by Christopher Sandford, but books no longer hand-printed

continued

Name	Founder	Dates	Output and notable books	Special features, etc.
GREGYNOG Newtown, Montgom.	Gwendolyn and Margaret Davies	1922-1940	Forty-two books published. First Herbert's *Poems*	Established to revive craftsmanship in Wales. Wood-engraving a strong feature. Managed by a series of distinguished 'Controllers'
NONESUCH Bloomsbury	Francis Meynell, Vera Mendel	1923 Restarted 1953	Nonesuch Bible, five volumes (1924-27)	"Significance of subject, beauty of format and moderation of price." Nearly all books machine-set, but to exacting standards, by various printers
DROPMORE London	Lord Kemsley	1945-c.1956	Wilson's Royal Philatelic Collection (1952), Holkham Bible Picture Book (1954)	Experimental work. Fine books of conspicuous literary merit

Collectors are recommended to study closely the books and prices in any sale especially devoted to the works from this selection of presses as well as from other presses, particularly if sound investment is a consideration. While there are inevitable deviations and eccentricities, such a survey is likely to give a fair indication of:

1 The reputation of one press compared with others. While fashion may play a small part, the overall picture will probably be a very sound reflection of the varying standards of craftsmanship and of the final judgement of shrewd buyers.

2 The difference in value, at one press, between its various books. This will depend partly on such factors as limitation of numbers, the nature of the binding and the standing of the illustrators; and partly on the fact that, with many presses, all the magic of the crafts, predictably or unpredictably, comes together in certain books and they produce masterpieces, minor or major.

3 The esteem in which certain authors and works are held.

4 The difference a particular artist can make.

5 The importance of format and condition, with even such small matters as the presence or absence of silk ties affecting the value.

Thus, a modest survey for the purposes of this chapter, of twelve presses from the foregoing list (Kelmscott, Doves, Ashendene, Essex House, Eragny, Vale, Shakespeare Head, Riccardi, St. Dominic's, Nonesuch, Golden Cockerel and Gregynog) featured in a recent fairly important sale, threw up the following facts:

In the price range £100-£1,000, no less than twenty-one of the twenty-two highest prices were paid for the products of six presses — Kelmscott (5), Doves (6), Ashendene (3), Golden Cockerel (2), Shakespeare Head (2) and Gregynog (3). Far ahead of the rest was a Doves Press Bible at £900, the next price being nearly £400 less. A Kelmscott Chaucer with an estimate of £4,000-£5,000 either did not reach its reserve or was withdrawn. The two-volume Doves Press edition of *Paradise Lost* and *Paradise Regained* with capitals by Edward Johnston and Graily Hewitt was also unsold, against an estimate of £300-£400.

The falsity of the impression that all private press books are expensive is demonstrated by the fact that fourteen examples from the Essex House (3), Vale (1), Shakespeare Head (1), Riccardi (1), Nonesuch (3), Golden Cockerel (4) and Gregynog (1) presses fell in the price range £18-£40, and the uniformity of some of the prices suggests that only protective reserves pushed them as high as that. The average price of these was a little over £26.

Surprisingly, perhaps, in an irreligious age, nearly a third of the highest prices were for works associated with the Bible, showing that, if the conclusion is not too naïve, respect and affection for it is still deeply ingrained and that, at least in fine editions, it is still a best-seller.

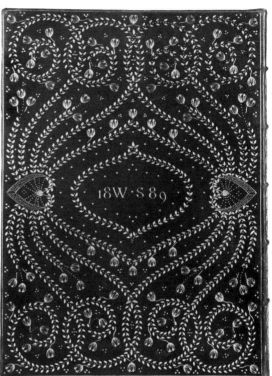

Cobden-Sanderson, co-founder of the Doves Press, was a celebrated binder as well as printer. This binding, executed in 1889, sold for £900 several years ago. Note the raised bands, spine in compartments, and gauffered fore-edge.

Old friends and established reputations still command the money — Shakespeare, Caxton, Milton, Swift, Keats, Swinburne and the rest. Modern writers and newcomers are not so much at home in the world of the major private presses.

Finally, in this small sample, a note might be made of the £520 paid for the *Descriptive Bibliography of the Books Printed at the Ashendene Press 1895-1935*, published in an edition of 390 copies signed by C.H. St. J. Hornby. All such bibliographies — and most reputable private presses have issued them — are of considerable value as sources of reference for booksellers and collectors and are paid for accordingly.

As for the modern scene, the collector can wander happily in a wonderland inhabited by presses with such names as the Cracked Bell, Happy Dragons, Shoestring, Ten Fingers, Apple Barrell, Vanishing and Toothpaste. He may meet the Pegacycle Lady or the Poltroon, rest beneath the Lilac Tree or in the Crabgrass. The ornithologically-minded will be well content because, for some reason unknown to me, birds figure very largely in the names of present-day presses, among them the Cygnet, Four Ducks, Night Owl, Tern, Waddling Duck, Heron and Whippoorwill.

The most recent list of private press books I have seen (for the year 1975, published by the Private Libraries Association, Pinner, in 1978) cited nearly three hundred publications from some 125 presses, at home and abroad. In this survey, I have elected to concentrate on English presses, in the belief that it is they that will be largely sought by English collectors; but I am much aware of the many fine examples in other

Title-page of a pirate press edition of an article by Max Beerbohm (no place or printer) on japan vellum; with, below, part of a letter from Beerbohm (1924) protesting at the piracy and endeavouring to find who was responsible.

THE DISCOVERIE
of the large and bewtiful Empire of
GUIANA

BY

SIR WALTER RALEGH

Edited
from the Original Text,
with *Introduction, Notes* and *Appendixes*
of hitherto unpublished
documents

BY

V. T. HARLOW, M.A., B. LITT.

Author of
*Colonising Expeditions to
the West Indies and Guiana,* 1924
A History of Barbados, 1926
etc,, etc.

1928

THE ARGONAUT PRESS
LONDON

An important function of the private presses has been to reprint rare works of historical and literary importance. The Argonaut Press printed 975 copies on japan vellum of this work of Sir Walter Ralegh's.

countries, not least in America, where such names as Bruce Rogers of the Riverside Press, Cambridge, Mass., Frederic Goudy of the Village Press, Park Ridge, Illinois (and later Marlborough, New York) and Daniel Berkeley Updike, who set up the Merrymount Press, will always be honoured. The last-named's *Printing Types: their History, Forms and Use* will be remembered long after many presses are forgotten.

Edwin and Robert Grabhorn, who founded the Grabhorn Press in San Francisco in 1920, worked so amicably together that it was said of them: "When Ed's away the shop goes to pieces; when Bob's away, Ed goes to pieces"; but it would be a mistake to think that relationships between printers were always so harmonious.

Cobden-Sanderson quarrelled with Emery Walker and, through the mediation of Sydney Cockerell, came to an agreement that Cobden-Sanderson should retain the Doves type for his lifetime, after which it should pass to the younger man. This promise he deliberately and ruthlessly broke, going out night after night in 1917 and hurling his load, punches, matrices and type, into the Thames from Hammersmith Bridge,[2] on one occasion missing a barge by inches.

This jealous guarding of types is not uncommon. Ricketts, too, pitched his types into the Thames when the Vale Press closed in 1904; and, fortunately for the river which, as Alan Thomas observed, must have been pretty well clogged with type, Lucien Pissarro chose the English Channel for the Eragny equipment.

But, whatever their idiosyncrasies and complexities, this highly individual body of printers served the book well and, if they sometimes failed in their human relationships, achieved in print a beauty and harmony that have been of inestimable benefit to us all.

For a comprehensive account on the subject of private press and press books, the collector is referred to such books as Roderick Cave, *The Private Press* (1971).

---

2 That this was no impulsive gesture may be seen from the last book to come from the Doves Press, the *Catalogue Raisonné* of 1916, in which he foretold exactly what he intended, so that the equipment of his press should be 'untouched of other use'.

Chapter 6

The Cult of the First Edition

Take care not to understand editions and title-pages too well.
It always smells of pedantry, and not always of learning.
> Lord Chesterfield, *Letters to his Son*

"Why do you collect first editions? I mean, isn't the print the
same in the second or third or fiftieth edition?"
   "Well, yes, but..."
   "Well why then?" Relentless.
   "It's difficult to explain..."
   "I see..." He does not see.
> Joseph Connolly, *Collecting Modern First Editions* (1977)

Two questions that are frequently asked are: how can one tell a first
edition? and why bother with it anyway?

The first, though the answer may sometimes be complicated, is much
more easy to deal with than the second, because in one case one is dealing
with fact and in the other with personal preference and feeling, which are
unpredictable and difficult to justify to the determinedly sceptical.

We can at least begin with a straightforward and incontrovertible
definition. An 'edition' of a book is the whole number of copies printed
from the same setting of type. After that, life becomes more complicated,
and perhaps I can best illustrate some of the points involved by taking a
number of books from my own bibliographical collection listed on the
following three pages:

This looks a fairly chaotic sort of table and one indicative of the
problems posed for the uninitiated in the matter of editions and the like.
But it is not as bad as it seems, and it is fairly typical for any dozen books
selected at random.

One facile answer I have heard, or read, to the question: How do you
tell a first edition? is: When there is no evidence that it is anything else.
There is, in fact, a basic stratum of truth in it; but there are so many
exceptions that the collector who took the dictum as gospel would make
many blunders and lose a great deal of money. It may be of some comfort
to read some words written recently by Gaby Goldscheider, an
experienced antiquarian bookseller, in the *Antiquarian Book Monthly:*

Book	Date or other information on title-page	Information on verso (back) of title	Other information
1 Plomer, *A Short History of English Printing*	1900	None	Preface undated
2 Partington, *Thomas J. Wise in the Original Cloth*	None	Copyright 1946	Preface dated 1945
3 Munby, *Portrait of an Obsession*	None	Copyright 1946 First published 1967	Preface dated 1967
4 Munby, *The Cult of the Autograph Letter in England*	1962	Copyright 1962	Preface dated 1961
5 Low, *With all faults*	1973	Copyright 1973	Preface undated
6 Prideaux, *A Bibliography of the Works of Robert Louis Stevenson*	1918 New and revised edition	None	Editorial note dated 1917
7 McKerrow, *An Introduction to Bibliography*	None	None	Page facing title states 'First Published 1927'. Second impression with corrections 1928

continued

Book	Date or other information on title-page	Information on verso (back) of title	Other information
8 Carter, *Taste & Technique in Book Collecting*	1970	First edition published 1948. Second impression (corrected) 1949. This edition reprinted from sheets of second impression 1970	Prefatory note dated 1969/70
9 Cotton, *A Typographical Gazetteer*	Second edition, corrected and much enlarged 1831	None	Introduction dated 1824. Advertisement to second edition dated 1830. Final advertisements dated 1885
10 Dore, *Old Bibles*	1876	None	Preface dated 1876
11 Blades, *The Biography and Typography of William Caxton*	1877	None	Preface (undated) refers to a two-volume edition 1861-63, the 'former edition', etc.

Book	Date or other information on title-page	Information on verso (back) of title	Other information
12 Jackson, *The Anatomy of Bibliomania*	1932	First published 1930. Second edition 1930. Third edition (revised) 1932	
13 Lowndes, *The Bibliographer's Manual of English Literature*	New edition, revised, corrected and enlarged	None	Publisher's notice refers to reissue in cheap form
14 Sharp, *Biographical Dictionary of Foreign Literature*	None	First published 1933	Preface dated 1933

We are, most of us, inclined to put first editions on pedestals. Antiquarian booksellers, like myself, and ardent collectors, feel it is all-important for a book to be a first edition and will sometimes pay the earth to buy such a treasure. Moreover, most of us seem to be so certain that a first edition is really a first edition. I may unnerve you by saying that many of us err in this. And it is not surprising when one considers that normally one detects a first edition simply by looking on the title verso for information. "Hurrah" I have frequently told myself in some second-hand bookshop, "I have found a valuable first edition for a mere song!" The reason why I have thought it to be so definitely a first edition is usually only because the title verso states: 'First published 19XX' or some such wording, and there is no mention about a second or third impression; or, because there was a date on the title page and a blank on the title verso; or the title verso had only the copyright date on it. In all these instances I could have been, oh, so wrong.

Let us begin by taking that important clutch of words 'edition', 'impression' and 'issue'. To elaborate a little on the definition I gave earlier, an 'edition' is any number of books, small or large printed from one setting of type. That type may then be broken up or 'distributed', if the publisher has decided to limit the first edition to a stated number, or if there is no demand for additional copies. If, on the other hand, the book proves popular, the publisher may order the printer to produce another 3,000 copies from the same type, perhaps making some very minor corrections. This is a 'second impression' of the first edition. With that impression exhausted, and demand continuing, the publisher may decide on another 2,000 copies, thus giving a 'third impression'. Each separate printing from the same type-setting is an impression, first, second, fifth or tenth; but they all add up to one edition.

Now we will suppose that the author has lighted on important new material or has had a significant number of errors in the first edition pointed out to him. His publisher may then decide that it is worth incorporating all the additions and corrections in another edition. This will inevitably involve a substantial resetting of type, and a second edition will result. If the demand holds there can also be second, third, fourth, etc., impressions of the second edition. Some books become such classics that they run on into innumerable editions and impressions, with the original so much extended, altered and corrected that there is scarcely a vestige of it left. A supreme example is the work familiarly known as 'Gray's Anatomy'. This medical textbook, by Henry Gray, was first published by J.W. Parker in 1858 and taken over by Longman in 1863. Gray died tragically early from smallpox when he had published a second edition; but willing hands carried on the work, and the 35th edition was published by Longman in 1973. This, of course, illustrates the vital necessity of keeping medical and scientific works up-to-date, and the fact that outmoded editions are worthless until they have attained the status of historical curiosities. The further back a collector goes, the more he will have to pay. A 'Gray's Anatomy' of the 1920s may well be found for less than £5. The first edition of the *Anatomy, Descriptive & Surgical* (1858) with 363 wood engravings, is likely to fetch around £200.

One curious example may have been noticed in the foregoing listing — that of the Rev. Henry Cotton's invaluable *A Typographical Gazetteer,* which is in the original binding. This is clearly stated to be the 'second edition, corrected and much enlarged' and the original, reprinted, Introduction establishes the first edition as 1824. At the end of the book, however, there are thirty-two pages of publisher's advertisements, dated 1885, which have not been tipped-in but bound in as an integral part. This can only mean that the University Press at Oxford kept the type of the second edition standing for over fifty years, or else had a large number of the second edition sheets left over and stored. This would by no means be a record. Stephen Pile's *Book of Heroic Failures* quotes David Wilkins's translation of the New Testament from Coptic into Latin, published in 1716 by the Oxford University Press, as having remained in print till 1907, by which time only 191 copies had been sold!

We have still to take the matter of editions a little further. If the second edition of a book contains revision material, it is the first revised edition. This does not alter the fact — and it is imperative to grasp this — that even if there has been no alteration or amendment whatever, and every word is identical, with exactly the same sort of type and format, a new edition is created every time there is a new setting of type.

We arrive at the vexed question of 'issue', which is something quite different from impression. A different or 'variant issue' can occur as part of the first edition when, after some copies have already been published, some alteration is made and even another title-page substituted. We then have two issues of the first edition. The term issue is normally used when it is possible to show beyond any reasonable doubt that the variations occurred after some of the edition had already been published, so that first and second issues (and even more) are recognisable. When priority is not clear and variant copies are, or were, on sale indiscriminately, it is more usual to talk about 'states'. Part of this confusion occurs because, particularly in early centuries, authors were allowed to visit the printers while their books were being run off and to make alterations.

It will be noted that, in the case of Lowndes's *Bibliographer's Manual,* No. 13 above, the publisher has used 'issue' in another sense. This is because the book trade has a habit of using terms less precisely than the bibliographer and collector. Since he was bringing out something in cheap and popular form, involving new type-setting and format, it was clearly a new edition, not another issue of the first edition.

At this point let us look back at our whole table of books and, in the light of our examination to date, try to draw some conclusions. It is completely safe to assert, from the evidence given, that half the fourteen books (Nos. 6, 7, 8, 9, 11, 12, 13) are not first editions because they carry specific statements about earlier editions and impressions. With another five (Nos. 3, 4, 5, 10, 14), I should regard the evidence that they are 'firsts' as entirely satisfactory because of the coincidence of dates on title, verso, preface, etc. If there were a great discrepancy it would be a matter for thought. This leaves only two (Nos. 1 and 2) where, without further checking, evidence might be considered too slight. Since I can find no copy in such sources as *Book Auction Records* bearing any other date, I am happy to accept Plomer; and, since I am not much troubled one way or the other, Partington will pass muster without further investigation. (As a matter of fact, a previous owner has pencilled 'First Edition' inside the cover, but, bearing Gaby Goldscheider's confession in mind, what the soldier said isn't evidence.)

There are one or two other important points to be borne in mind. As we know, some important and much-collected works were issued in 'parts', usually monthly, before they appeared in book form. It is not perhaps generally realised that this practice began as early as the late seventeenth century and that many of the splendid coloured aquatint books of the nineteenth century first reached the public in this way. Even the celebrated Mrs. Beeton's *Book of Household Management* (1859-61) was so issued.[1] But to book-collectors publication in parts is usually only a matter of much interest with such fiction writers as Dickens, whose *Pickwick Papers* (to give them their familiar short title) established a great new vogue in 1836-37. The description 'first edition in book form' normally means that the work was first published in parts or serialised in a magazine or newspaper. Usually, as with the aquatint books and with Thomas Hardy, it is the book form that collectors prefer; but with Dickens and Thackeray, among others, it is the original parts (if complete and with all covers and advertisements) that command big prices. A fair price for *David Copperfield* in book form (first edition 1850) would be £30-£40. A good set of parts could well be ten times that. Thackeray's *Vanity Fair* (first edition, first issue, 20 parts in 19, 1847-48) sometimes

---

1 Though her book is reckoned the classic work on how to prepare good food and run an efficient household, the picture of Isabella Mary Beeton (1836-65) as a vastly experienced hostess and housewife propounding her own recipes is entirely false. She was, in fact, only twenty-nine when she died and it is reckoned that she personally contributed only one recipe.

reaches £1,200-£1,500, whereas the first edition in book form can go on your shelves for perhaps £50-£80.

An expression that sometimes causes puzzlement is 'first published form', or something similar. This can be taken to mean that the work has already been printed for a limited number of people by private gift or circulation, but has not been published in the sense that it has been offered to the general public. 'First general circulation' has much the same meaning. The private circulation, because of its rarity (though it is also frequently better produced) normally commands a much higher price. One of the best examples is Lawrence of Arabia's famous *Seven Pillars of Wisdom*. So large was the first general edition of 1935 that you should easily find a copy for not more than £10. For the previous privately printed and limited edition of about 170 copies you will be fortunate if you are not parted from £2,000.

After a long pause for refreshment, we can return to the question we started with — how to tell a first edition. Despite problems and exceptions, the key to the situation is likely to be the combination of title-page and verso, plus dated prefaces, forewords and advertisements. If title-page and the information on the reverse agree as to date, and there is nothing to indicate earlier editions, then you may well have a 'first'. Whether it is the first impression or first issue of the first edition may be more difficult to establish, and you will be well advised to check from a standard bibliography. Do not be intimidated by the often unreliable burrowings of what John Carter called 'issue-mongers' and 'points maniacs'. A 'point' is an idiosyncrasy or peculiarity about a work which may be held to determine priority of edition, impression or issue. A number of these are entirely legitimate and cause great excitement among devotees, who will be found anxiously scanning the title of Pickwick to see whether Sam Weller's name on the inn sign-board is spelt with a W or a V; and, indeed, that particular work is notorious for the number of points a copy needs to score before emerging triumphant. It is much worse than a judge at Cruft's checking over the points of a Pomeranian or Pekinese, and you are more likely to be bitten. Points should never be worshipped to excess, and the unflagging zeal of bibliographical mudlarkers prodding for new ones should be mistrusted or at least treated with caution. Sir Walter Scott had some notable words in *The Antiquary:*

> Here were editions esteemed as being the first, and there stood scarcely less regarded as being the last and the best; here was a book valued because it had the author's final improvements, and there is another which (strange to tell!) was in request because it had them not. One was precious because it was a folio, and another because it was a duodecimo; some because they were tall, some because they

were short; the merit of this lay in the title-page — of that in the arrangement of the letters in the word Finis. There was, it seemed, no peculiar distinction, however trifling or minute, which might not give value to a volume, providing the indispensable quality of scarcity, or rare occurrence, was attached to it.

One of the best examples of the edition-impression-issue complex is that supreme nursery (and adult) treasure *Alice's Adventures in Wonderland*. The story was first told by Charles Ludwidge Dodgson (Lewis Carroll) to a group of his young Oxford friends. When he decided to publish it, in expanded form, he did so at his own expense. Probably fifty-odd were bound up (of which over thirty seem to have been sent to hospitals) before Dodgson learnt that Tenniel, the illustrator, was dissatisfied with the reproduction of the pictures, whereupon the author decided to abandon the publication and recall the distributed copies. These fifty or so gifts, of

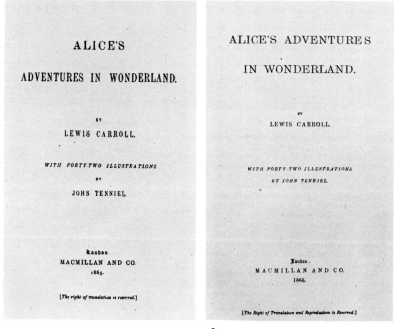

Left: Title-page of the extremely rare suppressed first edition of Alice in Wonderland *(1865).*

Right: Title-page of the 'ordinary' second, or 'first published' edition of Alice in Wonderland *(1866).*

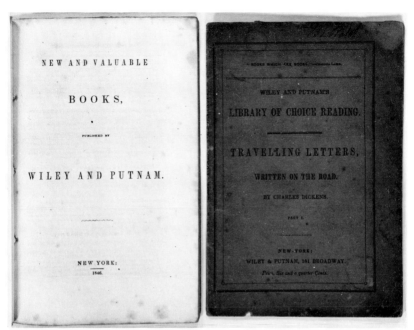

Advertisement and cover of the New York edition of Charles Dickens's Travelling Letters *and a choice subject for the 'follow the flag' debate. They reappeared in England later in the year in* Pictures from Italy.

which some twenty are known to have survived, constitute the true first edition of 1865. The next printing, of 1866, was from new type and was therefore the second edition, often, if not accurately, called the first published edition, on the grounds that, since so few of the 1865 copies were published and a number were recalled by Carroll, it was really a private printing and doesn't count. On the other hand, it can be argued more convincingly that it was fully intended to be an ordinary published edition before Carroll changed his mind.

The complications do not end there. Macmillan, the publisher, had a quantity of 'sheets' left over from the first printing and shipped them over to Appleton & Co., the American publishers. *Alice in Wonderland* (1865 printing) then appeared in America with a new title-page and the date 1866! The perspicacious reader will by now have decided that, if we accept the 1865 suppressed edition as the first, this American printing was the second issue of the first edition, since it was printed from the original setting of type. The so-called first published (English) edition is really the second edition. But before you finally make up your mind, you must

107

THE FOUR JUST MEN

By EDGAR WALLACE

£500 REWARD A Remarkable Offer is made in connection with this Novel. Apart from its interest as a most brilliant piece of story writing, Mr. Edgar Wallace has heightened its charm by leaving at the end one mystery unsolved. The Publishers invite the reader to solve this mystery and offer Prizes to the value of £500 (First Prize, £250), to the readers who will furnish on the form provided the explanation of Sir Philip Ramon's death. ✻ ✻ ✻ ✻ ✻ ✻ ✻

THE TALLIS PRESS
21, Temple Chambers, E.C.

Printed cover of a famous Edgar Wallace first edition. Perfect copies must have the competition form and the fold-out sectional view of 44 Downing Street.

decide where you stand in the 'follow the flag' controversy.[2] I personally gave that one up decades ago.

Two other minor aids to first edition detecting and one harsh rebuff. If you find such terms as 'Uniform Edition', 'Valima Edition', 'Border Edition' (and even 'Author's Edition') you will almost certainly be correct

2 The argument that still rages between sentimentalists and logicians over books first published outside the author's own country. Lamb's *Last Essays of Elia,* a very English book, was published in America five years before it appeared in London. Stevenson's famous *Doctor Jekyll and Mr. Hyde* in the U.S. edition beat the home publication by less than a week. Which, then, were the first editions? I need scarcely point out the horrors of the work of, for example, T.S. Eliot, born an American in 1888 and a British subject from 1927.

in deciding that the volume cannot be a 'first' but forms part of a, later, collected edition, all dressed up in a special format — a 'uniform', in fact. There are very occasional exceptions. Hardy's Wessex volumes, which are uniform, do include one or two first editions. You will easily spot them by carrying out the title/verso exercise.

In the absence of other evidence, a manuscript inscription, while not decisive, is sometimes a guide to, or confirmation of, date of publication, in such examples as 'Mary, the gift of her aunt, 7 February 1895'. Such inscriptions are useful in fixing, for example, Kate Greenaway books, which are often undated, and catalogues will quote them.

The rebuff is that, having painstakingly laid a firm foundation, I must, in all honesty, now kick part of it away by revealing that certain misguided authors and publishers (especially the latter) have unscrupulously omitted all the data we require, printing books without dates or any reference to previous editions. Collectors of such popular authors as G.A. Henty and Edgar Wallace will run into this sort of trouble. To quote an expert collector:

> As regards first editions...no author could have left behind such confusion in the classification of his novels as Wallace, although it would be fairer to say that the fault lay not with him but with his publishers. The rogues of the piece were undoubtedly the well established firm of Hodder and Stoughton, who seemed to have had an unusual and complex system of their own. Not only did they omit to date their editions, but they had almost identical books in the 7/6d [37½ p] and 3/6d [17½ p] category in cloth covers of a great variety of colours. They simply churned out dozens of reprints and impressions in a very short space of time to keep up with the ever growing demand by the Wallace clamouring public. While many of the 7/6d were firsts, some of the 3/6d issues also come into this category, and to make matters worse even some of the smaller red-backed 2/- [10p] editions with the designed covers were firsts.' W.O.G. Lofts, 'Collecting Edgar Wallace', *Antiquarian Book Monthly,* August 1977.

The only answer in this situation is to seek out the appropriate standard bibliography, if it exists, and to read expert articles in specialist periodicals. Another example is Beatrix Potter, who has recently undergone a great deal of research to establish which are truly 'firsts' and which are only reprints without any indication of the fact. Collectors, of whom there are understandably many, will find that one 'point' is the pattern of the endpapers!

Perhaps I should not leave our subject without a special mention of modern first editions, which have a special appeal to many collectors. I

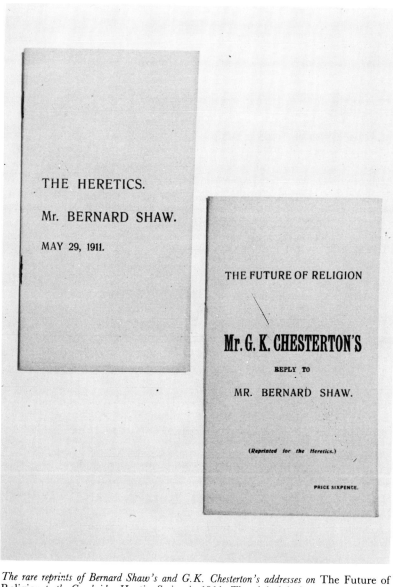

THE HERETICS.

Mr. BERNARD SHAW.

MAY 29, 1911.

THE FUTURE OF RELIGION

Mr. G. K. CHESTERTON'S

REPLY TO

MR. BERNARD SHAW.

(Reprinted for the Heretics.)

PRICE SIXPENCE.

The rare reprints of Bernard Shaw's and G.K. Chesterton's addresses on The Future of Religion *to the Cambridge Heretics Society in 1911. Though both had appeared in the press and are very slight pamphlets, they rank as first editions in book form.*

confess they have, for me, the serious drawback of requiring the collector to assume the mantle of prophecy as well as all the other gifts that are demanded. Perhaps that is the great fascination, the spice of risk, the lure of spotting a winner. With our Bacons, our Defoes, our Wordsworths, our Shelleys, our Austens and all the rest, we know where we are. Time has established their worth, which is now unlikely to alter substantially, either in terms of esteem or financial value. But the collector of modern first editions must perforce strive to anticipate the judgements of posterity, and that path is littered with blighted hopes and the debris of fickle fashion.

According to the edition, and sometimes with the aid of an inscription, Dylan Thomas (1914-1953) has been making £500 or more. In my opinion it would be a very rash collector who banked on him staying at that level. Will James Joyce, Ezra Pound, W.B. Yeats, Aldous Huxley, the Sitwells, Siegfried Sassoon, Henry Williamson, Edmund Blunden, Laurie Lee, T.S. Eliot, Evelyn Waugh, Tolkien, Virginia Woolf, Gertrude Stein, Harold Pinter, Sylvia Plath, Max Beerbohm, to name a haphazard miscellany, advance, hover uncertainly, or slowly fade into obscurity? I cannot answer. I know some are already on the slide. I know that when I see the books of a hitherto-collected writer being grouped in a catalogue in half-dozens and tens, instead of being offered singly, he is on the way out so far as the collecting world counts for anything.

'He pleases many, and he who pleases many must have merit.' On the basis of that opinion, Doctor Johnson might have backed his hunch and invested in John Pomfret. He would have been wrong. But undoubtedly he was right on the mark when he wrote in his essay on Thomas Parnell some words which might aptly be applied to many writers at present being collected:

> I can only say that I know not whence they came, nor have ever enquired whither they are going. They stand upon the faith of their compilers.

Substitute collectors for compilers and you have a fair estimate of the situation. Faith is perhaps the operative word for the collector of modern books, the type of faith displayed with such success by booksellers such as Bertram Rota who was recently called by another specialist in this field the 'master-mason of the modern first edition'.

I come to the hurdle which I confessed at the outset I might find difficult to clear: why collect first editions anyway, since the path is so littered with obstructions, difficulties and bibliographical rubbish, and the pilgrimage is often attended with so much expense?

It is a very good question, and if you are happy with your own charming and heterogeneous muddle of editions, impressions, issues and bindings, early or late, in good condition or bad, God bless you. I have no wish to disturb your contentment — a contentment which, as I look at my bookshelves, I must own I partly share.

There are three basic urges in first edition collecting — romanticism, acquisitiveness and snobbery. The genuine and most lovable *aficionados* are those who wish to possess the book in the very form in which it first reached its author's hands in the bleak parsonage at Haworth, the placid genteel home at Chawton, or that of 'The Great Unknown' north of the border. Drab and perhaps a little the worse for wear, sedate in unpretentious boards or cloth, they are cherished far more than copies reclothed and bedecked in elegant calf and morocco. Others want first editions from greed for rarity and will pay almost any price to secure it, and yet others because they want to put one over on other collectors.

One hopes that only the first group will inherit the earth.

They will have Macaulay's words written on their hearts:

> No substitute, however exquisitely formed, will fill the void left by the original. The second beauty may be equal or superior to the first; but still it is not she.

And on their walls, decorously framed, will be a paragraph from Ralph Waldo Emerson:

> They who make up the final verdict upon every book are not the partial and noisy readers of the hour when it appears...Only those books come down which deserve to last. Gilt edges, vellum, and morocco, and presentation copies to all the libraries will not preserve a book in circulation beyond its intrinsic dates...The permanence of all books is fixed by no effort, friendly or hostile, but by their own specific gravity, or the intrinsic importance of their contents to the constant mind of man.

✻✻✻✻✻✻✻✻✻✻✻✻✻✻✻✻✻

Chapter 7

Association Copies

> The sum is this: that varieties of association are excellent good
> for books as well as bookmen.
>
> Holbrook Jackson, *The Anatomy of Bibliomania*

I propose to devote a whole chapter to so-called 'association copies',
partly for the selfish reason that I am myself devoted to them and partly
because, looking at them as objectively as I can, they seem to me to offer
one of the most satisfying branches of book-collecting, especially to
anyone with the slightest sense of history.

An association copy can be a book which its author has inscribed to a
relative or friend. Obviously the more interesting the inscription, the
more valuable the book. At the bottom of the scale would be a copy
autographed by the author in some bookshop at the outset of a publicity
campaign. This is something coldly impersonal, whereas the essence of
real association is something much more intimate and interesting.

It can be a book which formerly belonged to some famous person,
preferably with some fair indication of that ownership, perhaps his
signature and, much better, marginal notes and comments. It could have
shared the owner's adventures and vicissitudes, occupied his leisure
hours, cheered his bleaker moments. One would treasure the copy of
Herodotus that Charles James Fox was reading by a roaring wood fire
when he had completed the squandering of £140,000 at the gaming table.
''What is a man to do?'' he asked. ''When he is miserable, egad, he must
keep good company!'' Perhaps one would have an even greater fondness
for the folio 1594 *Biblia Graeca Septuaginta* with which Doctor Johnson
knocked down his temporary employer, the bookseller Osborne, when he
accused his illustrious employee of negligence. The book was in the hands
of a Cambridge bookseller in 1812. Some wry amusement at the choice of
weapon could also be extracted from the folio Bible with which, according
to Anthony Trollope in his *Autobiography,* his father used to fell him
whenever he had been idle.

A special place of honour would be found for books having some close
connection with an important event in history and perhaps even helped to
shape it. One could fly no higher than the signal book that young
Lieutenant Pasco used at Trafalgar to send up the Immortal Signal. Yet,

Title-page of Ecclesiasticae Historiae Autores *(1549), inscribed by the translator Wolfgang Musculus ('little mouse') to Heinrich Bullinger, the friend of Calvin and Zwingli. Note the printer's device of Johann Froben (1460-1527), the great printer of Basle who commissioned Hans Holbein to design title-pages, borders and other decorations.*

Right: An unusual Doctor Johnson 'association' item: a manuscript ink and watercolour chart (much reduced) of the armies of Frederick the Great, drawn by an English soldier serving in the Emperor's Body Regiment and purchased in Berlin by Hester Piozzi (formerly Thrale), immortalised by her friendship with Doctor Johnson. Just before she left England for the travels during which she acquired this souvenir, Johnson tore up all her letters in his anger at her marriage with the Italian musician Gabriele Piozzi.

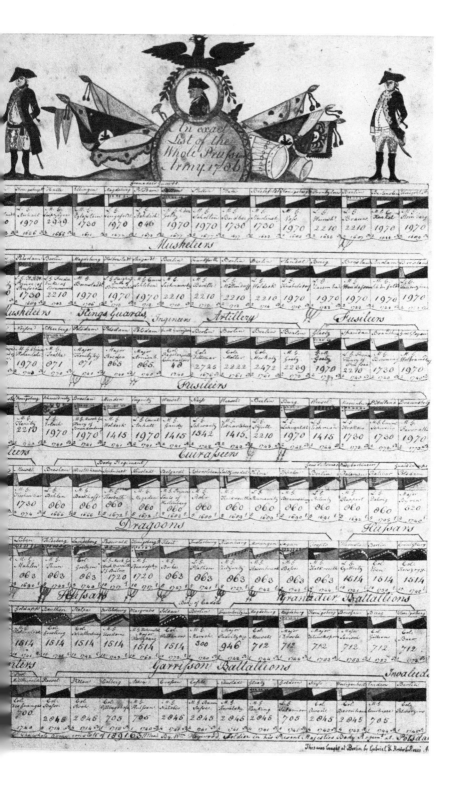

in another sphere of human activity, perhaps a book I examined recently in the library of Chichester Cathedral excelled it. It was a volume of the works of Hermann of Wied, Elector and Archbishop of Cologne, published at Bonn by Laurent Mylius in 1545. Hermann made great efforts to carry through reforms in his diocese and, as a result, was eventually summoned before both Emperor and Pope, deposed and excommunicated. His book, according to historians, was one of the chief sources consulted by Cranmer during the compilation of the *Book of Common Prayer,* first published in 1549 and revised in 1552, again by Cranmer. The Chichester copy carries the signature 'Thomas Cantuar' on the title; so that it was this very book that had such a significant influence on one of the noblest achievements of our literature and one of the greatest moulders of English life and character. If some slight evidence of that is required, the *Oxford Dictionary of Quotations* has over 550 entries for the Book of Common Prayer.

Nearly a hundred years ago there emerged from an obscure Suffolk parish an eight hundred year old manuscript book of the Gospels. In it was a faded inscription which revealed an astonishing story. St. Margaret, Queen of Scotland from about the year of the Norman conquest to 1093, was riding in a litter attended by a company of soldiers and a priest who read to her from a Gospel Book. As they crossed a stream the precious manuscript slipped from his hand and disappeared in the water. The horses were reined in and a man-at-arms plunged into the stream, presently triumphantly holding up the dripping book, which was returned to the anxious Queen. She, pious woman, had it carefully dried out and caused words of thanksgiving to God to be inscribed in it. Those words can still be read in the Bodleian Library, a priceless association with one of Scotland's greatest women.

Near me as I write are a number of volumes which I should like us to examine together in order to illustrate further the fascination of association books; this time not inaccessible treasures but items of the type that can come to every collector. I list them without bibliographical details, since these are largely irrelevant for our particular purpose; but I add what is more significant, the price paid for each, in or out of the saleroom, unless for some reason this is not known.

Book	**Association or inscription**
1 *The second Tome of Homilees. . . to be read in every parishe Church agreeably,* 1571. (6d or 2½p)	'Sacrario Ecclesia De Stansted Montfitchet in Com: Essexiae Sumptibus Parochiae'
2 Publius Virgilius Maro: *Opera,* 1572. (£60)	Signature 'Thomas Knyvett'

Book	Association or inscription
3 *The Bible. . . conteined in the Old and New Testament,* 1599	'For Mrs. Elizabeth Bernard my Deare Wife, whom god blesse'
4 Robert Taylor: *Miscellanea Medica,* 1761. (£75)	'P. Pott Ex dono Authoris 1761'
5 William Crowe: *Lewesdon Hill. A Poem,* 1788. (£90)	Accompanying autograph letter signed from the poet Edmund Blunden, thanking a friend for the loan of the book which has enabled him to compare the various editions, etc.
6 'Owen Meredith' (Edward Robert Bulwer Lytton, 1st Earl Lytton): *Lucile,* n.d. (£55)	'To Surgeon Major L.S. Bence in grateful remembrance of his kind attendance on the journey from Bombay to Calcutta, and with every good wish for his successful progress in the journey of life, this book is presented by the author. Lytton, Gov. House, Calcutta, 22 April 1876'
7 Lord Alfred Tennyson: *Works.* Vol. I only. Miscellaneous Poems, 1877. (£28)	'Alice Stopford Green from A. Tennyson, Dec. 13th 1877'
8 The Form and Order of the Service that is to be Performed and of the Ceremonies that are to be Observed in the Coronation of Their Majesties King Edward VII and Queen Alexandra in the Abbey Church of S. Peter, Westminster, on the 26th Day of June, 1902. (£30)	Inscribed by Organist and Director of Music at the Coronation: 'J. Frederick Bridge, August 9th (Coronation Day)'

With the aid of these books, let us see what glimpses of the past can be vouchsafed to us, what men and events we can recreate, what manner of 'association' is established.

1 *Tome of Homilees,* 1571

The first book sets us journeying in Essex, to a village grown into a town and the parish church of St. Mary. In Elizabeth I's reign (and, indeed, at other times) the standard of education and diligence among the clergy often left much to be desired. The evils of pluralism were rife, absenteeism was common and taken for granted. (In Henry VIII's reign, the great Dutch scholar Erasmus was given the benefice of Aldington in Kent and had it commuted for a pension of £20, charged on the living.) Presentations to livings could be made by totally unworthy patrons, often crooks and loose-livers who were not above putting in incumbents almost as bad as themselves. To remedy the worst excesses of lack of scholarship and poor teaching the Queen, following earlier examples, ordered Books of Homilies to be prepared for use in all parish churches. Eminent churchmen, among them Cranmer, Hooper and Latimer, co-operated in writing the books. The interesting feature of our book is that the title-page inscription gives the exact location and the method of purchase, translating: 'From the sanctuary of the church of Stansted Montfitchet in the County of Essex, bought from the parish chest.' Such are the adventures and travels of books that how and why it left its home are likely to remain a mystery. It was at one time in the library of Darcy Lever Hall, Bolton and in the 1930s it was rescued from a junk furniture shop in Kent. Perhaps, after four hundred years, it should go home at last; for, exhibited in a glass case in St. Mary's Church and with one significant gap, are all the rest of its Books of Homilies. Perhaps, too, the archaic words might for a brief minute live again:

> ...that we...may enjoye the continuance of thy great mercies towards us, thy right hand, as in this so in all other invasions, rebellions and daungers, continuallye saving and defendinge our Churche, our Realme, our Queene and people of England.

2 Virgil, 1572

Our second association item takes us to a late autumn in the next reign. ''About the previous Christmas...we brought our myne unto the Wall, and about Candlemas we had wrought the wall halfe through.'' Now the tunnelers were right through and ''there was placed under the Parliament house where the king should sit, some 30 barrels of gunpowder, with great store of wood, faggots and bars of iron.'' A figure carrying a hooded lantern moved among the barrels, laying the powder train that on the morrow, once it was fired, would send king, princes, bishops, judges, lords and commons to their reckoning in one gigantic blast intended to ''have ruined the whole estate and kingdom of England.'' Came a sudden clatter of feet on the stone steps to the cellars, torchlight on the steel of the men-at-arms, and Guy Fawkes, calling himself John Johnson, was caught in the act. Leading the discovering party was the Justice of the Peace for Westminster, Thomas Knyvet or Knyvett, later to become Sir Thomas Knyvet, Baron Knyvet of Escrick. His signature on the title of his copy of Virgil, probably written there in his quieter days at Jesus College, Cambridge, surely brings us much closer to that momentous day still celebrated in November and commemorated by the ceremonial searching of the cellars of the House of Commons.

3 Bible, 1599

The third example in our selected group, if the case is proven, must be reckoned the most precious. We can note in passing that the book is a ''Breeches' Bible, but that need not delay us here since the misunderstood version is discussed elsewhere (see Chapter 9). Much more important are the inscription and the bookplates of the Bernard family. In 1607 Shakespeare's daughter Susanna married John Hall, physician, of

Fly-leaf of a 1599 Bible perhaps inscribed by her husband to Shakespeare's last direct descendant, his grand-daughter Elizabeth Bernard.

Stratford-upon-Avon. Their only child, Elizabeth, was born a year later. Shakespeare was devoted to her and, in his will, left her 'All my Plate (except my brod silver and gilt bowl).' She later inherited the poet's house, New Place, and the rest of his entailed property.

Elizabeth married, first, Thomas Nash of Stratford in 1626 and then, in June 1649, John Bernard (or Barnard — both forms were used), later Sir John, of Abington, Northants. Both marriages were childless; so that Elizabeth was the last direct descendant of William Shakespeare. If this is the right Elizabeth, can we come much closer to him than through the loved child christened at Stratford 'Elizabeth, daughter of John Hall, gentleman' and her Bible, so tenderly inscribed by her husband?

4 Taylor, *Miscellanea Medica,* 1761

We take up the fourth book and find ourselves with a work which, if we are not Latin scholars and particularly interested in medicine, might seem a dull dog. But pause for a few moments with the two names it introduces us to — Robert Taylor, the author, and the book's recipient, Percivall Pott, whose characteristic signature it contains. Taylor (1710-62) had a large and popular practice in London, was President of the Royal Society and physician to George II. The redoubtable Pott (1714-88), who records the book as the gift of the author, was even better known. After being bound apprentice to the barber-surgeon Edward Nourse, he rose to become master of anatomy to the Corporation of Surgeons and, for nearly forty years, Surgeon to St. Bartholomew's Hospital. Your doctor today will tell you what Pott's Disease is and will probably delight in expounding upon Pott's Fracture. It is so-called because of the compound fracture of the leg which Pott himself suffered as the result of an accident in 1756. The surgeons shook their heads and unanimously recommended amputation. Pott would have none of it and, with the aid of his old friend Nourse, successfully set it himself. It was rumoured that Pott would not allow the bearers to take him to his own hospital, St. Bartholomew's, believing he would fare better elsewhere.

5 Crowe, *Lewesdon Hill,* 1788

Continuing our journey through the centuries we arrive at 1788 and a completely different type of association, linking past and present. *Lewesdon Hill* is a fairly rare work in its first edition. Though his name does not appear, it was written by William Crowe (1745-1829), who was at one time rector of Stoke Abbott in Dorset. Outside the village rises the noble hill of Lewesdon, neighbouring peak to Pilsdon Pen, beloved of Wordsworth when he lived at Racedown and first began to dedicate his life to poetry. Wordsworth much admired Crowe's poem, as did Coleridge and Samuel Rogers. Lewesdon climbs nearly nine hundred feet and, unlike Pilsdon Pen, which is bare and rugged, is thick with trees to its summit. Wrote Crowe:

> Up to thy furze-clad summit, let me climb;
> My morning exercise; and thence look round
> Upon the variegated scene, of hills,
> And woods, and fruitful vales, and villages
> Half-hid in tufted orchards, and the sea
> Boundless, and studded thick with many a sail.

Even poets must come down to earth and to the bottom of their hills, and the long poem ends:

> Of This enough:
> Tomorrow for severer thought; but now
> To breakfast, and keep festival to-day.

One can still climb Lewesdon through its aisles of trees and see the wide scene with its distinctive landmarks just as Crowe saw it, though the crowding sails of the ships of the line and the merchantmen have gone. But the book's greatest association interest is that another, and greater, poet found it worth studying for its content and craftsmanship. "I am returning the delightful Quarto edition of Crowe's poem, from which I have been able to observe what he did later with the piece. (I have edn. 3)." The two were less than two centuries apart, but it brings back to mind Flecker's verses *To a Poet a Thousand Years Hence,* which ends:

> I send my soul through time and space to greet you.
> You were a poet. You will understand.

6 Lytton, *Lucille*

On for nearly another hundred years, and we are with yet another poet, whose early work was written under the pen-name of Owen Meredith. Despite his aspirations to poetry, he became better-known as a prose writer in his minutes and despatches as a statesman, for 'Owen Meredith', better known to history as Edward Robert Bulwer Lytton, first Earl of Lytton (1831-91), became a distinguished diplomat, the climax of his career coming in 1876-80 when he served as Viceroy of India and in that capacity proclaimed Queen Victoria as Empress at Delhi in 1877. On the voyage out to take up his appointment he fell ill and, as the inscription in *Lucile* records, he was sustained by Major L.S. Bence and enabled to arrive in Calcutta in good shape.

Collectors of the Lyttons, father and son, have an inexpensive line of country and are to be congratulated if they can distinguish infallibly between the two without recourse to their reference books. Edward Robert Bulwer Lytton's father was Edward George Earle Lytton Bulwer-Lytton, first Baron Lytton as distinct from first Earl, and wrote some massive novels including *Eugene Aram* (3 vols. 1832), *The Last Days of Pompeii* (3 vols. 1834), *The Caxtons* (3 vols. 1849) and *The Last of the Barons*

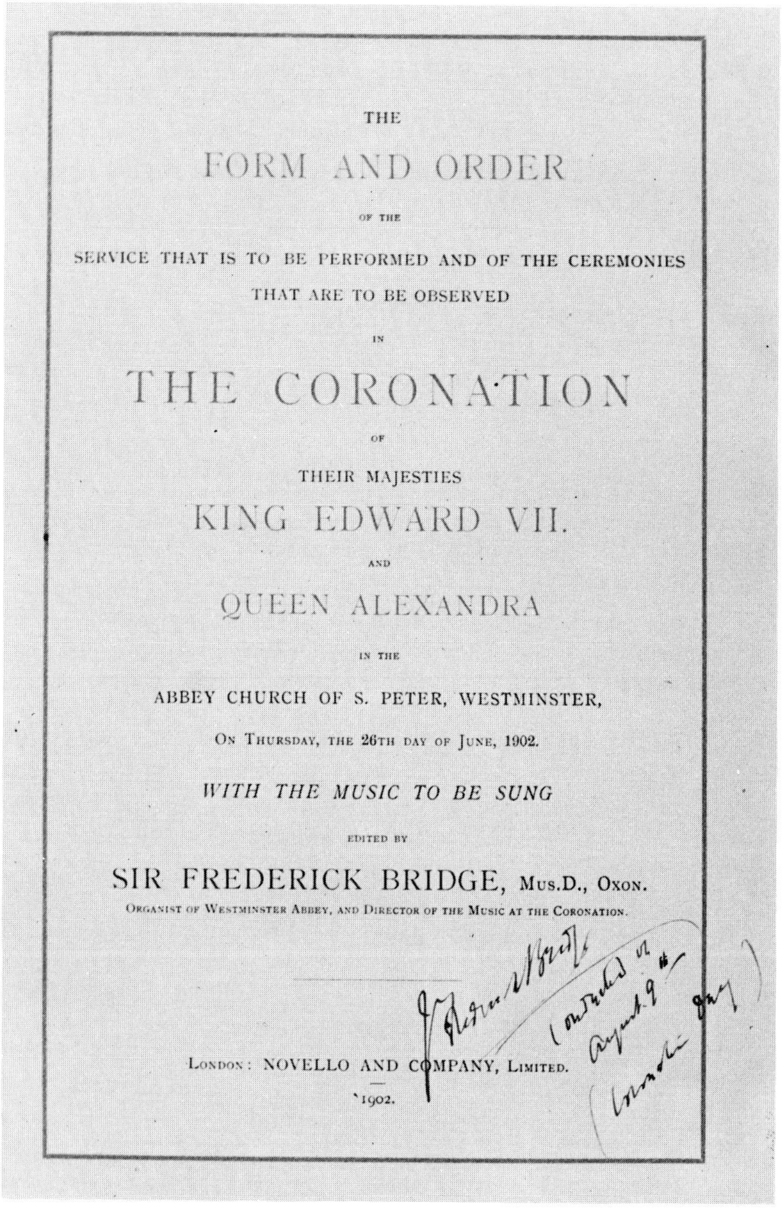

THE

FORM AND ORDER

OF THE

SERVICE THAT IS TO BE PERFORMED AND OF THE CEREMONIES
THAT ARE TO BE OBSERVED

IN

THE CORONATION

OF

THEIR MAJESTIES

KING EDWARD VII.

AND

QUEEN ALEXANDRA

IN THE

ABBEY CHURCH OF S. PETER, WESTMINSTER,

ON THURSDAY, THE 26TH DAY OF JUNE, 1902.

WITH THE MUSIC TO BE SUNG

EDITED BY

SIR FREDERICK BRIDGE, Mus.D., Oxon.

ORGANIST OF WESTMINSTER ABBEY, AND DIRECTOR OF THE MUSIC AT THE CORONATION.

LONDON: NOVELLO AND COMPANY, LIMITED.

1902.

(1843). I confess that I give pride of place to the story of his children on the occasion they organised a charade displaying a Crusader knight returning from the wars. ''At his gate he was welcomed by his wife to whom he recounted his triumphs and the number of heathen he had slain. His wife, pointing to a row of dolls of various sizes, replied with pride, 'And I, too, my lord, have not been idle.' '' George Russell, *Collections and Recollections,* 1898.

7 Tennyson, Miscellaneous Poems, 1877

On to the Poet Laureate, Lord Tennyson and Volume I only of his *Works,* a book which ordinarily, as an odd volume, might well have been sold for £1 or less had not the inscription on the title turned it into a desirable association item. The poet gave it to Alice Stopford Green wife of that frail and 'singularly attractive' priest of St. Philip's, Stepney, who awoke one day to find himself famous with the publication of his *Short History of the English People,* one of the most vivid and colourful of histories, first issued in 1874 and later (1877-80) expanded to four handsome illustrated volumes. His wife was a historian in her own right, an ardent Irish home ruler and a member of the Irish Senate. Among her other political activies, she sympathised with the Boers and visited St. Helena when it was used to house prisoners from the South African War.

8 Order of Coronation Service, 1902

This meander among association books ends with a royal occasion — the coronation of King Edward VII and Queen Alexandra in August 1902. The vigilant will, I hope, have noticed the discrepancy in dates. The printed date of the coronation is 26 June 1902, but Sir Frederick Bridge, organist at Westminster Abbey and Director of Music for the occasion, has written 9 August. The already elderly Prince of Wales was called to the throne on 22 January 1901, and his coronation, on a magnificent scale, was set for 26 June 1902. To the dismay of his countless subjects and, doubtless, of the organisers of the pageantry, two days before the king was forced to bow to his surgeons and undergo an operation for perityphlitis. He made an excellent recovery, and the postponed coronation took place on 9 August, a dramatic sequence of events which this association volume faithfully records.

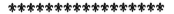

Left: Title-page of The Form and Order of the service. . . in the Coronation of Edward VII and Queen Alexandra, *inscribed by the Organist and Director of Music and carrying the original and postponed dates.*

123

Chapter 8

Provincial Presses

> If stationary men would pay more attention to the districts on
> which they reside...from such materials might be drawn the
> most complete county histories.
>
> Gilbert White, *The Natural History of Selborne*

I feel there can be few more worthy objects for the book-collector who is
suitably placed geographically than gathering the printed products of his
town or city through the centuries. The provincial presses, though they
may lag behind their metropolitan brothers in equipment and technique,
have a great story to tell. Not only do they record the history of their
localities, they are themselves the product of history, played on a far wider
stage.

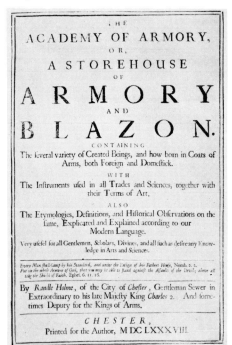

*Left: Title-page of what was
probably the first book printed in
Chester.*

*Right: Title-page of the Oxford
printing that saw Doctor Johnson's
first appearance in print, a
translation into Latin of Pope's
Messiah, included without
Johnson's permission.*

Thus, the first book we know of printed in Norwich was in Dutch, for the benefit of the refugees who had fled there from the persecutions of the Duke of Alva in the Netherlands. When Charles I went north at the beginning of the rebellion that was to cost him his head, his Lord General sent to Robert Barker, the King's Printer, to bring a press to Newcastle-upon-Tyne, from which could be disseminated royalist proclamations and pamphlets. Barker complied with the request by sending his son-in-law John Legatt. The only piece of provincial printing in Queen Mary's bloody reign of five years came from Canterbury in Kent.

Numbers of novelists, poets, essayists and artists had early work printed by provincial presses. Many woodcuts of Thomas Bewick's were used by Catnach at Alnwick, in Northumberland. Doctor Johnson's first appearance in print (without his permission) was at Oxford in an

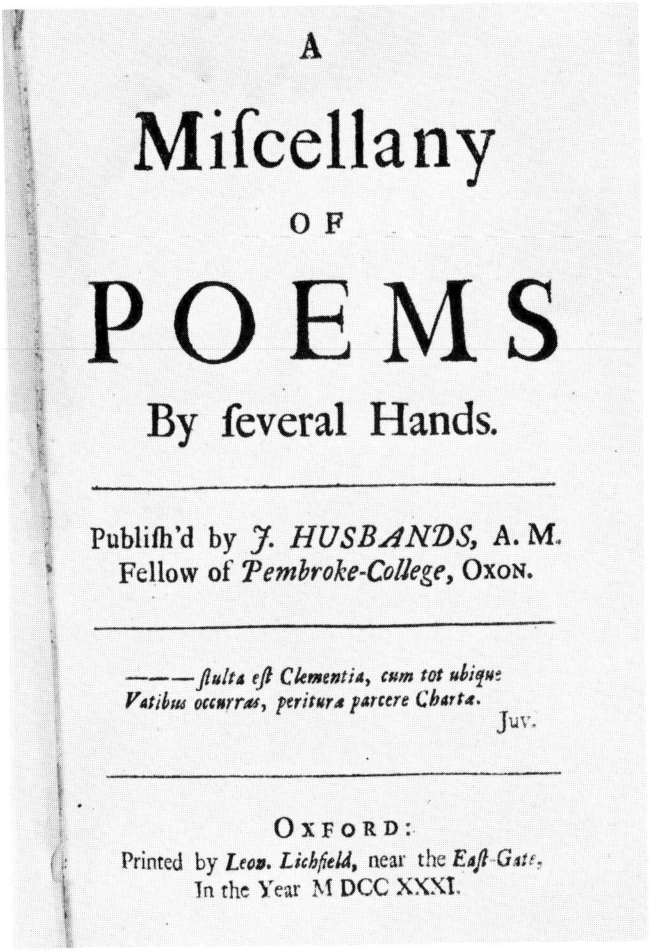

A

Miſcellany

O F

POEMS

By ſeveral Hands.

Publiſh'd by *J. HUSBANDS*, A. M.
Fellow of *Pembroke-College*, OXON.

———*ſtulta eſt Clementia, cum tot ubique*
Vatibus occurras, peritura parcere Charta.
Juv.

OXFORD:
Printed by *Leon. Lichfield*, near the *Eaſt-Gate*,
In the Year M DCC XXXI.

125

WOOD ENGRAVINGS

FOR

THE HIVE

OF

ANCIENT AND MODERN LITERATURE.

BY T. BEWICK AND L. CLENNEL.

NEWCASTLE: PRINTED BY S. HODGSON.

1805.

Title of a Newcastle printing of Thomas Bewick of 1805. The great majority of his work was produced by provincial presses.

ORIGINAL POETRY;

BY

VICTOR AND CAZIRE.

CALL IT NOT VAIN:—THEY DO NOT ERR,
WHO SAY, THAT, WHEN THE POET DIES,
MUTE NATURE MOURNS HER WORSHIPPER.

Lay of the Last Minstrel.

WORTHING:

PRINTED BY C. AND W. PHILLIPS,
FOR THE AUTHORS;
AND SOLD BY J. J. STOCKDALE, 41, PALL-MALL,
AND ALL OTHER BOOKSELLERS.

1810.

TITLE PAGE OF SHELLEY'S FIRST PUBLICATION IN VERSE

The most famous (and rarest) book to come out of Worthing, by Shelley and his sister Elizabeth. No copy was known till 1898. Only about one hundred copies had been circulated when Shelley asked for the destruction of the rest of the edition.

anthology of miscellaneous poems published by his tutor. *Lyrical Ballads* was printed by Biggs and Cottle at Bristol. Shelley's *Original Poetry,* by Victor and Cazire, saw the light at Worthing in Sussex. Byron's second published work was at Newark. Examples could be multiplied. Many of these works, because they were printed in small numbers at obscure presses, are among the rarest books in our literature. There may be little or no hope of finding those particular items, but there are many others to be collected, some as yet unrecorded. There is the added attraction that, since little is known of publishing in many places, items are not always recognised as rare or significant, and are therefore comparatively inexpensive.

Starting overleaf is a list of some first or very early provincial printings in England, Scotland and Wales. There is still a great deal of study necessary for anything like a full history.

Provincial printings from Shrewsbury, 1848-52 and Hafod, 1803-10, the latter being Thomas Johnes's translation of Froissart's Chronicles.

Note: in some cases earlier printings have been recorded but no copy has ever been traced.

Place	Date	Printer	Publication
Aberdeen	1622	Edward Raban	*The Pope's New Years Gifts*
Abingdon (Monastery of the Blessed Virgin)	1528	John Scolar	*Breviary for the use of the Benedictine Abbey of Black Monks there*
Alnwick	c.1795	John Catnach	*Beauties of Natural History selected from Buffon's History of Quadrupeds* (sixty-seven woodcuts by Bewick)
Bath (without Westgate)	1733	Felix Farley	*To the Fore-Chairman that carried Her Majesty, February 1732.* By a Gentleman of Bath
Bedford	1785	B. Hyatt	Bedfordshire Directory
Birmingham (near St. Martin's Church)	1717	Matthew Unwin	A Sermon preached on 30th January; A Loyal Oration
Bradford	1785	W. Portch	Wingrove's Hymns
Brecknock (above old Christ College School)	1772	Evan Evans	*Sion Llywelyn, Caniadu*
Bridgwater	1790	S. Symes	*Carriages*
Bristol (Tower Lane)	1695	William Bonny	John Cary, *Essay on the State of England, in Relation to its Trade, its Poor, and its Taxes*
Cambridge	1521	Johann Lair, known as John Siberch	Henry Bullock, *Oratio ad Thomã Cardinalem archiep. Ebor.* (speech made when Wolsey visited the University)

Place	Date	Printer	Publication
Canterbury	1549	John Mychell	*The psalter poynted or Psalms of David*
Carlisle	1746	Thos. Hams	*Genuine Dying Speech of the Rev. Parson Coppock*
Carmarthen	1721	Nicholas Thomas	*Pedwar Ugain*
Cirencester	1718	Thomas Hinton	*Cirencester Post* or *Gloucester Mercury*
Colchester	?1648 (reputed)	Unknown	*Choak-Peare for the Parliament*
	1733	John Pilborough	Rev. John Tren, *Two Discourses*
Coventry	1721	S. Davis	*A Ratiocination upon Voting*
Darlington	1771	J. Sadler	M. Raine, *English Rudiments*
Devizes	1744	T. Burrough(s)	*America vindicated from the High Charge of Ingratitude and Rebellion*
Douglas	1783	J. Briscoe	*The Acts of Tynwald*
Durham	1733	J. Ross	*Durham Cathedral as it was*
Edinburgh	1508	Walter Chepman, merchant, and Andrew Millar, 'a mere workman'	*A curious volume of poetry* (a collection of ballads, including Chaucer's *Maying and disporte*)
Eton	1610	Melchisidec Bradwood	Sir Henry Savile, Vol. I of Works of *Chrysostom* (completed 1813)
Exeter	1645	Thomas Hunt	Thomas Fuller, *Good Thoughts in Bad Times*
Glasgow	1638	George Anderson	Thomas Abernethie, *The Abjuration of Poperie*

Place	Date	Printer	Publication
Gloucester	1772	Robert Raikes & Wm. Dicey	*The Gloucester Journal;* John Blanch, *History of Great Britain from the Tower of Babel*
Gosport	1708	James Philpot	Gosport Churchwarden's Accounts
Great Milton, Oxon.	c.1715	Matthew Williams	*A Book of Psalmody*
Greenwich	1748	Thos. Henderson	Rev. John Butley, *A Sermon*
Halifax	1759-60	P. Darby	*A Pocket Companion for Harrowgate Spaw; A Treasury of Maxims*
Hereford	1721	W. Parks	*Pascha; or Dr. Prideaux's vindication of the Rule and Table for finding Easter*
Horsham	1784	A. Lee	*Journal from Bassova to Bagdad*
Ipswich	1547	Anthony Scholoker	*The just reckenyng or accompt of the whole number of yeares, from the beginnynge of the world, unto this present yeare*
Isle of Man (Whitehaven)	1769 1773	John Ware & Son	Prayer Book (in Manx dialect); Old Testament (first Manx version)
Kendal	1731	Thos. Cotton	*Kendall Courant*
King's Lynn	1740	Wm. Garratt	*The Curiosity, or Gentleman and Ladies Repository*
Leith	1651	Evan Tyler	*Discovery after some search of the sinnes of the ministers*

Place	Date	Printer	Publication
Lewes	1745	Wm. & Arthur Lee	*Sussex Weekly Advertiser*
Lincoln	1729	William Wood	*Articles of Visitation*
Ludlow	1719	W. Parks	S. Jones, *Sermons*
Maidstone	1704	?R. Wilson	E. Brettoneau, *The Life of James II*
Malton, Yorks.	1750	Joshua Nickson	Rev. Thos. Comber, *Modest and Candid Reflections*
Newcastle-upon-Tyne	1639	John Legatt (son-in-law of Robert Barker)	*Lawes and Ordinances of Warre...and other royalist proclamations and pamphlets*
Northampton	1720	Robert Raikes & Wm. Dicey	*Northampton Mercury*
Norwich	c.1566	Anthony de Solemne or de Solempne	*Der Siecken Troost, Onderwijsinghe om gewillick te sternen* (in Dutch for refugees from Netherlands)
Nottingham	?1711	Wm. Ayscough	*Remarks on the several paragraphs of the Bishop of Salisbury's Speech in Relation to the first article of Doctor Sacheverell's impeachment*
Oxford	1478	No printer's name (Theodoric Rood?)	T. Rufinus, Bishop of Aquileia, *Expositio sancti Ieronimi in simbolum apostolorum* (date wrongly set by printer as 1468)
Reading	1723	D. Kinnier & Wm. Parks	*Reading Mercury*
Rochester	1648	Unknown	*The Kentish fayre, or the Parliament sold to their best worthe*

Place	Date	Printer	Publication
St. Alban's	1479	The School-master printer	Augustinus Datus, *Augustini Dacti scribe sup. Tullianus eleganciis & uerbis*
St. Andrew's	1552	John Scot	Archbishop Hamilton, *Catechism*
Salisbury	1715	Samuel Farley	*Salisbury Post-Man*
Sheffield	1736	William Ward	*Sheffield Public Advertiser;*
	1737 onwards		Chapbooks
Sherborne	1737	Wm. Bettinson & G. Price	*Sherborne Mercury*
Stratford-on-Avon	1745	T. Pasham	Wm. Baylies, *Short Remarks on Dr. Perry's Analysis made on the Stratford Mineral Water*
Taunton	1718	W. Norris	F. Squire, *The Lawfulness of Taking Oaths*
Tavistock	1525	Thomas Rycharde	Boethius, *De consolatione philosophiae*
Tewkesbury	1760	Sam. Harward	Chapbooks, first of which was probably *Love in a Barn*
Trefhedyn (Cardiganshire bank of R. Teifi)	1748	Isaac Carter	Two ballads. (First press on Welsh soil)
Waltham	1748	William East	*Musarum Brittanicarum Thesaurus*
Warrington	1731	John Eyres	*A broadside*
Worcester	1549	John Oswen	Henry Hart, *A Consultorie for all Christians*

Place	Date	Printer	Publication
Yeovil	1749	Robert Goadby	*Western Flying Post*
York	1509	Hugo Goetz	*Aelius Donatus, Directorium Sacerdotum, Donatus Minor cum Regio,* and *Accedence.*

Testimony to the interest and importance of this field of collecting occurred in October 1980, when Sotheby, Beresford, Adams of Chester held an auction almost exclusively devoted to provincial presses. Items printed and published in over 350 localities in the British Isles were sold, and the cataloguer wrote:

> One of the greatest fascinations of provincial printing in Britain is the diversity of localities where presses were set up, often, for example, along the line of canals, where labour was cheap and plentiful. . . another fascination being that this is a relatively unresearched area, its local beginnings in the eighteenth century often more obscure than the highly recorded beginnings of early printing.

Chapter 9

Bibles

> No man was a greater lover of books than he [Shelley]. He was rarely to be seen, unless attending to other people's affairs, without a volume of some sort, generally of Plato or one of the Greek tragedians. Nor will those who understand the real spirit of his scepticism be surprised to hear that one of his companions was the Bible. He valued it for the beauty of some of its contents, for the dignity of others, and the curiosity of all.
>
> Leigh Hunt, *My Books*

If it seems odd to devote a chapter to one book, however important and significant, it must be appreciated that numerically it is by far the most commonly found book and one which has been published over such a long period that the collector will see it more frequently than any other.

Speaking only from a base financial standpoint, there is probably no book of which people hold higher hopes than the Bible, and none where they are more doomed to disappointment.

Few days go by without booksellers and auctioneers being offered, for instance, some imposing nineteenth century edition with brass clasps and bright chromolithographs; or a 'very rare' Breeches Bible, the latter almost inevitably rather battered and with a number of pages torn or missing.

I do not write derisively, only factually. For the truth is that few Bibles produced over the last 370 years have any substantial value, neither have a great many from the period before that. There is one obvious reason. In crude terms, value normally depends on rarity, and no book can show a greater number of editions than the Bible. It is astonishing to think that in the forty-odd years after the invention of printing, no fewer than ninety-four editions came off the presses of Europe; and that for four centuries there has been almost no year in which a new edition has not appeared in England. In many years there were several. It was the earliest best seller. Of an edition of Luther's Bible printed in Wittenberg in 1534, it is estimated that 100,000 copies were sold in forty years. Add to these statistics that translations have now appeared in some 850 languages and it will be apparent that, except in a few notable cases, rarity is not often a factor to be reckoned with.

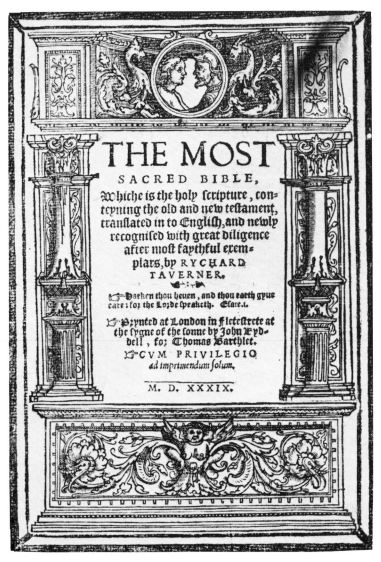

Title-page of Rychard Taverner's edition of the Bible, 1539, partly adapted from Matthew's version and partly translated by himself. It was soon superseded and complete copies are very rare. Of the ten copies sold at auction in the last eighty years, only one has been perfect.

Since it has already been mentioned, let us take the case of the so-called Breeches Bible, from the reading in Genesis iii.7 "and they sowed fig leaves together, and made themselves breeches." It seems to be an invincible belief that this edition is both scarce and valuable, whereas it is neither.

To begin with, this was not the first use of the curious rendering. It had appeared in Caxton's edition of Voragine's *The Golden Legend* (1483) and in Wycliffe's translation of about a hundred years before; but the sobriquet is reserved for the Geneva version of the Bible, first printed there by Rouland Hall in 1560. This was the first English Bible printed in Roman type and with verse divisions, which are among the reasons why it was enormously popular and, for the next fifty years, the most commonly owned and read version in England. Dore, the historian of the Bible, tells us that "from that date [1560] until 1612 no year passed without one, two, or more editions being issued from the press." In fact, up to the outbreak of the Civil War in 1642, some 150 editions had appeared.

For some strange, probably mildly salacious, reason, it is the 'breeches'

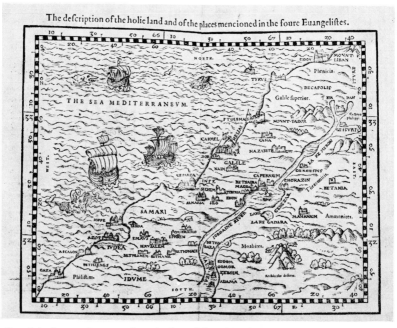

The description of the holie land and of the places mencioned in the foure Euangelistes.

One of the five woodcut maps from the first edition of the Geneva Bible in English, printed at Geneva by Rouland Hall in 1560. This was the edition most commonly used in England till the publication of the Authorised Version in 1611 and is often known as the 'Breeches' Bible from the rendering in Genesis iii.7.

that popular interest has fastened on though, etymologically, there are other words of equal interest. For example, in the Gospel of St. Luke, ii.16, we find "So they came with haste, and found both Mary and Joseph and the babe layd in the cratch." The word cratch was until recently in common use in Yorkshire for a large basket, and its antiquity is shown by the fact it occurs in a gloss in the Gospels written about the time of the Norman Conquest.

I have said enough, I think, to show that the version is a very common one and of small commercial value. Often the title page has disappeared in the course of the centuries. If so, the breeches and cratch references will establish the version. Any edition of it, in good condition, will suit the collector, who should not be persuaded to pay a high price for it. The only two comparative rarities are Hill's first edition of 1560, and the first English edition of the Geneva version, printed by Christopher Barker in 1576.

Of course, there are very valuable Bibles, both from the point of view of rarity and from their place in the history of literature and the troubled progress of religious belief. In the service of no book have so many suffered exile, persecution, hardship and death. No book bears the imprimatur of so many great names — Caedmon, Bede, Wycliffe, Tyndale, Coverdale, Cranmer among them; so that a collection of Bibles can be a worthy and exciting thing, even though the first editions of a number of landmarks will almost certainly be denied you. A single leaf of the Gutenberg (or Mazarin) Latin Bible of c.1456 is likely to cost from £2,000-£3,000; even an imperfect copy of Coverdale (which is the only condition in which it occurs) will probably fetch from £5,000-£10,000 according to the nature of its deficiences; and a reasonable copy of the first issue of the first edition of the Authorised Version would be hard to find for less than £2,000-£3,000.

Apart from these and some other editions and issues remarkable in one way or another, the collector can expect to have an easier time financially than in many other fields of collecting. Sawyer and Darton put the position accurately and succinctly in *English Books 1475-1900:* "Certain editions are valued for their peculiarities, their rarity or their beauty of production, but not, from a collector's point of view, so highly or so often as the amateur who possesses an old volume believes."

Let us pick up that word peculiarities. I have already cited one example — that of the Breeches Bible — of an edition having an undeserved reputation because of an eccentricity of translation which, in fact, was not an eccentricity at all, having very respectable antecedents. There are several others with oddities of translation, but many more with careless, and even horrifying, mistakes by printers. Justifiably or not, these have their place among the desiderata of some collectors. Some are reasonably common, and therefore should be reasonably priced, some are fairly rare and correspondingly costly, and some are so scarce that, short of divine intervention, they will not be found in a lifetime. I include them for their interest as sidelights on history, because a number, for the benefit of the collector, have been faithfully printed in facsimile, and as a reminder that, despite the plethora of them in our daily newspapers, printer's blunders are not the prerogative of our own day. One of the craft was in a mighty hurry when he set Judas for Jesus at John vi.67, as happened in 1609; and so was his descendant in 1653 when, at Corinthians vi.9, he pronounced that "the unrighteous shall inherit the kingdom of God", which must have been a great comfort to a considerable number of citizens under the Commonwealth.

To take a selection in chronological order:

The first complete Bible in the English language, translated by Coverdale, was published on 4 October 1535. So far as I am aware, no perfect copy is known. It contained the reading at Psalm xci.5: "So yt thou shalt not nede to be afrayd for eny bugges by night." This translation is found in a number of later editions, so that the assiduous collector may well be able to ferret out a 'Bug' Bible. The word probably derives from the dialect boggart for bogies and other unpleasant denizens of the night. Edmund Becke's 1549 revision of the so-called 'Matthew' version (Thomas Matthew being a fictitious name adopted to cover the true identity of the translator) was also a Bug Bible; but it is also known as the 'Wife-beater Bible' because of Becke's annotation at I St. Peter iii.7. The Authorised Version has: "Likewise, ye husbands, dwell with them [i.e. wives] according to knowledge, giving honour unto the wife, as unto the weaker vessel, and as being heirs together of the grace of life." Becke's revision reads: "He dwelleth wyth his wyfe accordinge to knowledge, that taketh her as a necessarye healper, and not as a bonde servaunte or a bonde slave." Then, provoked by we know not what domestic disaffection, he adds: "And yf she be not obedient and healpfull unto hym, endevorethe to beate the feare of God into her heade, that therby she may be compelled to learne her dutie and do it."

Doubtless because of strong objections from the distaff side, Becke's truly Christian comment was not repeated in later editions.

A number of editions of Coverdale's translation contain the curious reading at Jeremiah viii.22: "there is no more Triacle [treacle] at Gilead", which we are more familiar with as "no balm in Gilead". Find one of these copies and you will have added a 'Treacle' Bible to your store.

At one period in our history the Whig party was alleged to consist of 'place men', i.e. politicians willing to forsake any principle in order to secure a 'place' or Government appointment. A 1562 edition of the Bible

138

ousted the peacemakers from their inheritance and, at Matthew v.9, proclaimed "Blessed are the place makers." It is not surprising that this has become known as the 'Whig' Bible. The same edition made the unfortunate error of substituting 'condemneth' for 'commendeth' in the St. Mark xii paraphrase "Christ commendeth the poore widdow."

In 1568 Matthew Parker, Archbishop of Canterbury, published a revision of what is usually known as the Great Bible, of nearly thirty years earlier. So many august prelates assisted him that it is called the 'Bishops' ' Bible. In Psalm 45 is a well-known reference to the gold of Ophir, the legendary and unidentified treasure house celebrated in Masefield's poem:

> Quinquireme of Nineveh from distant Ophir
> Rowing home to haven in sunny Palestine...

There has always been much speculation about the site of this region, guesses including East Africa, Abyssinia, Arabia, Spain, Armenia and Peru. One of Parker's coadjutors contributed a remarkable note: "Ophir is thought to be the Ilande in the west coast, of late founde by Christopher Columbo frõ whence at this day is brought most fine golde."

The year 1599 was a bewildering one for Bibles. Of the ten or so editions bearing that date and the London imprint 'by the Deputies of Christopher Barker' (the Queen's printer, who held the monopoly of printing Bibles) most were printed abroad in centres such as Amsterdam and Dort and, probably, later than 1599. They show slight variations, for example in the woodcut decorations. One, on the separate title page of the Metrical Psalms, has the motto 'God is my helper' and the device of a goose, from which it derives its nickname of the 'Goose' Bible.

In 1631 came an edition, from 'R. Barker and the Assigns of Bill', which stirred up more trouble than most, particularly for the printers. From the commandment in Exodus xx.14: "Thou shalt not commit adultery" they made the catastrophic error of leaving out the word not. It has been suggested that this was a deliberate fix to discredit the royal printer. If so, it was very successful, for the incensed Bishop of London reported the matter to Charles I, who had the offenders brought before the Court of High Commission, where they were reprimanded and heavily fined. Peter Heylyn gives an account in his *Cyprianus Anglicus* (1668):

> His Majesties Printers, at or about this time, had committed a scandalous mistake in our English Bibles by leaving out the word NOT in the Seventh Commandment. His Majesty being made acquainted with it by the Bishop of London, Order was given for calling the Printers into the High-Commission, where upon Evidence of the Fact, the

whole Impression was called in, and the Printers deeply fined, as they justly merited.

Since the whole edition was of only one thousand copies and only a small number had been circulated when the suppression was ordered, this is obviously a rare book and one that is likely to be costly unless the seller is ignorant of its history. It is appropriately known as the 'Wicked' Bible.

An even rarer item is the 'Souldiers Pocket' Bible of 1643, a collection of short passages, mainly from the Geneva version, for the use of Cromwell's troops in the Civil War. It was not positively identified till 1854, when an American collector described one. Some other copies have emerged since, but it remains very scarce indeed. The book had a strange subsequent history in that five distinct editions, totalling perhaps 50,000 copies, were reprinted for use by the Federal troops in the American Civil War (1861-65), more than two hundred years after the other Civil War. With that number about little more than a century ago, it might be thought an easy matter to run one to earth. Don't count on it.

Fifty years after the 'Souldier's' Bible had been carried in the pockets[1] of the Roundheads to inspire them at Marston Moor and Naseby, appeared a reprint with some additions and alterations. Published in 1693 by R. Smith ('under the Piazza of the Royal Exchange in Cornhill') with the title *The Christian Soldier's Penny Bible, Shewing from the Holy Scriptures the Soldier's Duty and Encouragement. . . fit for the Soldier's or Seaman's Pocket,* it is thought to have been produced for our troops in Flanders. Either they were very careless or it was a singularly destructive campaign, but there is only one copy known, in the British (Museum) Library.

Before we leave this troubled century, it may be worth noting an edition of the Bible printed in 1652 by John Field, 'Printer to the Parliament of England'. This is the first in which Parliament is mentioned on the title. In 1682 a printer gave a boost to cannibalism by substituting ''if the latter husband ate her'' instead of hate her in the verses on the Mosaic law of divorce at Deuteronomy xxiv.3.

Progressing to the next century, we arrive at an edition which might well satisfy one of Sawyer and Darton's criteria, that of beauty of production. This was published at Oxford by John Baskett a printer of obscure origins who was able to acquire the patent as Royal Printer, the most lucrative monopoly in the kingdom, in 1709. He was also astute enough to obtain a twenty-one year lease from Oxford University for their printing privilege. In 1716-17 Baskett produced his masterpiece, a two-volume folio Bible characterised by splendid large type and fine steel engravings. Unfortunately the fidelity of the typesetting was not

---

1 Or was it their boots? Cf. ''Men of the new religion, with their Bibles in their boots'', G.K. Chesterton, *The Secret People.*

commensurate with the dignity of the design, with the result that Baskett suffered the mortification of having his edition labelled 'A Baskett-ful of Errors'. One occurred in the headline above Luke xx, which read 'The Parable of the Vinegar' instead of Vineyard. It has since been christened the 'Vinegar' Bible and would be a fine (and weighty) addition to a collection, probably costing in the £200-£400 bracket. The type, Roman and italic, is described in Baskett's stock list as "A very large ffount of Double Pica, new, the largest in England."

Oxford, of course, holds a very important place in the story of the printing of the Bible since, apart from earlier editions, the copyright for printing the Authorised Version of 1611 (which, strangely enough, was never authorised in any official sense), and the Book of Common Prayer, is granted by charter to Oxford and Cambridge University Presses (and by licence to the Queen's Printers, Messrs. Eyre and Spottiswoode). In 1881 Oxford produced 'the rarest book produced at Oxford since the 15th century'. Known as the *Golden Gospel*, it was St. John printed in gold letters on dark olive paper. Aspirants to possession will have to rely on criminal entry, since only three copies were run off.

It is perhaps understandable that, the nearer we approach modern times, with their greater technical proficiency, the number of 'curious' editions should diminish. At the same time, typographical excellence and beauty of design are easier to find. We must not leave the eighteenth century without mention of the great typefounder and printer of Birmingham, John Baskerville (1706-75), who not only designed the famous type that bears his name but greatly improved the general standard of English printing and gave us, in 1763, one of the most splendid editions of the Bible. This was produced in Baskerville's capacity as printer to Cambridge University, an office he held for ten years. The original price to subscribers was four guineas unbound, but it did not sell well and was remaindered at 36s. a copy. In a good contemporary binding it is unlikely to fetch less than £1,500-£2,000 today. Much cheaper is the subsequent Birmingham printing of 1769-71, which will normally hover between £100 and £200. The first issue was in 130 weekly parts at 2½d. each, but apparently no complete set is recorded.

Passing to our own day, fine editions include the Nonesuch Press issue of 1924-27, in five volumes with engraved titles and head-pieces by Stephen Gooden; but many will give pride of place to the Doves Press *The English Bible containing the Old Testament and the New,* published in 1905, also in five volumes. It was limited to five hundred copies and afterwards the type was destroyed.

I have omitted much in this survey of the centuries. The collector must obviously have the Revised Version of 1881-95, and some other notable attempts (not, in everyone's view, attended with much success) to

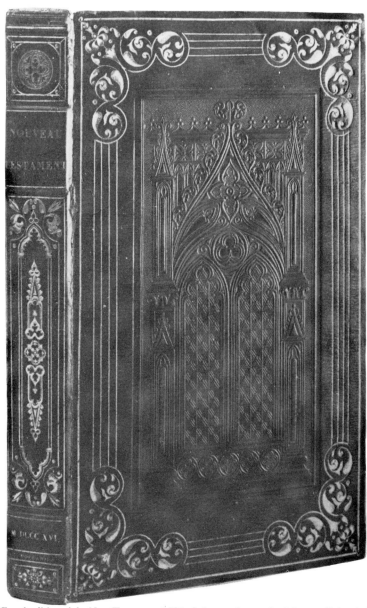

A French edition of the New Testament, 1826. It is a good example of the so-called cathedral binding, i.e. one decorated in a Gothic architectural style, often incorporating a rose window. In France the design was often blocked on the cover, i.e. imposed by a heated engraved plate set in a blocking or arming press.

improve on the Authorised Version. He may also wish to take in such oddities as the Bible in shorthand and, if he can find them, the portions published in the dialects of Cornwall, Cumberland, Dorset, Durham, Devonshire, etc., most of them privately printed for Prince Lucien Bonaparte, who included the Song of Solomon in twenty-four dialects among his list of nearly eighty publications, his English agent being Bernard Quaritch of 15 Piccadilly.

Whichever way his tastes lie, and whatever the capacity of his purse and his bookshelves, it is certain that no other single work offers to the collector such variety of choice, experience and discovery as four and a half centuries of the book of which Lord Chief Justice Sir Matthew Hale (1609-76) wrote to one of his sons who had just recovered from smallpox:

> I have been acquainted somewhat with men and books, and have long experience in learning, and in the world: there is no book like the Bible for excellent learning, wisdom, and use; and it is want of understanding in them that think or speak otherwise.

Chapter 10

Completeness and Condition

> Students who...may require this vast sea of books...may suffer many shipwrecks.
>
> Isaac D'Israeli, *Curiosities of Literature*

> The condition of a book must be seen to be realised, and condition more than anything else nowadays dictates value and will continue to dictate it.
>
> Michael Sadleir

I have so far dealt only with what might be considered extraneous matters which are of little concern to the non-collector, who can read and enjoy a book without worrying about endpapers, half-titles, advertisements and the rest; though even the ordinary reader must reach a point where bibliographical matters begin to impinge. Nothing can be more exasperating to the borrower of library books than to find a vital page or two missing from the dénouement of his thriller. Even so, he is in better plight than the collector, for he can at least attempt to supply the deficiency from his doubtless fertile imagination. No such remedy is open to the dedicated book man. His pearl is fatally flawed, and to supply the missing leaf, or leaves, in facsimile, even of the right size and type, is a desperate measure acceptable only in cases of extreme age or rarity. He would doubtless suffer this blow to his esteem in a First Folio or a 1532 Chaucer, given half a chance, but in lesser books the wound is too serious.

The collector, then, will always examine the evidence that his book is complete in every respect and, as well as all the trimmings with which we have temporarily been preoccupied, will carefully test the completeness of the text itself. This may seem a fairly straightforward task. Are not all the pages numbered and therefore readily checked? This is the most elementary method, which may serve in most modern books, but it can never be relied on with earlier examples. Our printing forefathers were notoriously careless about their pagination. To cite only one example, the collector following page numbers in the first edition of Walton's *Compleat Angler* will find that in one run of twelve pages the typesetter begins happily with 69, 80, 81, 72 and finishes with 77, 88, 89, 80.

However, the page numbers are usually not the only numbers in the text. Look down at the foot of the page and you will probably find others, occurring not so frequently but with regularity and at fixed intervals. If there are no numbers, there will almost certainly be letters instead; and often a combination of both. These are 'signatures' and, if, in early books, the printer has set them out in sequence right at the end, perhaps with the colophon, he has supplied the 'register of the signatures'. Since they were provided to enable the binder to collect the various gatherings or sections in the right order before putting the covers round, much more

An unusual printer's note to the binder regarding signatures, from Richard Baxter's **A** Holy Commonwealth, *(1659).*

To the Binder.

THough fignature *L* and *C c*, *D d* be not, yet the Book is perfect.

The Price of this Book is 3ˢ Bound.

care was exercised with them than with the page numbering. That is why they are a more reliable guide to completeness.

In front of me is a Tudor Bible, 'Imprinted at London by the Deputies of Christopher Barker, Printer to the Queenes most excellent Maiestie' in 1599. It is a thick volume measuring approximately 8½ ins. by 6½ ins., squarish, and for everyday purposes might be described as a quarto.

Ignoring all the preliminary pages ('prelims') and reaching the 'First Booke of Moses called GENESIS', I find in the bottom right-hand margin the capital letter A. The next leaf is number A2. Continuing on, the signatures run (I have put 'ns' where there are none):

A	A2	A3	A4	ns	ns	ns	ns	B	B2	B3	B4
ns	ns	ns	ns	C	C2	C3	C4	ns	ns	ns	ns
D	D2	D3	D4	ns	ns	ns	ns	E	E2	E3	E4

This numbering and lettering continues systematically till the alphabet runs out in the Book of Job and a new pattern begins with the Psalms:

Aa	Aa2	Aa3	Aa4	ns	ns	ns	ns	Bb	Bb2	Bb3	Bb4
ns	ns	ns	ns	Cc	Cc2	Cc3	Cc4	ns	ns	ns	ns
Dd	Dd2	Dd3	Dd4	ns	ns	ns	ns	Ee	Ee2	Ee3	Ee4

By the end of the Old Testament the printer had again reached the end of the alphabet and started all over again, this time with Aaa Aaa2 Aaa3, etc., till he finally ran out, at the end of the Book of Revelation and the 'Table', with the Rrr signatures.

It will be observed, in running through the complete signatures of a book, that there is no J, no U and no W — an indication of what sticklers for tradition we are. In early manuscripts and books using the Latin alphabet J and U were written I and V as capitals and there was a good deal of indiscriminate use even in the lower case (e.g. Maiestie above). There was no W, since it was not reckoned a proper letter in its own right, but only a double U, which is how we pronounce it.

There are exceptions to this practice. American books often used the whole alphabet, but were not consistent, some printers being faithful to their origins, some insisting on independence.

Returning to our table of signatures, what do they teach us about this particular Bible? It is apparent that they are running in groups of eight, the workman 'signing' the first four in each case. He had folded his sheet three times, giving himself eight leaves (sixteen pages) in each section or gathering. Thus, despite the temporary appraisal by eye, the book is an octavo, not a quarto — a fact established by checking the signatures. By chance, this is a very tidy 'signing'. Often it will be found that a text starts with the B signatures, the preliminaries rarely being so obliging as to add up to a complete signature.

A LILLVSTRISSIMO

ET ECCELLENTISS: SIG.

ALESSANDRO FARNESE
P·R·I·N·C·I·P·E
DI PARMA ET DI PIACENZA.

 OSTRA ECCELL.ᵃ haue
rà potuto facilmente intende-
re, chi fia ftato il Commenda-
tore Annibal Caro già mio
zio : & quanto & di che quali-
tà Seruitore egli fuffe de la Ill.
Cafa Farnefe: dico che l'haue-
rà potuto intendere; perche fe bene egli fi tirò tan
to innanzi con gli anni, che V. Ecc. l'hauerebbe po
tuto molto ben uedere, & conofcere per fe medefi
ma; nondimeno l'effere ella ftata per lo paffato di
troppo tenera età, & lontana da l'Italia, & da'fuoi;
& egli appreffo l'Ill. Sig. Car. Farnefe; & in queft'
ultimo de la fua uita, inuecchiato molto più da le in
difpofitioni, & da le fatiche, che dal tempo; è ftato
cagione, ch'egli non habbia potuto darfi a conofce
re a lei, come ha fatto a tutti gli altri fuoi. Il teftimo
nio de'quali ancor che fia baftante à metterlo in có
fideratione de l'Ecc. V. per quello ch'egli fù tenu-
to da loro, con tutto ciò maggior laude farebbe fta
ta la fua, & maggior fatisfattione la mia, ch'ella po

* 2 teffe

A signature at the foot of the dedication in a book from the press of Aldus Manutius, Venice, 1569. Since this is part of the preliminaries, the page, as was frequently the custom, was signed with an asterisk instead of a letter, the letters beginning with the main text.

CHAP IV.

The most accurate Methods for erecting Conservatories, GREEN-HOUSES, *and* ORANGERIES : *With the Culture and Management of* EXOTICKS, PERENNIAL GREENS, *and other tender Plants.*

THE Preference that is given to *Exoticks* beyond our *Domestick* Plants, and the Observations I have made relating to those Vegetables, occasion me to treat concisely of them ; flattering my self, that a short Chapter on this Head will not be unacceptable to the curious. These Plants are acquir'd and propagated with no small Trouble, and at a necessary Expence : But the Beauty of the *Orange* and *Lemon* only, when they are ripe and in their full Glory, (which they will arrive to in a few Years, with an exact Culture and Management,

Page from Charles Evelyn's The Lady's Recreation. . .the Art of Gardening Improv'd *(1717), showing at the foot a typical catchword. The syllables 'nagement' are repeated in the first line of the next page.*

I open another book, this time William Camden's *Remaines of a Greater Worke, concerning Britaine...* (1605), where the printer had rather more trouble at the outset. This time, following the free endpaper and title-page, we have: A3 ns B B2 B3 ns C C2 C3 ns D D2 D3 ns E E2 E3 ns and so on, till we eventually finish at Hh2.

This time, each sheet had been folded twice to give four leaves (eight pages) in a gathering, and the book is therefore a quarto (4to). If further confirmation is needed, the chain lines are running horizontally and the watermark is hovering in the centre of the page on the inner margin.

As a matter of interest, the printer's pagination in one place runs 65, 66, 76, 68, 69, 70 — reinforcing the statement that signatures should be relied on rather than page numbers when it is important to be completely sure.

I have given here only a superficial account of the business of signatures but sufficient, I hope, to indicate something of their history, use and worth. Those who delight in complexities and wish to pursue the matter further will find a number of adequate textbooks and sources of information which will be pointed out with fiendish delight by any qualified librarian, since he has had to run the whole gamut in preparing for his examinations.

There is one ancillary, but useful, method of checking completeness, which is by the 'catchwords', not often used today, but formerly courteously provided at the lower right-hand corner of each page of a book, below the last line. This is the same as the first word on the next page. If, therefore, the catchword and first word do not agree, there is likely to be something wrong. Catchwords are particularly vulnerable when the pages are being trimmed and may have been removed by clumsy cropping.

Confusion sometimes arises over the use of the words 'book' and 'volume', normally regarded as almost interchangeable, but taking on a special meaning, often indicated by the title-page, when applied to the make-up of a complete work. One which is too large to be housed conveniently between one pair of covers is often split into two, four, six, eight or ten volumes each separately bound. If you have shelf room, there is a 1784-89 set of Voltaire in seventy volumes, and Bell issued an attractive edition of the Poets (usually called Johnson's) in seventy-five small volumes.

Sometimes the original number of volumes is found to be inconvenient and a work is compressed, and so that we can get 'four volumes in two', 'eight volumes in four', etc. Both make-ups can be available at the same time and, so far as value goes, there is nothing to choose between them. Thus, a great work such as William Daniell and Richard Ayton's *Voyage Round Great Britain,* mentioned in Chapter 4, is offered either in eight

Mathematical Magick;

OR, THE

WONDERS

That may be performed by

Mechanichal Geometry.

In Two BOOKS.

CONCERNING

Mechanical { *Powers.*
{ *Motions.*

Being one of the moſt eaſie,
pleaſant, uſeful (and yet moſt neglected) part of *Mathematicks.*
Not before treated of in this Language.

By *J. Wilkins,* late Lᵈ Bᴘ of *Cheſter.*

Τέχνη πρατυμιν ἂν φύσει νικώμεθα.

LONDON:

Printed for *Edw. Gellibrand* at the *Golden
Ball* in St. *Pauls* Church-yard. 1 6 8 o.

One volume, but two books: title-page of Mathematical Magick *(1680), which described
four methods of flight: (1) by spirits or Angels; (2) by the help of fowls; (3) by wings fastened to
the body; (4) by a flying chariot.*

volumes or in four ('eight volumes in four'), even though the title-page may still say 'in eight volumes'.

Books, in the special sense, are a different matter. On the title-page 'in five books' or 'libri V' means that the author has divided his work into five main sections, all of which can be contained in one volume. Though each volume of a work will normally have a separate title-page, each book will almost certainly not. Chapman's famous translation of Homer, which sent Keats into ecstasies, is in twenty-four books, but they are contained comfortably in one folio volume.

One very simple little point, surprisingly often overlooked: if you find 'Finis' or 'The End', you will know that the goal is reached. If it says 'End of Vol. 1' or 'End of Vol. 5' you will know there is more to come and the set is not complete. Often the publisher will make all clear by putting 'End of fourth and last volume'. Though separate volumes sometimes have their own index, it is more usual to have a complete index at the end of the final volume, and the presence of this can sometimes be a useful guide.

Only in a very few cases can incompleteness be acceptable. You will sometimes see in a catalogue, or noted by a bookseller inside the cover, 'All published'. This means that, although it was originally intended to publish a longer work, it was never completed and that the three volumes out of the planned six, or some other combination, are all that will ever be available, unless some other author is eventually commissioned to complete the job. In such cases, the publication has status and will be priced accordingly. H.S. Lecky got less than half way through his *The King's Ships* (1913-14), giving a history, in alphabetical order of name, of the ships of the Royal Navy. But it is still a valuable work, and will be listed as 'all published'.

We must, of course, go further than the signed pages when dealing with an illustrated work. 'Plates', that is, whole page illustrations printed separately from the main text, and often on different paper, are not part of the original gathering and are therefore not signed. Sometimes, but not always, the author has supplied a list of plates and where they should appear in the book; sometimes, but not always, this can be relied upon, since plates apparently missing have an odd habit of turning up in some other spot; sometimes, but not always, the plates themselves are numbered, which makes life easier. You will often find, usually at the end, the optimistic author's 'Instructions to the Binder' for placing the plates; and, as frequently, discover that the disobliging fellow, doubtless resenting such autocracy, has made up his own mind about it.

More crimes are committed with illustrated books, especially in certain categories, than with any others, owing to the operations of the 'breaker', the dealer (and sometimes, regrettably, the collector) who will ruthlessly

JACOBI BREYNII
GEDANENSIS
EXOTICARUM
aliarumque
MINUS COGNITARUM
PLANTARUM
C E N T U R I A
PRIMA,

cum

FIGURIS ÆNEIS SUMMO
studio elaboratis.

Divinitas

Utilitas & Delectatio

Cum Sac: Cæsareæ Majest: Privilegio

Jacob Breyn

GEDANI·

Typis, fumptibus & in ædibus AUTORIS,
Imprimebat
DAVID-FRIDERICUS RHETIUS.
Anno cIɔ. Iɔc. LXXIIX.

An example of 'all published', from Dantzig, 1678. Note (1) the Emperor's licence to print, contained in the rectangular frame; (2) the unusual arrangement of Roman numerals (see Appendix I). Another uncommon feature is that the author has signed the title.

THEATRUM CHEMICUM
BRITANNICUM.

CONTAINING

Severall Poeticall Pieces of our Famous

English Philosophers, who have written

the *Hermetique Mysteries* in their owne
Ancient Language.

Faithfully Collected into one Volume,

with Annotations thereon,

By ELIAS ASHMOLE, *Esq.*

Qui est Mercuriophilus Anglicus.

THE FIRST PART.

Serpens & Bufo gradiens sup terrā, Aquila volans, est nostrū Magisteriū.

LONDON,

Printed by *J. Grismond* for NATH: BROOKE, at the
Angel in *Cornhill*; MDCLII.

Another example of 'all published', though 'the first part' on the title would normally lead one to expect more. Even unfinished, since it is an important alchemical work, it is probably worth £5,000-£6,000.

destroy a perfectly good book because the total value of the separate plates or maps, sold individually, is more than the intact volume would ordinarily be. Take, for example, a good copy of Camden's *Britannia,* Gibson's 1695 edition with its fifty fine double-page maps by Robert Morden. It regularly fetches £400-£600. Its fifty maps, according to county (and especially when attractively coloured) will fetch anything from £30 to £200 each, there being a greater demand for the Home Counties and certain others. If we take an average selling price of £50, the breaker stands to make £2,500, a tempting proposition. This sort of book is regularly stolen, despite security precautions.

The same treatment is accorded to fine hand-coloured and aquatint plate books containing noteworthy topographical views and military and sporting subjects. Book-destroyers of this kind, especially when they blatantly advertise their wares as suitable for breaking and framing for an inn, a billiard room or boudoir, act only in the cause of financial gain and have no respect for the qualities to be found in a complete book. I recall a fine falconry work where some plates had been extracted by the owner for this purpose, a Peter Pan Portfolio despoiled by a feminine hand, and a number of other examples.

I have just seen in a saleroom catalogue a single manuscript leaf from an early fourteenth century Bible, patiently and diligently written by a scribe in Southern France, illuminated, historiated and decorated[1] in gold, red and blue. Its whole history is known and is a sad example of cupidity overriding respect for beauty and history. For years it was in the library of a Spanish noble house, from whence it was acquired by Thomas Thorp (1791-1851), a baker who took to bookselling in Bedford Street, Piccadilly and Henrietta Street, Covent Garden. He specialised in gathering historical, topographical and genealogical documents and manuscripts, so was a great source of supply for Sir Thomas Phillipps (see pp.29-30) who at one time owed him £3,000. Phillipps bought the two-volume monastic Bible from him and it acquired the Mill Hill number MS 2506. In January 1921 it was purchased privately from the Phillipps collection by Sir Alfred Chester Beatty (1875-1968), the mining magnate whose chief hobby was the collection of manuscripts conspicuous for their calligraphy and decoration. In 1955 the Bible was exhibited at Trinity College, Dublin. After the Chester Beatty sale of 1969 it passed into the hands of a well-known London bookseller, Alan G. Thomas (who in 1975 published a fine book, *Great Books and Book Collectors*). He sold it to an American bookseller, who broke up the historic volumes that had survived the hazards of more than six centuries. Separate leaves have been appearing and reappearing since, the current value of good

---

1 See Chapter 13 for an explanation of these terms.

specimens being £200-£400. Even more recently a whole catalogue has been devoted to single leaves and cut-out miniatures from despoiled manuscripts.

In condemning such acts of desecration, I am of the opinion that the only exception that could be made is in the case of books already seriously incomplete and in bad condition, when the completion of its unhappy disintegration may be forgivable. Such a book, along with the executioner himself, is called a 'breaker', and will normally be sold w.a.f. ('with all faults').

There is a small category of books where incompleteness, for one reason or another, is almost the rule, so that it is accepted as the norm. Thus, a cataloguer can write with a reasonably happy heart, of Ackermann's *History of the University of Cambridge* (1814): "81 plates, including 15 of costume, but lacking the 32 supplementary portraits of the Founders", knowing that he can still be comfortably sure of his £1,500-£2,000. James Jenkins's *The Naval Achievements of Great Britain* (c.1820) has a splendid array of coloured aquatints, but can almost never be found with the two portraits of Nelson and Howe. Even without them, it is still worth in the region of £2,000.

The importance of general condition cannot be overstressed. Completeness and condition are two different things; for a book can be complete but in very poor condition and, conversely, incomplete but otherwise in very good state. The booksellers' and auctioneers' vocabulary concerning condition is a very extensive one and varies greatly from cataloguer to cataloguer. I offer the following as a partial guide:

> Sound: past its prime and beginning to show it.
> Suitable for rebinding: very badly in need of it; alternatively, wanting £40 spent on a £10 book.
> Reading copy: fit for nothing else.
> Working copy: not likely to withstand further toil.
> Sophisticated: dressed-up, faked-up and with face lifted.
> Honest copy: not attempting to hide its many imperfections.

The true collector should never allow himself to be beguiled into buying an unworthy copy of a book. He should take a very good look at it and, even more important, handle it. Is the binding loose? Are the hinges beginning to weaken? Has some moron tried to strengthen them with yellowing tape? Are the spine and boards badly scuffed or rubbed? (the euphemistically-minded cataloguer may say 'chafed', the French, more elegantly, 'tired'). Are the bottom corners bruised and in need of building up? Has the book been rebacked? (not a serious fault if the work has been expertly done. It should be almost imperceptible). When the book is opened, does it lie comfortably flat or is there marked constraint,

Chipped and hinges weakening: seventeenth century volumes feeling their years.

Rubbed and rebacked .

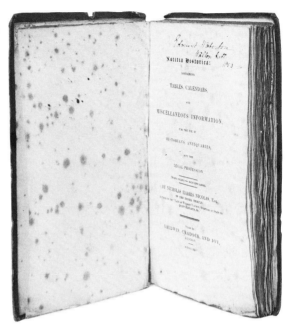

A bad attack of foxing.

Two volumes of Bohn's edition of Lowndes's Bibliographer's Manual, *the headbands betraying rough handling.*

indicating a plethora of new glue somewhere? Even the great binders can occasionally be at fault. The collector Frederick Locker Lampson once protested to the famous Bedford that one of his bindings was too tight. Doubtless with his tongue in his cheek, Bedford replied: "But Mr. Lampson, you must have been opening the book."

The plates and text should be scanned to see if 'foxing' is unacceptably bad. Foxing was a term first used in about the 1840s, probably because the brownish-yellow spots and blotches reminded some fox-hunting bibliophile of his quarry in the countryside. They are caused by micro-organisms feeding on the size and cellulose fibres and seem to attack certain types of books more than others, perhaps because of the quality of the paper or some fault in its manufacture. Certainly damp and bad ventilation foster it. It will be an unusually dishonest catalogue that does not have to mention it somewhere. 'Foxed as usual', 'margins foxed but plates clean', 'badly foxed in Vol. I', 'light foxing only', will be the sort of descriptions encountered.

The buyer has two courses open to him — he can live with the foxing or try to have it removed. The pages can be immersed in a solution of hypochloride and bleached till the stains, if they are not too recalcitrant, have disappeared. Then the paper will be washed clean with running water; and, if a proper job is to be made of it, resized and even retoned. It should be clear that such a restoration is not to be undertaken lightly, and it should be entrusted only to a skilled professional. There can be little doubt that the process tends to alter the original character and 'feel' of a book, and only the owner can decide whether this should be accepted as part of the price for turning a blighted copy into a reasonably healthy one. Don't look too surprised if you see an experienced bookseller sniffing an old book of very good appearance. He is not engaged in some new and unnatural vice. If you have a sensitive nose, you yourself will be able to detect if some washing operation has been carried out, since the chemicals used tend to leave a lingering smell, especially along the inner margins.

Worm holes are another blemish which should be noted by cataloguers, even though their presence will not normally be taken as a good reason for returning a book. They are almost in the category of honourable scars, and even some testimony to the quality of the text, since the larvae of the several types of beetle engaged in the battle seem to have thrived best on old and scholarly works, especially incunabula. Report has it that they have now virtually committed racial suicide, declining to accept the deplorable standards of modern literature and paper. The recommended treatment for infested books is to put them into a sealed tin with a jar of paradichlorobenzine for a week.

To sum all this up, if, on inspection, a book scores low marks and is a reasonably common item, have nothing more to do with it. There is a better copy round the corner or at the next sale. There is nothing more depressing than a collection of so-called first editions and rare items displaying faded spines, mull bursting through cracked hinges, scarred leather inadequately treated with greasy polish, mending tape of various hues round the spine, head and tail bands hanging forlornly and, perhaps worst of all, a badly lettered brown paper cover holding the whole thing together. Better ten books in good condition than a hundred cripples.

There are very occasional exceptions to this round condemnation. There are certain books, in almost any field, that are so rare that the collector is very unlikely to find a copy in good condition and, perforce, will have to make do with second, third, or tenth best. To take the most extreme case, the first English comedy is generally reckoned to be Nicholas Udall's *Ralph Roister-Doister* (date uncertain, but c.1560). The only copy known in the world is the one at Eton College, where Udall was headmaster, and that has no title-page. Clearly, if you or I should happen to chance on a second, battered and with a dozen pages adrift, we should be happy to buy it for a modest sum. There are many other books, even if they are not in quite so exclusive a category, that are unlikely to be found in any form at all; to take a miscellaneous selection, Wordsworth's and Coleridge's *Lyrical Ballads* (1798); the suppressed first edition of *Alice in Wonderland* (1865); the first edition, first issue, of Fergus (Ferguson Wright) Hume's *Mystery of a Hansom Cab* (1886), John Bunyan's *Book for Boys and Girls: or, Country Rhimes for Children* (1686) and Edgar Allan Poe's *Tamerlane* (1827). Of Tennyson's *The Lover's Tale* (1833) only six copies were printed. Of some books which are known from records and letters to have existed, no copies at all are known to have survived. So that, in assessing condition and completeness, the question of rarity must play an important part. Rarity is caused by a number of factors — the passage of time, the small number printed, the obscurity of the publisher and printer, suppression by authority or the author himself, accident, or deliberate destruction. Volumes I and II of the four-volume second edition of John Hutchins's *History and Antiquities of the County of Dorset* are very rare owing to a disastrous fire. According to the Brontë sisters, Aylott and Jones, the publishers of their *Poems* (1846), sold only two copies. According to another report, many of the sheets of Hume's *Mystery of a Hansom Cab* were blown away from a street barrow. Some early Thomas Hardy was remaindered by the publisher.

You will come across many definitions of rarity and, judging from catalogues and the like, surprisingly many different standards in assessing it. As John Carter has observed, such attempts at definition are a favourite game among bibliophiles. My personal effort is: "A rare book is one I can't find, and can't afford when found."

✳✳✳✳✳✳✳✳✳✳✳✳✳✳✳✳✳✳✳

Chapter 11

The Care of Books

> ...neither suffer them through negligence to mould and be moth-eaten or want their strings and covers.
>
> H. Peacham, *The Compleat Gentleman*

> Let no book perish, unless it be such an one as it is your duty to throw on the fire. There is no such thing as a worthless book, though there are some far worse than worthless; no book which is not worth preserving, if its existence may be tolerated; as there are some men whom it may be proper to hang, but none who should be suffered to starve.
>
> Hartley Coleridge, *Biographia Borealis*

It is a sad thing that so many so-called book lovers are book spoilers in some degree or other, through carelessness, neglect or indifference. They have earned their special opprobrium in the word biblioclast (book destroyer).

The famous are not exempt from blame. Johnson, in his periodic spring cleanings, had a habit of donning large gloves and lustily banging his books together amid clouds of dust before returning them to their shelves shaken and contused. As I have noted elsewhere, Shelley was known to tear out fly leaves in order to make paper boats. William Morris threw a fifteenth century quarto, so valuable that he would permit no one else to handle it, at the head of someone who annoyed him. Charles Lamb, an inveterate reader at the table, confessed that his copy of Milton might be found "in certain parts dirtied and soiled with a crumb of right Gloucester blacked in the candle." As has already been noted, James Thomson opened his books with a candle-snuffer, and Wordsworth with a greasy butter-knife. Edward Fitzgerald, who translated Omar Khayyam, tore out from his books pages that did not please him. Charles Darwin would cut a heavy book in halves to make it more convenient to handle, and fix broken sections together with strong metal clips.

I take leave to assume that none of my readers belong to this scapegrace company, but wish to cherish their possessions. A good deal of the care of them is common sense, but it is extraordinary what an uncommon quality that is when it comes to books.

When a book is opened, and either held in the hand or placed on a table, the front cover and hinge are immediately subjected to strain, especially if the volume is a thick and heavy one. Be merciful. Whichever hand it is held in, ensure that the fingers are supporting the other cover. If you have visitors who let the cover droop helplessly, like a child raised by one arm and dangling in mid-air, cross them off your visiting list so far as your books are concerned. If the volume is laid on desk or table, place another book, or something of equivalent thickness beneath the upper cover.

Many bookcases and sets of shelves displayed in furniture shops were never designed by a 'book man or anyone well acquainted with books, especially where sizes are concerned. If you are ordering, designing or making shelves, take the precaution of measuring a fair sample of your collection. You will find that a large proportion of them need a good ten inches between shelves, not forgetting that there must be ample room for them to be gently eased out and not hooked by the headband. A quarto is likely to need all of twelve inches, a folio correspondingly more, if you are not to be reduced to laying it on its side. There are very few books that are comfortable with less than eight inches.

Remember that books are weighty things. Shelves, if made of wood, will need to be at least three-quarters of an inch thick and preferably a little more; and they should be supported every three feet or so. Nothing looks more lamentably depressing than shelves sagging wearily in the middle, with decent books struggling to maintain a dignified upright posture. I have said nothing of metal, believing it to be offensive to any right-minded book lover, at least in his own home.

Remember that books need to breathe. Give them room to be taken easily from their shelves, not wrenched and twisted from their tightly packed companions. Desirable though they may be in special circumstances, I have always conducted a personal vendetta against glazed cabinets and patented bookcases with evil and malicious sliding and lifting glass panels. Nothing can be finer for honest books than to stand unashamed and free to the air. A soft feather duster need be their only guardian; and, anyway, a thin layer of dust keeps off other dust.

Damp is a formidable enemy and too much warmth as great a one, especially where leather bindings are concerned. Central heating can be as serious a scourge to fine old books as it is to fine old furniture. Vellum can become harsh, brittle and buckled. Calf and morocco can dry out to become lifeless and lustreless, instead of sprightly and glowing. Remember that they are made of the hide of good beasts and still appreciate feeding, even after three or four hundred years. Toilet lanolin, obtainable from any chemist, with its base of an oily substance extracted from wool, is an adequate curative, rubbed well into the leather and polished off after several days. Even better, after gentle cleaning, is a

Frontispiece of Thomas Moule's Bibliotheca Heraldica Magnae Britanniae *(1822) and, right, the title page of the same book showing the shadowy off-set of Moule's portrait.*

BIBLIOTHECA HERALDICA

MAGNÆ BRITANNIÆ.

AN

𝕬𝖓𝖆𝖑𝖞𝖙𝖎𝖈𝖆𝖑 𝕮𝖆𝖙𝖆𝖑𝖔𝖌𝖚𝖊 𝖔𝖋 𝕭𝖔𝖔𝖐𝖘

ON

GENEALOGY, HERALDRY, NOBILITY, KNIGHTHOOD, & CEREMONIES:

WITH A LIST OF

PROVINCIAL VISITATIONS, PEDIGREES, COLLECTIONS OF
ARMS, AND OTHER MANUSCRIPTS;

And a Supplement, enumerating the principal

FOREIGN GENEALOGICAL WORKS

By THOMAS MOULE.

London:

PRINTED FOR THE AUTHOR,
Duke Street, Grosvenor Square.

PUBLISHED BY LACKINGTON, HUGHES, HARDING, MAVOR, AND LEPARD,
FINSBURY SQUARE; J. MAJOR, SKINNER STREET; AND
R. TRIPHOOK, OLD BOND STREET.

....

1822.

preparation known as Boots C1590, compounded of lanolin, hexane, cedarwood oil and beeswax. I have known a derelict country house collection rescued with it and have seen ancient college and cathedral libraries brought back to serene life after decades of neglect. The British Museum formula (which is non-proprietary) using these ingredients is:

Anhydrous lanolin	7oz.
Cedarwood oil	1 fluid oz.
Beeswax	½ oz.
Hexane	11 fluid oz.

If you attempt the brew yourself, the beeswax should first be dissolved in the hexane, then the lanolin added and, finally, the cedarwood oil. **The hexane is very inflammable and neither it, nor the resulting thin yellow cream, should be used near a flame.** The mixture should always be well shaken before use. When life and substance have been restored, an occasional polish with a microcrystalline wax will keep a good sheen on calf bindings.

Parchment and vellum should be approached with great caution, since they are not likely to respond to ordinary cleaning methods; but the firm Archival Aids, of High Wycombe, Bucks, which specialises in the safe treatment of early records, has marketed a non-abrasive powdered rubber which may be applied with safety and will remove at least surface dust and dirt.

Tempting though they are, books should not be regarded as natural repositories or presses, especially for botanical specimens. The book-collector becomes familiar with the 'off-set', which is the accidental transfer, in a rather tasteful brown shade, of ink from a printed page or illustration to the opposite page. Vegetable juice is even less desirable, and the resulting plant print rarely has any relevance to the text. Elizabeth Barrett Browning gave us a gentle reminder in *Aurora Leigh:*

> Silly girls
> Who plant their flowers in our philosophy
> To make it fine, and only spoil the book!
> No more of it, Aurora.

So far as actual repairs to defective books are concerned, I hope I have said enough in earlier pages to discourage collectors from attempting them, unless they submit themselves to attending one of the excellent courses arranged in some centres of education. If a professional binder is employed, make very sure that he is what he sets out to be and has all the qualities of sensitive craftsmanship the work demands. It is unfortunately all too common an experience to see so-called expert work resulting in a garish meretriciousness quite unsuitable for, and unworthy of, the original book.

Hartley Coleridge, already quoted at the head of this chapter, had the rights of it:

> The binding of a book should always suit its complexion. Pages, venerably yellow, should not be cased in military morocco, but in sober brown russia. . . How absurd to see the works of William Penn in flaming scarlet, and George Fox's Journal in Bishop's purple!

❋❋❋❋❋❋❋❋❋❋❋❋❋❋❋❋❋

Chapter 12

Ephemera

> To sift the good from the bad in the daily onset taxes all our
> wits...no use battling against such a stream; all the shouting,
> the crying and the spluttering of all times have not arrested it,
> nor will they, for rubbish is necessary...thistledown blown
> hither and thither by the wind.
>
> Holbrook Jackson, *The Anatomy of Bibliomania*

Literally speaking, ephemera are things that last only a day; in the more
accepted sense, things destined to endure only a short time; but, by a
curious paradox, in the most modern sense, things which have, in fact,
long survived their predestined span.

Though, doubtless, man has always been a jackdaw, a snapper-up of
unconsidered trifles, the recognition of ephemera as a legitimate and
respectable sphere of collecting is a comparatively modern phenomenon,
its devotees now having their own Society and special sales organised by
reputable auctioneers who not long ago would have looked down their
noses at the trivia they are now, in the name of Mammon, glad to
catalogue.

I have hesitated about including a small section on this sort of material
in a volume on book-collecting, since the ephemera umbrella seems to
cover an extraordinary variety of objects; including music hall songs,
palm prints, cigarette packets, orange wrappers, 'peep' eggs, bridge score
cards, menus, embroidery patterns, watchmaker's labels, tram tickets
and commemorative tins; to say nothing of posters proclaiming the merits
of various soaps, female herbal pills, bilious and liver medicaments.

On the other hand, I note that sales include material which is the
legitimate concern of the book-collector, such as official proclamations,
periodicals, almanacks, children's exercise books and writing sheets,
albums, Acts of Parliament and broadsides.

Although there is some laxity in the use of the term, 'broadside' or
'broadsheet' should properly be applied only to a complete, undivided
large sheet, printed on one side. In fact, the description 'single sheet' is
sometimes found. Interestingly enough, broadside probably derives from
the naval tactic of firing all the guns from one side of a ship of war at once,
without giving the recipient the necessity of awaiting instalments. Such

Bowden's Indestructible Battledore.

GAINSBOROUGH: PRINTED BY J. W. BOWDEN.
PRICE THREE HALF-PENCE.

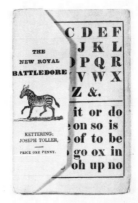

THE
NEW ROYAL
BATTLEDORE

KETTERING:
JOSEPH TOLLER,

PRICE ONE PENNY.

C D E F
J K L
O P Q R
V W X
Z &.

it or do
on so is
of to be
go ox in
oh up no

A B C D
E F G H
I J K L
M N O P
Q R S T
U V W
X Y Z &

FOR A GOOD
CHILD
AT SCHOOL.

Price One Penny.

CASTLE CARY:
Printed and Sold by S. Moore,

ELEPHANT AND CHILD.
A woman dying, who had been
very kind to an Elephant, and who
used to lay her infant near him;
the animal was so fond of the child,
that he seemed uneasy when it was
out of his sight; and would not eat
unless the nurse laid the cradle between his feet. When the child
slept he drove away the flies with
his trunk, and when it cried he
would rock the cradle till it fell
asleep. Some are 15 feet high.
PRICE ONE PENNY.

A group of provincial 'battledores' from Gainsborough, Kettering, Castle Cary, etc. Descendants of the earlier hornbooks for the instruction of children, they were usually printed on coloured card.

sheets are of historic importance, since they date back to the sixteenth century, when popular poems and ballads were issued in this form; and royal and official proclamations took to the streets in this guise almost from the first days of printing. Through the centuries politicians, protestors and agitators of every sort found them invaluable for smiting the public eye; and, in their most debased form, they were used by such printers as James Catnach (1792-1841) of the Seven Dials, London, to convey to sensation seekers scaffold speeches by murderers and other criminals, often before the rogues had uttered a word or given any sign that they intended to.

A point of typographical interest is that the printers of broadside notices and ballads continued to use the old 'black letter' or Gothic founts of type long after they had been discarded in favour of the Roman letter for printed books; so that many of them can take us back in spirit and atmosphere to the Gutenberg Bible and Caxton working at the Sign of the Red Pale in Westminster. The term 'black-letter' ballad is sometimes found.

At the peak of their literary importance, broadside sheets were used for poems by men of such eminence as John Dryden (1631-1700), and publications of this nature could certainly find a fit home with any book-collector. A single sheet printing of Dryden's *The Epilogue. . . Spoke before His Majesty at Oxford, March 19, 1680* has fetched nearly £1,000.

An attractive broadside group are the so-called Beadle and Bellman's Verses, addressed in the first half of the nineteenth century to such town and city dwellers as 'the worthy inhabitants of the Parish of Barnes, Surrey' or 'the worthy masters and mistresses of the Holborn End Division of the Parish of St. Giles in the Fields' and designed to be proclaimed by the public crier or parish bellman. With such decorations as Christmas scenes they often brought an additional touch of jollity at special festivities.

Other 'collectables' are the single sheet almanacks of the tradesman and workshop variety, and the products of the perennial 'Old Moore' who, possessed of the secret of eternal youth, began prophesying in 1699 and is still going strong. The original was Francis Moore, a versatile citizen of Lambeth who was at once schoolmaster, astrologer and physician. He was probably the first 'weather-man', using the medium of the broadsheet instead of television and radio. Their comparative accuracy has never, to my knowledge, been studied.

The broadsheet idea, or at least the name, was borrowed by *The Times* newspaper in the First World War, when it organised the printing and distribution of literary extracts, reminiscent of home, for the comfort of the troops. Printed on thin single sheets, suitable for enclosing in an envelope, they were a considerable success. They were truly ephemeral

A 1624 broadside publication of Nicholas Breton's The Shepheard's Delight *and Thomas Deloney's* A pleasant new Ballad of Daphne; *black letter on a single folio sheet.*

An early nineteenth century broadside naval recruiting poster, original size approx. 24ins. by 14½ ins.

and complete sets are now very rare. Another venture which resurrected the broadside idea was the Flying Fame Press founded in 1912 by Holbrook Jackson, Claude Lovat Fraser and Ralph Hodgson. It printed prose and verse in broadside and chapbook form till its activities were cut short by the War.

A recent auction sale brought to my mind the fascinating subject of tally sticks, which could make a wonderfully interesting and historically interesting collection. Unfortunately they make admirable firewood, and vast numbers have been destroyed deliberately or by accident. In 1834 reforming zealots destroyed a vast collection of Exchequer tallies in the furnaces of the House of Lords, and through the centuries they have been thoughtlessly thrown out and destroyed in the same way that, after a period, we ourselves dump old bills and receipts. Essentially, this is what tallies were, wooden sticks used in accounting and common all over Europe. When, for example, money was paid into the Royal Exchequer, a stick was notched and split into two parts, payer and payee retaining one each. In cases of dispute the two halves would be matched to see if the notches corresponded. We still complain that accounts and statements do not 'tally'. One half of the stick was known as the 'stock', the origin of our modern word in 'stocks and shares'. Notches on tallies were an early way of scoring in cricket matches, and people are still said to 'notch up' a good score, just as one can still hear a commentator say that a free-scoring batsman is 'in good nick'. Surprisingly, the last official tally-making at Westminster was as late as 1826. In 1909, almost by accident, the 'stocks' of about 1,300 medieval Exchequer tallies were discovered.

The old official tallies were about 9ins. long, though I believe the Bank of England treasures one majestic example of 8ft. 6ins. At the auction sale mentioned above, a tally stick belonging to Sir Thomas Phillipps and recording the delivery of horses and waggons of hay at Carlisle for Edward I's Scottish campaign of 1306, along with five relevant documents, fetched £2,400 against a pre-sale estimate of £400-£600.

A section of printed ephemera with its own special charm is that consisting of the small mementoes which a number of printing houses struck off to amuse and honour visitors. The name and date were inserted in a decorative framework, this probably being kept standing for immediate use when sightseers arrived. The visitor was often allowed to pull the press and, at least in some places, in return for watching the setting of the type and the privilege of carrying away the souvenir, was expected to buy beer for the workmen. The Sheldonian Theatre in Oxford was one popular centre for this *divertissement* and Celia Fiennes, who chronicled her seventeenth century journeys, records that she was there in 1694 and printed her name several times. Most surviving examples date from the eighteenth century, by which time the decoration became

A group of nineteenth century greeting cards and valentines, types of ephemera now a popular field of collecting.

Nineteenth century ephemera, including table games, playing cards, a hieroglyphic card (one where small pictures are substituted for a number of letters or syllables) and (centre) a 'zoetrope' or 'wheel of life', an early motion-picture toy.

Upon the F R...
B Ehold the Liquid
  That ltely S H
Here You may P R I...
'Cauſe numb'd with (
And lay it by ; Th
May ſee what T H I

Mr. John Ma
in Long-Buck

Printed on the I(
Hithe, J A N (

Souvenir of the great freeze of 1740, printed 'on the Ice upon the Thames at Queen-Hithe'.
The elaborate allegorical framework was left standing. John Matcham's name was set by the
printer and the 'woollcomber' pulled the press. Of this 'unheard of frost' one chronicler
recorded that "Men felt so oppressed that days passed by unheeded. One... could hardly

Year 1739-40.

ow frozen o'er !
y Burden bore.
, tho' cannot Write,
with great Delight.
t to come
ICE were done.

Voollcomber,
hamptonſhire

Thames at Queen-
2d, 1739-40.

speak; one sat and thought, yet could not think. . .the trees split asunder. Not only beer, but wine in cellars froze. . .No bread was eatable, for it was as cold and hard as a stone." Note the 1739/40 dating. For an explanation, see Appendix II.

increasingly elaborate and stylised. In the next century the practice petered out, though it was still occasionally revived for particularly distinguished visitors, who might expect to have their names recorded on silk or satin rather than plebeian paper. Perhaps the last feeble kick of this lust to print one's name was the station platform and amusement arcade machine where, on inserting a penny, one was able to punch one's name on a metal strip, which the contraption disgorged on the pull of a handle.

Oxford, in fact, houses one of the best collections of printed ephemera, assembled by Doctor John Johnson, printer to the University from 1925-46. His profound scholarship is reflected in his catalogue of Greek and Roman papyri in the Rylands Library at Manchester; but he also found delight in small and simple things produced by more humble establishments than University Presses, such as cotton-reel labels, trade cards, valentines, playbills, almanacks, grocery bags and much else.

Among printers' mementoes, one should not forget the special examples, in the nature of things not easy to find because of the infrequency of the occasions, produced by presses set up on frozen rivers, such as the Thames and Severn. In 1684 Croom, a printer of Bride Lane had such a press which was patronised by Charles II[1] and his court mingling with the crowds on the ice. John Evelyn records of the same occasion:

> January 24th. The frost continuing more and more severe, the Thames before London was still planted with booths in formal streets, all sorts of trades and shops furnished and full of commodities, even to a printing press, where the people and ladies took a fancy to have their names printed, and the day and year set down when printed on the Thames.

Since they have their own Society and Journal, collectors of bookplates may object to them being categorised as ephemera, but they are certainly among the periphera of interest to book-collectors. Often known as *ex libris* ('from the books of. . .'), they are divided by experts into a number of well-defined categories, according to style and period. A less elaborate version is the book-label or book-ticket, which is smaller and often carries only the owner's name.

Bookplates, attached to the front paste-down or, less frequently, to the free endpaper, are often readily detachable. If they originate from some person of eminence they have, of course, additional prestige; but they are prized in their own right because many are beautiful in themselves and are representative of their time and place. Since they can be removed,

---

1 Charles II had the names of himself and his family printed on a piece of paper measuring 3½ins. by 4ins. Among the names he included 'HANS INKELDER', a matter of some puzzlement. But the humour of the Merry Monarch was probably in play since 'Hans in Kelder' is Dutch for 'Jack in the Cellar' and Princess Ann of Denmark was pregnant.

Bookplates of Richard Towneley (an early dated example), Queen Victoria and Horace Walpole's Strawberry Hill.

they can also be inserted, and any book that carries a distinguished plate should be scrutinised with care to see if there are signs of an earlier bookplate beneath or of recent addition. Forgeries of coveted plates, such as George Washington's, William Penn's and Lord Nelson's are not unknown and, since a number of the original copper-plates have survived, later 'strikes' have been common. There are also special plates printed by auctioneers when they are selling off the library of some eminent man, or put in by librarians to denote a special gift or legacy of books. Sometimes a descendant has resurrected the bookplate of an ancestor and used it in later books, if necessary cutting off the original name.

Gordon Craig once said that "a bookplate is to the book what a collar is to the dog" — a wisecrack not wholly true, since the purpose of the plate is not to enable a book to be led round by its owner, or even for it to be returned by the police when lost. True, some plates seem to have been designed as a reminder, sometimes polite, sometimes far from it, that the volume has strayed from its proper home. Brian North Lee, in *British Bookplates* quotes a label printed 'From a bedroom in Arundel Castle'. Such a book could conceivably be returned openly with only a modest blush; but another labelled 'Stolen from. . .' would necessitate a more surreptitious means of restoration to its owner.

Bookplates have an ancient and honourable history both in England and on the Continent. Albrecht Dürer designed them as early as 1500 or before. Cardinal Wolsey used one, 1515-34, as did Sir Nicholas Bacon, father of Sir Francis. France, Holland and Italy can all claim early examples. In America the first so far discovered dates from 1674, but the most prized plates, e.g. those of Washington and Paul Revere, occur a hundred years afterwards. Their charm and variety are endless, depicting, as they do, alluring piles of books, scholars at their labours, proud armorial bearings, ancestral homes, gardens, landscapes, allegories, even the likeness of owners, as in the case of Samuel Pepys and James Gibbs, the architect. You may see the location of Ellen Terry's cottage at Winchelsea, the billowing sail of Captain Locker's ship (see p.200-201), the Tower of London (as used on the Public Record Office plate), the crest of Charles Dickens, to which he was not entitled, having annexed it from a 1625 grant to William Dickens, and the forty quarterings of the arms of Sir Francis Fust. Famous artists have contributed, Holbein, Hogarth, Bewick, Bartolozzi, Vertue, Kate Greenaway, Reynolds Stone. The characteristic styles of great architects and designers may be seen clearly reflected — Chippendale, Sheraton, Adam and Hepplewhite.

One of the attractions of bookplate collecting is that it can be relatively inexpensive. Leaving aside the famous names, which will inevitably be

Bookplates of Lord Rodney, Robert Harley of Brampton Castle and Mr. Cumberland (designed by William Blake).

An early Australian photograph, c.1885, typical of topographical ephemera now much sought after.

more costly, great numbers of obscure and humble folk have chosen this friendly and attractive method of identifying their precious books and have thereby secured a small niche in the history of bibliophily. Considerable collections can often be acquired in a single auction room lot.

Among book ephemera I must also spare a paragraph for the modest bookmark, much neglected and too little chronicled.[2] I do not, of course, refer to improvised examples such as scraps of brown paper and bacon rinds, but to the commercially produced strips of silk, paper and card, some of them elaborately lettered and decorated, deckled, frilled, tassled and ribboned. Some of the best were produced at Coventry in the last century. The best collection I ever knew had cost its owner not a penny. He was a Nottingham bookseller who, over the years, had abstracted from the volumes that came into his shop countless examples reflecting an extraordinary diversity of art, quotation and opinion, good and very bad. He had unfortunately proceeded to mar them by fastening them to strips of card with paper clips, which had rusted and left their foul trail on the bookmarks. As one who, to the detriment of temper, finger tips and nails,

---

2 But see A.W. Coysh, *Collecting Bookmarkers,* David & Charles, 1974.

has removed them in their thousands from letters and archives, I implore mercy from any like-minded custodians.

A note on a field of collecting which shows every sign of becoming more than a passing fad — that of old cheques. The book-collector can obviously fight his corner here with examples from well-known authors and historic figures who either drew the cheques or were at the receiving end. £20-£40 is at present the going rate for good examples.

The value of early photographs has also risen sharply in recent years, especially those of topographical significance.

Handwritten ephemera have a special interest, bringing as they do a

Bill presented by George Cruikshank, 1848 (see overleaf).

sense of intimacy, of closeness to the people concerned, that does not belong to the printed word. Tradesmen's bills, recipes, nurserymen's lists of plants, school prospectuses, old exercise books and writing sheets, programmes and invitations, all the domestic and commercial trivia from before the days of typewriters, are typical.

From my own collection I cherish a small bill presented by the artist George Cruikshank (1792-1878) in the form of a tiny letter which, when folded, measures only about 1½ ins. by 2ins. and is marked 'wait' on the outside. Opened up, it contains only a rapid sketch of the artist's hand holding a supplicatory top hat, above the characteristic signature.

I was fortunate to find between the leaves of a large book an exquisitely penned transcription of the Commandments and the Lord's Prayer, all embraced in a delicate architectural framework, dating from the late eighteenth century. It was by the celebrated Matthew Buchinger, born in Germany without legs and only short stumps of arms without hands. He settled in London and astounded the country by the extent to which he was able to overcome his disastrous physical handicaps. As well as becoming a superb calligrapher, he was an expert conjurer, performed on musical instruments, played a variety of games and could thread a needle with the best. He also contrived to marry several times, on one occasion to a shrewish wench who so exasperated him that he leapt upon her and gave her such a beating that she held her peace thereafter. Apart from originals from his pen, which are rare, printed broadsides illustrating his feats were popular.

I treasure a torn and spotted letter, valueless from the autograph point of view, dating from the late eighteenth century and endorsed on the back 'This Letter was found by Lord Lewisham in a Haberdashers Shop.' I quote it in full, in tribute to the whole glorious regiment of women shoppers, firm of purpose and knowing exactly what they want:

> Sir,
>
> If you please to send me a scarlet Cardinal [a short red cloak], and let it be full yard long, and rather longer than a yard long, and let it be full, for it be for a large Woman, they tell me I may have a long one, and a handsome one, for 11s but I shou'd not be willing to give more than 12s, but if you have any as long as that, either duffil or cloth, if it is cheaper, I shou'd like it as well, for I am not to give but 12s for it. I shou'd like a cloth one best if you please — I beg of your Sir to be so good as not to fail me this Cardinal by Wednesday, without fail, but let it be full yard long I beg, or else it will not do fail not on Wednesday, and in so doing you will very much oblige me.
>
> Hampton   M. Vins

PS   I hope you will charge your lowest price for it, and if you please not to send a duffil one, but a cloth one, full yard long, fail not on Wednesday, please to send it by Mr. Field the Waterman, who comes to the Beehive, at Queenhithe, pray don't send a duffil one but a cloth one. I have altered my Mind; I should not like it cloth, but duffil, let it be cloth, and not to be more than 11s at most, and full yard long, and two if you please, both of a length, and both large ones, full yard long, both of a price, they both be for one Woman — they must be exactly alike for goodness and price — fail not on Wednesday — and full yard long.

Magazines — deriving their name from the word in several languages for 'storehouses' — are increasingly becoming a recognised field for the collector. 'Periodical' may be regarded as almost synonymous, but seems to be increasingly reserved for the more literary types. Though earlier examples may be found, those of the eighteenth century are more likely to come to hand fairly often, e.g., *The Tatler,* begun in 1709, *The Spectator* (1711) and *The Guardian* (1712). John Wilkes's *North Briton* has its own brand of excitements, and a complete run of the *Gentleman's Magazine,* from its inception in 1731, will occupy a good deal of shelf room and, probably, a decade or two of happy searching. Long runs can, of course, be purchased at a price in the saleroom, but odd volumes picked up here and there should be inexpensive. The next century saw the emergence of such revered names as the *Edinburgh Magazine,* the *Quarterly* and *Blackwood's,* and soon the presses engaged in a helter-skelter race to put a remarkable variety of magazines, at every educational level and from every popular viewpoint, on to bookstalls and into reading rooms. It is a daunting task to compile an adequate list, but it has been successfully attempted in such publications as Crane and Kaye's *Census of British Newspapers and Periodicals, 1620-1800* (1927), and the Library Association's *Subject-Index to Periodicals.*

The chief disadvantages for the collector are the vast amount of space needed to house anything like a representative collection, and its far from attractive appearance, except with bound runs. Outhouses are usually the only answer. Many will restrict themselves to such magazines and periodicals in which their chosen authors made significant appearances. Conan Doyle, Thomas Hardy, Rider Haggard and Evelyn Waugh are among them. Charles Lamb can be found sheltering modestly over the initials 'C.L.' in Hone's periodic publications. The collectors of boys' and girls' magazines need neither justification nor encouragement. Tom Merry, Bob Cherry, Billy Bunter and all their peers bid fair to join the immortals, only a little lower than Falstaff, Gulliver and Long John Silver.

I have left till last what may well be considered by book-collectors one of the most charming fields of ephemera collecting — that of the chapbook, so called from the chapman or pedlar in whose pack so many of these small publications found their way through the shires of England. Had he not plodded his way to the fairs and markets, to the countless isolated communities in villages and hamlets, the English race would have been immeasurably poorer in its literature, its recreations and its memories of the past.

We must try to imagine these little worlds, with no public libraries or mobile vans, no bookshops or post offices, no magazines and even an old newspaper a rare event. Periodically through the dust and the rutted mud came the laden pedlar, on his feet or the back of a donkey; and from his strapped load presently spilled the trifling, precious wares of his trade — the cheap gloves and laces, the toys, trinkets and gee-gaws, the lengths of material — and, most important of all for our purposes here, the ballad sheets, broadsides and booklets that brought news of the wider world and stories and verse to give pleasure round the hearth in the long winter evenings.

Curiously enough, since by definition a stationer 'stays put', they are variously described on their publications as the 'walking', 'running' and even 'flying' stationers; and there is adequate testimony to their activities and to their influence.

Roger Ascham (1515-68), tutor to Queen Elizabeth, wrote in *The Scholemaster:*

> In our forefathers' time...few books were read in our tongue, saving certain books of chivalry, as they said for pastime and pleasure...As one, for example, 'Morte Arthur', the whole pleasure of which standeth in two special points, in open manslaughter and bold bawdry...What toys the daily reading of such a book may work in the will of a young gentleman, or a young maid...wise men can judge and honest men do pity.

George Wither (1588-1667), poet and pamphlet-writer, complained in *The Scholler's Purgatory:*

> They [the Stationers] have so pestered their printing-houses and shops with fruitless volumes that the ancient and renowned authors are almost buried among them as forgotten...so they who desire knowledge are still kept ignorant; their ignorance increaseth their affection to vain toys; their affection makes the stationer to increase his provision of such stuff, and at last you shall see nothing to be sold amongst us but...Bevis of Southampton or such trumpery.

John Bunyan (1628-88) pictured himself in his unregenerate youth as saying: "Give me a ballad, a news-book, George on horseback, or Bevis of Southampton."

Richard Baxter (1615-91) warned his readers "of the writings of false teachers, which would corrupt your understandings: and of vain romances, play-books, and false stories, which may bewitch your fantasies and corrupt your hearts."

Leaving aside the single sheet publications, which we have already discussed, the most desirable of the chapman's wares for the collector are the sheets folded to make a booklet of eight or twelve pages. Often they carry crude woodcuts (which may have little or no relevance to the contents). They perpetuate the great romances and adventure stories of the Middle Ages, setting down in simple and unadorned sentences the songs and tales formerly carried by minstrel and troubadour; tales of the Seven Champions of Christendom, the great Bevis of Southampton (twice quoted above), with his steed Arundel and his invincible sword Morglay, Arthur and his company of the Round Table. Here, too, are the less lordly but much-loved Robin Hood, Tom Hickathrift, Lob-lie-by-the-Fire, the Wise Men of Gotham, Jack the Giant Killer, Puss-in-Boots, Dick Whittington, and a hundred more. Fairy tales, fables, moral and religious stories, alphabets, songs and poems, all were grist for the stationers' presses.

Sir Thomas Malory's *Noble Histories of King Arthur and of Certain of his Knights* — 'open manslaughter and bold bawdry' — was printed by Caxton in 1485. Malory was a thief, a cattle-rustler and a despoiler of sacred things, a knight who tarnished his vows and broke the code of chivalry. But in prison he perhaps recaptured some of his lost knighthood in telling the heroic stories of the Round Table. There was another edition of them in 1554, then they do not seem to have been reprinted for nearly three hundred years. How then were they kept alive and fresh in the hearts and minds of English folk, if not through the chapman?

As we have seen, Queen Elizabeth's Roger Ascham, in many ways broadminded and tolerant, thought the stories immoral and mischievous; and other high-minded people pronounced them wanton and unworthy of reading. But the people of England knew better and continued to read and delight in their chapbooks. Even a later and more sophisticated age continued to enjoy them. Leigh Hunt (1784-1859) wrote in *My Books:*

> The oldest and most worn-out woodcut, representing King Pippin, Two Shoes, or the grim Soldan, sitting with three staring blots for his eyes and mouth, his sceptre in one hand, and his five fingers raised and spread in admiration at the feats of the Gallant London Apprentice, cannot excite in me a feeling of ingratitude.

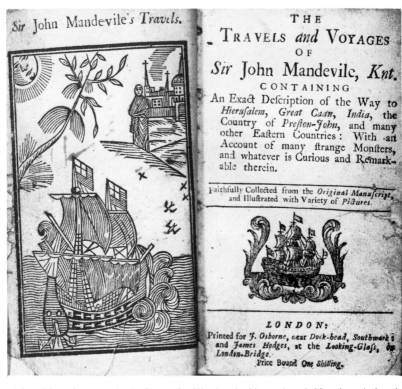

The following text appears within the illustration:

Sir John Mandevile's *Travels.*

THE
TRAVELS *and* VOYAGES
OF
Sir John Mandevile, *Knt.*
CONTAINING
An Exact Description of the Way to *Hierusalem*, *Great Caan*, *India*, the Country of *Preston-John*, and many other Eastern Countries: With an Account of many strange Monsters, and whatever is Curious and Remarkable therein.

Faithfully Collected from the *Original Manuscript*, and Illustrated with Variety of *Pictures*.

LONDON:
Printed for *J. Osborne*, near *Dock-head, Southwark;* and *James Hodges*, at the *Looking-Glass, on London-Bridge.*
Price Bound One *Shilling.*

A late eighteenth century chapbook type of publication, in this case bound. Note the typical crude woodcut illustration, probably resurrected from an earlier publication.

Such men as Joseph Crawhall of Newcastle, Andrew Tuer and Claud Lovat Fraser have striven to revive them and imitate them, with their woodcuts, their simple stories and their irresistible humour. Their predecessors are still to be found, sometimes cheaply with those who do not know their true significance and worth. As Sawyer and Darton wrote so tellingly in *English Books:* ''The Running Stationers, as they were at the last called, bore a light but precious fardel: just the Short History of the English People — no more.''

✱✱✱✱✱✱✱✱✱✱✱✱✱✱✱✱✱✱

Chapter 13

Autograph Letters and Manuscripts

> The best of the autograph collectors would not have accepted for one minute that their pursuit was the poor relation of manuscript collecting proper. Indeed they would have argued — and perhaps with some justice — that theirs was a more refined branch of the art: for did it not demand to a quite exceptional degree a sense of the romance of the past and a feeling for an evocative relic?
>
> A.N.L. Munby, *The Cult of the Autograph Letter in England*

This is a book about books; but some small space must be found for that art, and its products, which preceded printing by many thousands of years and without which there would have been no books at all — that of handwriting.

Books, letters, documents, manuscripts — in my mind they are all indissolubly linked, members of one great family; but it is far from the general feeling. I know booksellers who regard the written word with the utmost suspicion, profess that they do not understand it, and will have nothing to do with it; dealers who specialise in autograph material, but will not touch books — unless, of course, they happen to be on the subject of autographs; and many who maintain an ambivalent attitude, preferring to keep their options open and, if they can afford it, employing some eccentric especially to deal with this awkward material.

I find all this difficult to understand, perceiving no dichotomy; though I must confess to some predilection for the original letter or manuscript. For me, there is an immediacy about them, an intimacy, that can bring me closer to the writer than anything else. The hasty note, the spluttering pen, the exasperated correction, the careful clerkly hand, the grandiloquent flourish, the obsequious subscription, the torn seal, the glint of sand still held in the writing from the hand that strewed it centuries ago — all these and much else bring me into close company with the past, more than the rooms in which men sat, the streets they walked, the clothes they wore or the trinkets that adorned them. I make an exception, of course, of the books they owned.

As ever, we must begin by getting our terms clear, beginning with the much misused word 'autograph'. This is both noun and adjective. As the man in the street normally understands it, the noun autograph means 'autograph signature'. This is the sense in which the mere autograph

DATE	NAME	ADDRESS	REMARKS

Page of the visitors' book to a famous, though short-lived London bookshop, the Bermondsey Bookshop (1921-30), founded "to bring books and the love of books into Bermondsey." It was a fashionable haunt of the literary set, the above page showing the signatures of Laurence Binyon, Richard Church, A.E. Coppard and Clemence Dane among others.

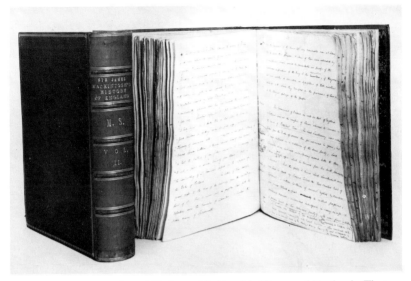

The 'holograph' manuscript, of Sir James Mackintosh's History of England. *The term holograph (from the Greek 'whole' and 'I write') is often used of literary MSS as distinct from autograph letters and documents.*

collector uses it, the boy who triumphantly proclaims that he has secured the hastily scribbled signature of his favourite footballer.

More care should be exercised in the use of the adjective, as in 'autograph manuscript', than is sometimes the case. Let us imagine that we are fortunate enough to find, written in Robert Browning's hand, a copy of his famous song from *Pippa Passes,* beginning ''The year's at the spring, And day's at the morn...'' This is the, or at least an, autograph manuscript of *Pippa,* meaning that it is genuinely in the poet's hand. But supposing Browning for some reason has copied out some lines from his wife's almost equally well-known *A Musical Instrument,* beginning ''What was he doing, the great god Pan, Down in the reeds by the river?'' This is not the autograph manuscript of the poem, but it is an autograph manuscript of Robert Browning's, since it is in his hand.

Unless it refers to something of antiquity, beauty of handwriting or decoration, as in ''illuminated manuscript', the term manuscript (literally 'written by hand') usually implies a literary composition of some sort. Sometimes an early manuscript contains more than one hand, the additional words, marginalia or even whole paragraphs and columns, being explanations of, or comments on, the original. These are known as 'glosses'. A document, as distinct from a manuscript, implies something official or designed to set out facts or points of view. In a handwritten document, the main body will normally have been written by a scribe or secretary, but signed by the person, or persons, issuing it. Thus, 'GEORGE III. Document signed. . .' means that only the signature itself is the hand of the king. Similarly, 'GEORGE III. Letter signed', as distinct from 'Autograph letter signed', means that the letter has been written by a clerk or secretary but that the king has added his signature. Another important convention should be noted, as in: '[Henry II]. A collection of deeds. . .etc.' The use of square brackets would normally mean that there is nothing in the hand of the king, not even a signature, but that the material is contemporary with him and belongs to his period.

A number of standard abbreviations are in common use in catalogues and should be interpreted in the light of some of the explanations give above:

> AL Autograph Letter in the hand of the person to whom it is attributed, but unsigned.
>
> ALS or ALs Autograph Letter signed.
>
> DS or Ds Document signed.
>
> Holograph An up-market word for a manuscript entirely in the author's handwriting.
>
> LS or Ls Letter signed (i.e. the main text is in another hand).
>
> MS A single manuscript, MSS more than one.
>
> TLS or TLs As above, but typed.
>
> The same type of abbreviations will be found for postcards.

Reverting to early manuscripts, especially those of monastic origins, there is a small group of words often encountered in their description. If a book or manuscript is 'illuminated' it is lit up with hand-painted initial words, capital letters and borders in colours, gold and silver. This is a general term covering the whole field of decoration. Not all the work was done in religious houses. From about the fourteenth century lay artists became more prominent, sometimes travelling and sometimes settled in urban workshops near wealthy patrons. The term illuminated has, of course, been borrowed for books printed in colours in medieval style.

If a book or manuscript has headings or the first capitals of paragraphs painted or printed in red, the rest of the text being black, it is said to be 'rubricated'. The rubricator, usually a specialist in the work, put in his capitals when the rest of the manuscript or printed book had been completed. It is not uncommon to find the spaces still blank in early books, the scribe not having arrived before the books were put on the market. An early printed book which has escaped the attention of the illuminator or rubricator is often described as 'untouched'. If certain capital letters incorporate coloured drawings representing scenes in the text, they are said to be 'historiated'. In the world of manuscripts, 'miniature' has come to have a rather puzzling significance. To 'miniate' originally meant to use minium or red lead (usually mixed with, e.g., egg white and water) for rubrication and illumination. Thereafter confusion set in and, from scenes of events, groups of figures, etc., presented on a very small scale, the term has come to mean elaborate pictures, much more ambitious than the historiations and sometimes extending to the whole of a large page. The value of illuminated manuscripts depends very much on the nature, quality and size of all these pictorial decorations, with the textual content and beauty of the calligraphy often playing a comparatively minor role. This was, in fact, the same scale of values that initiated the work, since wealthy patrons were at liberty to specify the number of historiations and miniatures and paid accordingly.

An opening from the Hours of the Virgin *written and illuminated c. 1516-47 for Guillaume de Bracque, Abbot of the Benedictine Abbey of St. John the Baptist in Valenciennes, Flanders. It contained, as well as the magnificent borders, twenty-five small miniatures, often up to half a page in height, and eleven full-page miniatures. Noteworthy are the fine flower and fruit paintings, and the early pictures of children's games. The left-hand miniature shows the Visitation against an architectural and landscape background. Framed in the initial capital 'D' on the right-hand page are the arms of de Bracque, surmounted by his abbot's crozier. The handwriting in this case is of a type known as batarde, i.e. mongrel or mixed in style.*

As an example, in about 1500 Nicolas von Firmian, member of a noble Tyrolese family, commissioned a Book of Hours from a Flanders scriptorium. It contained twenty-two large initials with elaborate borders and a number historiated; fourteen fully historiated borders; forty-eight small miniatures; and fifteen full-page miniatures. As was often the practice, the paintings included portraits of the noble and his family. When this manuscript came up for sale in London in 1980, its estimated value was £40,000-£60,000.

Such splendour is not for most of us, either as patrons or purchasers; but, if he is content to appreciate the diligence of the scribe rather than luxuriate in the extravagancies of the illuminator, the collector can assemble single leaves from a wide variety of manuscripts at modest cost. From time to time he may be able to supplement his hoard with pieces of fine scribal work culled from early printed books, where they were often used by printers to serve the menial office of strengthening hinges or even acting as a paste-down.

The majority of collectors of autograph and manuscript material will not concern themselves with these early periods or with anything much before the sixteenth century. Official documents and those concerned with the lease, sale and transfer of land and other property, survive in considerable numbers from medieval times, but these are usually only of much interest to the topographer and county historian. Many of them find their way, as they should, to local record offices which, staffed with trained archivists, now exist in every part of the British Isles.

Domestic and personal correspondence from the same period is extremely rare, which is fortunate for the collector, who will not have to bother himself with palaeography, the deciphering of ancient hands. Apart from certain legal hands, the most difficult he will need to master will be the so-called 'secretary' hand used for much of the Tudor period. This, as practised by ordinary mortals rather than professional scribes, can cover everything from neatness to wild illegibility — much as handwriting does today among our nearest and dearest. Elizabeth I, it will be remembered, could use either a singularly beautiful humanistic style (common to all the carefully instructed Tudor children) or what she herself called a 'vile skrating hand'. Despite the initial shock of being confronted with a typical Elizabethan letter or manuscript, the collector may be assured that, once he has troubled to master the unfamiliar forms of a number of the letters, their consistency will ensure that he will have no more — and sometimes less — trouble than he has with some of the missives that find their way to his desk or doormat today. Help may be found in a number of places, the most generally useful probably being in Appendix Eight to McKerrow's *An Introduction to Bibliography* where he analyses with admirable clarity, and with illustrations of all the minuscules and capitals, a letter written by Thomas Kyd, the Elizabethan dramatist, to Sir John Puckering, Lord Keeper of the Great Seal.

By the beginning of the seventeenth century the secretary hand had been almost entirely superseded by the 'Italian' hand, introduced in Henry VII's reign by his Latin secretary. Since this is the direct ancestor of modern handwriting, and is usually much superior to it in clarity, there should be no further difficulties.

The scope for the collector of autograph letters, manuscripts and historical documents is enormous and offers opportunities for even the most modest purse. It is comforting that requirements of condition are not so exacting as in the printed book world. If five hundred or five thousand copies of a book have been printed, we have a right to insist, among so many, on a high standard in the one we purchase. But every letter is unique and even a retained copy, the equivalent of a modern carbon, does not detract from that essential quality: so that criteria are not so stern. A fragile letter from Nelson with a tear in the fold is a letter from Nelson and nothing can detract from its lustre. The gap in the paper where it has been torn away from the seal is a desirable human touch rather than a blemish. Unevenness of style, poor quality ink and paper, erasures and alterations,

Tudor and Stuart manorial records, the open volume written in a 'secretary' hand.

these are all part of the writer and his circumstances, and we would not have it otherwise.

There are, however, shortcomings the collector will wish to avoid. A letter which has been 'mounted' or stuck down to another sheet is not as desirable as one that is free. Less offensive is one that has been 'inlaid' or let into a stronger leaf so that both sides of the letter or document are visible by means of this window. A particularly precious or tender example may have been 'silked' by an expert hand, that is placed between two sheets of fine entirely transparent gauze. This is an asset rather than a defect, since its preservation is assured.

Collections can be built round an individual, a county, a town, a political party, a period in history, a social movement, a ship, a battle or campaign, a family, a building, a pet hobby, expeditions, law suits, theatres, royal houses, gardens — the list is endless, the opportunities plentiful. Whatever men and women have been interested in, concerned about, preoccupied with, either in the line of duty or on the domestic and recreational fronts, they have communicated it in letters, notes, diaries, journals, files, log books and the like.

Despite this wealth, or perhaps because of it, enthusiasm should be tempered and caution exercised. Avoid detached signatures, unless they are of extreme rarity and unimpeachable authenticity. Old, even centuries old, pieces of paper are fairly easily come by, and the unrighteous find no great problem in copying an acceptable signature thereon. Sometimes genuine letters are offered without the vital signature, some rabid autograph hunter having removed it at some period. Unless the main text is of particular importance, these, too, are to be passed by. The Victorians were fond of detached envelope 'fronts', written by celebrities or 'franked', that is signed by members of parliament, bishops and innumerable nonentities to ensure free passage through the post. Hundreds of thousands of them were hunted, exchanged and mounted in large albums. Whatever their attractions then, they are worthless now.

It cannot be too strongly stressed that the subject of letters is all-important and that, even though they may be complete with the signature, they are of little virtue or worth unless they say something of at least modest significance. Tennyson turning down one of the countless invitations to tea with which he was plagued is one thing. Tennyson explaining how he came to write the *Idylls of the King* is another.

Be wary of some people in high places whose duties involved them in prolific correspondence. They sometimes had secretaries who could imitate their master's hand so perfectly that it is difficult to tell one from t'other. The Duke of Wellington is a case in point. A man who was Commander-in-Chief, First Lord of the Treasury, Chancellor of the

University of Oxford, Lord High Constable, Lord Warden of the Cinque Ports, Constable of the Tower, Commissioner of the Royal Military College and Military Asylum, Chief Ranger and Keeper of Hyde Park and St. James's Park and, when he had a week or two free, Home Secretary, Foreign Secretary and Prime Minister, deserved a little respite when it came to correspondence. At least one French monarch employed an official scribe with a special aptitude for imitating the royal hand.

In one way the collector of autograph and manuscript material is at a disadvantage compared with his bibliophile brother, in that it is much easier to forge a letter than a book. Many famous writers and historical characters, from Julius Caesar to Bernard Shaw, have received this sort of unwelcome attention. A certain Major Byron, who claimed to be the son of the poet, specialised in Keats, Shelley and his putative father. The publisher Moxon went so far as to put out an edition of the Shelley forgeries, with an introduction by Robert Browning.[1] The volume, which is now itself a rarity, was recalled shortly after publication, when Moxon discovered his blunder. In 1893 a clerk named Alexander Howland Smith, more familiarly known as 'Antique' Smith because of his activities, received a sentence of twelve months' imprisonment for his forgeries of a wide range of letters, including some from Carlyle, Thackeray and Mary Queen of Scots. I have no space to dilate on the rascality of these and other forgers through the centuries — or on the extreme gullibility of some purchasers.

One other possible area of danger is that of good facsimiles, which are more likely to be met with from time to time than competent forgeries. Many have been produced in all honesty as book illustrations or in celebration of some interesting event or anniversary. There is little to fear from them if they can be closely examined, though they can be rather more deceptive when framed and covered with glass. The paper will nearly always be quite untypical of its period. The handwriting will be much too smooth and even in appearance, showing none of the alterations of thickness, pressure and overall individuality of an ordinary letter.

Coming back to handwriting, the price of safety in autograph collecting, like that of freedom, is eternal vigilance. There are superficial and obvious checks that can be made. For instance, if the paper is water-

---

1 "The art of forging letters purporting to be relics of men of literary celebrity, and therefore apparently possessing a commercial value, has been brought to a rare perfection by those who have made Mr. Shelley's handwriting the object of their imitation. Within the last fourteen years, on no less than three occasions, have forged letters been presented to our family for purchase . . . on the most careful inspection we could scarcely detect any difference between these and the originals; for some were exact copies of documents in our possession. The water-mark on the paper was generally, though not always, the mark appropriate to the date; and the amount of ingenuity exercised was most extraordinary."

Lady Shelley, *Shelley Memorials*', 1859

An authentic Shelley manuscript poem.

Part of a forged Shelley letter. Comparing this with the genuine example of the poet's handwriting above, some of the discrepancies in the forgery will be obvious — the over-flourished 'd's, the tilted crossing of the 't's. Note, too, less obvious but important details, such as the dotting of the 'i's, in general much too high in the forgery; and the dissimilar form of the ampersand.

Menu of the historic dinner given to General Jan Christiaan Smuts in the Royal Gallery of the House of Lords, 15 May 1917. The handwritten note is by his military secretary.

I was the only "non-member" present. The dinner was got up largely by Freddy Guest - a Gost whip -. It was quite unique and special Royal authority had to be secured to use this Gallery as a dining Hall. Never has such a dinner been given before to an "overseas" statesman. The speech itself has been printed widely over 1,000,000 copies being sold in the English language.

Royal Gallery, House of Lords.

DINNER

given in honour of

Lt.-Gen. The Rt. Hon. J. C. SMUTS

by

MEMBERS OF THE

HOUSES OF PARLIAMENT

Tuesday, May 15th, 1917.

Smuts's own notes for the great speech he made on the occasion of the dinner in the Royal Gallery (see above), of which over 1,000,000 copies were sold in the English language alone. It was conspicuous for his use of the historic phrase 'British Commonwealth of Nations'.

marked, does it agree sufficiently with the supposed date of the letter and do the circumstances and events it deals with coincide with the known facts? I was once offered a John Wesley letter which had the slight blemish of being written on paper watermarked some thirty years after the evangelist died, and on another occasion a letter from a supposed Trafalgar seaman, mentioning officers and members of the crew who were not on the muster roll of the ship concerned. I remember a stately home which proudly displayed a Nelson letter the original of which was in the National Maritime Museum.

But, quite apart from simple precautions, the answer in the end must lie in sensing the difference between a natural flowing hand and the stilted and lifeless exactitude of a painstaking copy. Spontaneous handwriting has a life and character of its own, conveyed to it by a busy brain through easy fingers. If the forger tries to write quickly and naturally he loses accuracy. If he writes slowly and with extreme care, he forsakes natural rhythm and ease of style.

Then, too, the forger will not find it easy to come across the right paper. Mistrust a single torn off sheet. It may be genuine, but is likely to have come from a bifolium or double sheet. Mistrust even more two leaves that have been joined together to fabricate a bifolium. Old paper was usually sized to make it take ink smoothly. Size will evaporate in the course of the years, and new writing will blur and spread at the edges. Efforts to stain paper artificially to give an appearance of age have little hope of withstanding careful scrutiny. Handle all the genuine letters and documents you possibly can and you will soon find that eyes and finger tips make very efficient detectives. A reliable dealer will, of course, have taken all these precautions for you and you can safely rely on his judgement and experience.

The collector of signed letters by modern statesmen faces an additional hazard in the form of a machine which not only reproduces signatures exactly but holds a fountain pen or biro to accomplish them.

Let none of these warnings and precautions put you off the adventure and excitement of collecting in this field if you have an inclination that way. There is far more genuine material about than there is false or suspect; and much is of such a nature that there is no temptation for anyone to forge it. Only the most illustrious names hold out the lure of considerable profit; but many thousands of unknown men and women have left behind them a legacy of written material that will never be illicity copied and imitated yet will yield a rich store of history, and throw light on their place and period, life and labours, which are every bit as important, in the ultimate scale of things, as the antics and accomplishments of those who contrived to hit the headlines. John Masefield began his collected poems with a consecration declaring that he was not concerned with the princes and prelates, the bemedalled commander, the 'potentates goodly in girth', but rather with the humble and unknown folk, the losers and rejected, the common sailor and soldier, the servant rather than the master. G.K. Chesterton had the same message in *The Secret People,* who had never spoken yet. There is some sort of lesson there for the autograph collector, who need not despair if the great names are beyond his aspirations and his purse.

❋❋❋❋❋❋❋❋❋❋❋❋❋❋❋❋❋

Chapter 14

The Adventure of Collecting

> The evening being come, I return home and go to my
> study...I pass into the ancient courts of the men of old,
> where, being lovingly received by them, I am fed with that
> food which is mine alone; where I do not hesitate to speak with
> them, and to ask for the reasons for their actions, and they in
> their benignity answer me; and for four hours I feel no
> weariness, I forget every trouble.
>
> Niccolo Machiavelli in exile, writing to
> Francesco Vettori, December 1513

Books, autograph letters and documents can be the end of a quest. They
may, even more excitingly, be the beginning of one; and some of the most
interesting hours of my life have been spent in searches, encounters and
adventures initiated in this way. As I approach the end of this book, I sit
in my study much as Machiavelli did and reflect on all the figures and
families from the centuries I have in some sense come close to through
collecting, some famous, some unknown, but all with their individual
charm and magic. Indeed, it is often the humble and insignificant that
have the most allure. So much is already known of the great and
illustrious; but the people of the quiet streets and remote villages, of the
farm and workshop, of the river and inshore waters, of the ranks and the
lower deck, so often have had no chronicler that, through their letters and
documents, and painstaking researches on the part of collectors, they
forsake their long anonymity and live again their everyday occupations
and frivolities, their trials and happinesses, their loves and hates.

*   *   *   *   *

Beside me as I write are some papers I found in a small antique shop in
Totnes. I asked the owner if he had perchance any old letters or
documents and, after looking dubious, he went to a cupboard at the back
and produced a battered cardboard box, obviously of small value or
interest to him.

To me it was a small argosy, for through it and its contents I met the
Dew family, substantial landowners, at the end of the eighteenth and
beginning of the nineteenth century, in Essex, London and where they

Prospectus of one of the schools attended by the Dew sisters.

lived at Whitney Court, near Hay-on-Wye. I came to know very well the cheerful, indolent Armine and her uncertain-tempered sister Ann; their admirably methodical mother who, on her first husband's death, took over the management of the estates and preserved copies of all her correspondence; and their villainous stepfather Colonel Powell, who might have stepped straight out of a Victorian melodrama. I have related their history elsewhere, but did not add the ghost story that came my way.

At one stage in their careers the two high-spirited girls were sent to London to be 'brought out' by a gentle lady named Jane Partington, an old friend of their mother's, who clearly didn't know what she was letting herself in for and who breathed a tremulous sigh of relief when the coach finally rolled away with her troublesome charges. Jane lived, with her husband Miles, at 57 Lower Brook Street, now just Brook Street. I consulted the wonderful collection of material on old London at County Hall, Westminster Bridge, and discovered that, since the Partington's day, the street numbering had been altered and that the old number 57 was now 23. I found the house, very near New Bond Street, where what Jane contemptuously called 'two-legged puppies' were to be seen strutting. The wall carried one of the blue plaques set up by the authorities to mark houses associated with the famous. Surely my errant Armine and Ann did not come within this category?

I crossed over to read it. It bore the name of George Frederick Handel, who had lived at 23 for over thirty years before, half a century later, the house was invaded by the noisy and mischievous Dew daughters. Did they know of, or ever faintly hear in their sitting room, the majestic soaring chords of the Messiah, composed there by Handel in just twenty-four miraculous days, sometimes with the tears running down his face and splashing onto the manuscript?

I climbed the stair down which had so often rushed the feet of Armine and Ann, anxious to seat themselves in the dashing curricles and phaetons that came to call, watched by an anxious and hovering Mrs. Partington. I wandered through the rooms, now occupied by a famous textiles firm who had gone to great pains to furnish and maintain them appropriately.

Back again with the receptionist, I asked jokingly: "Have you ever seen a ghost?" The reply was not as light-hearted as I had expected.

"Strange that you should ask. We never have, but a little while ago a charwoman came downstairs looking very flustered and said that there was an old man like a judge in one of the rooms. She wouldn't work for us again."

Like a judge? To whom else would an ordinary London cleaner liken Handel in his great full wig?

*   *   *   *   *

I move up the social scale a little, to demonstrate that the collector-researcher in full cry can sometimes add his modest mite to known history. This time I was burrowing in the archives of the great Earls of Northumberland, of whom it was said that the north knows no king but Percy. My quarry was Sir Henry, ninth Earl (1564-1632), who, because of his scientific experiments, was known as the 'Wizard Earl' and who, because of his alleged complicity in the Gunpowder Plot, was tried for misprision of treason and condemned to life imprisonment in the Tower. The main foundation of the charge was that he had financed the plotters.

It was true that his cousin and steward, Thomas Percy, had collected his northern rents and fled south with them, but the Earl denied all knowledge of this.

In the household accounts for 4 November, 1605 I found a small slip of paper detailing the charge made by a Thames waterman for conveying the Earl's ermine robes from Sion House to the House of Lords in readiness for the opening of Parliament. Does a man do this if he expects the place to be blown sky-high the next day? Alas, I was too late to give evidence.

* * * * *

At a small house sale in the Isle of Wight I bought a small folder of watercolours dating from the early nineteenth century. They were not particularly skilful, but had an impish charm and some gift for caricature. A number were concerned with Malta and showed fashionable ladies and their beaux riding in carriages or in boxes at the opera, brightly uniformed army officers, priests and peasants at their various occupations. In many of the drawings the same puckish face peered out, bespectacled and with a turned-up nose, as though the unknown artist had chosen an amusing way to sign himself, though there was also an actual signature, that of J. or John Locker, a name that in that geographical context meant nothing to me. Notes and inscriptions on the reverse of the watercolours were few and uniformative: only one leapt to the eye, and that could have meant nothing at all — 'From poor Nelson's book.' Nelson, after all, is a common enough name, both as a Christian and surname.

But here was a small covey of clues that might be worth following up. Could any connection be found between Malta, a John Locker and — dare one hope — Lord Nelson?

The first port of call, as so often, was the *Dictionary of National Biography,* and here was a promising group of Lockers, five of them, and all related. Genealogically it worked out as:

John Locker (1693-1760)
Miscellaneous writer
|
William Locker (1731-1800)
Captain in the Navy
Lieutenant-Governor of Greenwich Hospital
|
Edward Hawke Locker (1777-1849)
Commissioner of Greenwich Hospital

Frederick Locker (1821-95)   Arthur Locker (1828-93)
Clerk in the Admiralty   Novelist and journalist

More detailed information was, of course, available, but even on this simple evidence a pattern was emerging. There were clearly strong naval links and Greenwich Hospital was a strong factor. There was even a John, but his dates were too early for my purposes. What was more important than anything was the establishment of a strong Locker-Nelson connection which, above all, I suppose I had been hoping for; for some reading of biographies and Nelson's collected letters revealed the exciting fact that Captain William Locker had given young Horatio his first command — a small captured vessel that Nelson immediately renamed *Lucy* in honour of his commander's daughter. In after years, when Nelson was famous, he acknowledged in generous terms his debt to the man who had schooled him: ''I have been your scholar; it is you who taught me to board a Frenchman...it is you who always told me, 'Lay a Frenchman close and you will beat him.' ''

William Locker did not live to see Trafalgar, his pupil's crowning glory, but he must have rejoiced at the news of the Battle of the Nile in 1798, that brilliant feat of seamanship which destroyed the French fleet and isolated Napoleon in Egypt. Two years after Locker died and Nelson, paying a last tribute to the friend he had honoured and corresponded with for so many years, wrote to the family, addressing his letter to John Locker, another son, who did not attain sufficient position and reputation to justify a place in the *Dictionary of National Biography*. Indeed, details of his career are elusive, but I managed to establish that he was an Admiralty agent in Malta, so that the chain was complete. Despite his failure to hit the headlines, I have always felt that the chuckling face, peering out so shrewdly from my watercolours, belonged to one of the most lovable members of the family.

A distinguished group it was for, as well as that of Edward Hawke Locker, who, obviously sharing his brother John's gifts with brush and pencil, published *Views in Spain* (1824) and established the great gallery of naval pictures at Greenwich, my small genealogical table shows a name which every book-collector should delight to honour — that of Frederick Locker or Locker-Lampson, he having added his second wife's maiden name in 1885. A discriminating and cultured man of letters, his library at Rowfant, in John Carter's opinion, ''was possibly the most revolutionary in its influence upon following generations that the whole century produced''; and the bibliograher Graham Pollard wrote that Locker:

> Formed in two small book-cases such a gathering of first editions of English imaginative literature that the mere catalogue of it produced the effect of a stately and picturesque procession...the compactness and unity of this small collection, in which every book appears to have been bought for a special reason and to form an integral part of the whole, gave it an artistic individuality which was a pleasant triumph

for its owner, and excited so much interest among American admirers of Mr. Locker's poetry that it may be said to have set a fashion.

The poetry to which Pollard referred was, of course, the famous *London Lyrics* which began life as 'unpublished' and later attained enormous popularity. Light and amusing of touch, in verse as well as conversation, Locker gave us such couplets as:

> Some men are good for righting wrongs —
> And some for writing verses.

> And many are afraid of God —
> And more of Mrs. Grundy.

> The world's as ugly, ay, as sin,
> And almost as delightful.

London Lyrics was followed by more lyrics in 1881 and *London Rhymes* in 1882. The Rowfant Club in Cleveland, Ohio, published *Rowfant Rhymes* in 1895. The many editions of his work were illustrated by Cruikshank and Richard Doyle among others. Collectors will wish to add his anthologies *Lyra Elegantiarum* (1867) and *Patchwork* (1879), as well as his autobiographical *My Confidences* (1896).

A Locker family collection can prove expensive or moderately cheap, according to good fortune or where you choose to shop. Edward Hawke Locker's *Views in Spain* will not normally be less than £200-£300. His son Arthur wrote some novels, such as the three-decker *Sir Goodwin's Folly* (1864), which are rising in value. The catalogue of the Rowfant Library, published in 1886, with the 1900 Appendix, should be yours for less than £50.

The plant once set, the tendrils reach out and out. One of Frederick Locker's close friends was Kate Greenaway. She designed his bookplate and used as a frontispiece to *Little Ann* (1882) a charming frontispiece of his four children. Several years ago a visitor came into my office with a complete set of Kate Greenaway Almanacks, every one inscribed to one of Frederick Locker's daughters, and with a copy of *Little Ann.* Pointing to Maud, the little girl in Kate's frontispiece, she said "That is my mother." Only this year there came to me Frederick Locker's personal volume of notices, reviews, etc., of *London Lyrics* with his modest autograph note: "I am half ashamed of myself for allowing these cuttings to be collected. Let those who come after me go thro them & destroy all they like to destroy. I was very green at that time, green as an author."

Thus, an interest in the Lockers has burgeoned from that chance purchase of a few watercolours more than thirty years ago, and I am grateful to the artist, John. Good fortune led me to lunch more than once

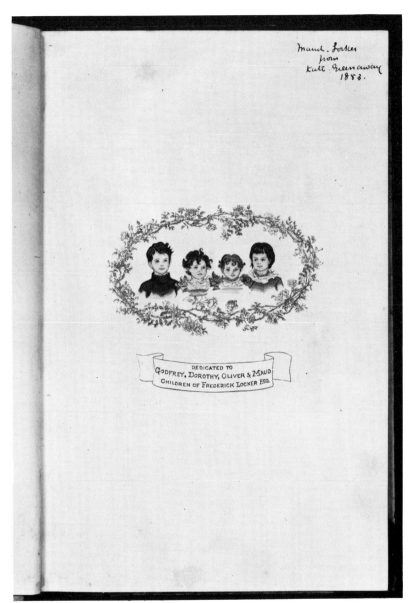

Kate Greenaway's dedication leaf to the Locker children in Little Ann, *inscribed by her to Maud, the girl on the far right. Kate Greenaway's books are rarely dated, and this is a case where the inscription aids the collector and bibliographer.*

in the house at Greenwich where he had grown up while his father was Lieutenant-Governor. To it had come a battered one-eyed, one-armed sailor to have his portrait painted by Lemuel Abbott and be helped from his cloak by John and the other children. The story may therefore be reckoned complete enough. But I still do not know what 'poor Nelson's book' was. It is not too late. In the adventure of collecting, while breath lasts, it is never too late.

*   *   *   *   *

Turn again, back to the seventeenth century and a small vellum-covered manuscript book of recipes,[1] dated 1658-72 and with the contemporary ownership signature 'Arch. Palmer, 1658.' Recipe books, which many judicious people choose to collect, are plentiful from the nineteenth century, fairly common from the eighteenth century, and increasingly rare before that, especially when they cover important periods such as the Great Plague of London and are likely to include suitable specifics. Arch. Palmer's book was therefore likely to be of some interest.

The first thing was to attempt to identify him and to trace his origins — often, in such cases, very difficult or, lacking any clues whatever, impossible. Here, however, were one or two promising leads. There were, for example, references to Cambridge, including one to 'Mr. Moses, Mr. [Master] of Pembroke Hall' at whose table the writer had apparently partaken of the asparagus for which Cambridge colleges are still famous, and to 'Onelep' (with other spellings) in Leicestershire.

The invaluable source for tracking down any early Cambridge student is John and Archibald Venn's *Alumni Cantabrigiensis* and, by good fortune, gold was struck immediately. There was a Palmer with the unusual Christian name of Archdale admitted to Pembroke College at the age of fifteen in 1627/8, and his son, another Archdale, migrated there from Sidney Sussex in 1657/8, the exact date of the recipe book. Furthermore, on the evidence of the manuscript, the writer was well acquainted with William Moses, who was Master of Pembroke.

Had these Palmers any connection with Leicestershire, and, in particular, with any place looking or sounding like Onelep? The luck held. Five miles north of the city of Leicester, beside the River Soar, was the village of Wanlip (earlier Onelep, Anlep, etc.) and John Nichols's great *History and Antiquities of Leicestershire* (eight volumes 1795-1815) revealed that the Palmer family had been associated with the place since about 1630, when the manor was sold by Lord Aston of Forfar to 'Mr.

---

1 The old spelling was usually receipt, which is still heard and occasionally read today. Which of the two is right is still debated, though Fowler opines that either word is as good as the other. Recipe is a Latin imperative, meaning 'take' and was the first word of prescriptions in Latin.

William Palmer, citizen of London.' Nichols obligingly gave a detailed genealogical table of the family, an engraving of Wanlip Hall, their armorial bearings and particulars of their memorials in the church. With all this evidence, there could be no doubt that the compiler of the recipe book was Archdale Palmer of Wanlip, High Sheriff of Leicester in 1641. With the dating of the asparagus recipe so exactly given as 8 April 1659, and his son's entry to Pembroke on 5 April that year, it is legitimate to suppose that father Archdale went to Cambridge and, as an old member of the College, dined with the Master, ensuring at the same time that his offspring was properly settled in.

Of the recipe book, several significant things may be noted. It was unusual for a man outside the medical profession to keep such a book, which was normally the duty of the women of the household. It was important both historically and medically, for it showed not only the thought and practice of common folk, but also that of well-known physicians and surgeons at a time when some of the greatest English practitioners had made, or were making, their mark. Furthermore, it is abundantly clear that he did not copy recipes from other sources, but normally obtained them direct from the users and by word of mouth. I was glad to see that a tapster at the Mitre Inn in Fleet Street had passed on a recipe at a time when Pepys might well have been crossing the threshold; and that Charles II was thoughtful enough to send his Lord Mayor a remedy against the Plague. From a servant, a useful gossip as always, he extracted what he claimed was the recipe for the first coffee brewed in England.

To quote detailed recipes would be to stray outside the purpose of this book; but I cannot resist giving my readers, in case of need, the best way to deal with 'a bone or a pinne in ye throate':

> Given me by Mr. Hollis a Minister in Northamptonshire, Cousin Travel's Acquaintance 13 May 1663 yt dined with him this day at my house.
> Take a Thimblefull of Gunpowder puttinge it into a spoone, wetting it with a little Beere & bruising of it well together & so drinke it & after let ye pty drinke a good spoonefull of Beare or 2 after it.

* * * * *

One more example and I must have done with this aspect of collecting.

I once lived in a district where one of the great Kentish families had been landed since the late seventeenth century. On the female side they had descended from Oliver Cromwell and had been prominent in Whig politics. Their great estates had disappeared and the male line had died out, and in the sole remaining small house a country sale was held. I not

Part of the page from David Polhill's manuscript journal, mentioning the accident to the portrait of Oliver Cromwell.

only bought several of the portraits, but a manuscript journal kept by David Polhill (c.1674-1754), one of the famous 'Kentish Petitioners' associated with Daniel Defoe, High Sheriff, and five times Whig member of Parliament. He was an engaging character, a good landlord and master, described by one of his sons as "this good man and most Excellent parent...He never got over the death of my Brother Thomas who was killed by a fall from his horse on Westminster Bridge."

I read his letters, studied his journal minutely, walked in his village and in his great garden, now given over to the operations of a nurseryman. He was descended from Bridget Cromwell, to whom I found the Protector had given, along with his other daughters, a copy of his portrait, and I was naturally especially interested to read the following entry:

> Mr. Gouge a Painter, a papist yet a good man for mending
> an original picture (half length) of Cromwell. The picture was
> defaced by some Tory who came to see my house when i was

from home, by thrusting the feiril [sic] of a cane thro the left eye. £4.4s. n.b. my housekeeper was a Jacobite then unknown to me.

The portrait of Cromwell was not with the rest of the family pictures at the sale I attended and I learnt that it had probably been sold some time before, to whom I could not establish.

Here is a quest not completed. Somewhere in the country is a half-length portrait of Cromwell with a repaired left eye, and the original damage probably still visible on the back of the canvas. Where are you, my Lord Protector? Where are you, Copper Nose?

* * * * *

I hope I have written sufficient to persuade at least some collectors that there is more to the pursuit than just the accumulation of books, letters and documents. There is often more joy in travelling than arriving; and, for those who choose, any destination is only a taking-off place for another journey.

✵✵✵✵✵✵✵✵✵✵✵✵✵✵✵✵✵

Chapter 15

Sources of Supply

> Some hold that book-hunters lack time even for idle vices, and
> of all classes of men they cause least concern to the state. He
> stalks his prey through noble shops, poor wheelbarrows, by
> scent, by the bait of a good catalogue, by mere chance. He
> emerges at last, into a place where pride and covetousness are
> no longer deadly sins, but the austere restrained virtues of the
> true lovers of good books.
>
> > Charles J. Sawyer and F.J. Harvey Darton
> > *English Books 1475-1900*

The book-collector has many avenues through which he may seek his
treasure — book shops, junk shops, charity shops, book fairs, church
bazaars, market stalls, advertisements and auction sales among them.
Wheedling books out of unsuspecting relatives is not on the accredited
list, and I must confess to some pusillanimous scruple about charity
shops, not wishing to be confronted by an ethical dilemma should I
discover a valuable book in the shilling box. My conscience is also a little
tender in those events organised by admirable ladies in aid of the church
spire, new hassocks for the pews and the roof of the village hall, though
one can always add a few shillings or even a pound or two if the find
warrants it. Otherwise, it is all fair game, and the devil take the hindmost.

It may be sensible at the outset to clear up one or two legal points that
collectors may encounter from time to time.

In the case of trade advertisements you are well protected by law and by
such reputable bodies as the Antiquarian Booksellers' Association
(founded in 1906) and even by the Advertising Standards Authority. But
beware of the small classified advertisement. The law does not protect
deals between private individuals. Christopher Ward, in his delightful
How to Complain, warns us about "the small-ad seller who offers you a
parrot with a vocabulary of two thousand words." Be similarly wary of
anyone who philanthropically offers you an unlikely book bargain.

Study the small print in auction sale catalogues. One ingenious
auctioneer of some prominence has adopted the (to him) useful device of
describing his books as 'not collated'. Whatever the precise definition of
that term (and there is more than one), the onus of deciding on the

completeness and good state of the item has been transferred fairly and squarely to the buyer. But most top auctioneers have a stated period during which goods found to be defective may be returned and a refund obtained. Note, however, that this saving clause does not normally cover such defects as minor binding damage, missing or imperfect blank leaves and advertisements (vital in a number of first editions), stains, foxing and worm holes. Certain categories of items, such as atlases, periodicals, and books where the binding is more important than the contents, are often sold 'not subject to return'.

Here is an extract from one well-known auctioneer's Conditions of Sale:

> In addition to the general Conditions of Sale, the following special conditions shall apply to printed books, historical documents, manuscripts and autograph letters.
>
> Unless listed in the catalogue as 'not subject to return' or 'with all faults' (w.a.f.), printed books which are found to be defective in pages or illustrations (provided these have not already been noted in the catalogue) may be returned by the purchaser and the sale set aside within two weeks of the conclusion of the sale, the said items being in the same condition as at the time of sale.
>
> The above condition of sale shall apply only to text and illustrations. No book shall be returned, neither can the sale be set aside, because of damage to bindings, inscriptions, worm holes not materially affecting the text, foxing or other stains, missing or defective blank leaves or advertisements; nor for any question of authorship or such disputative matters as first edition 'points'. No unnamed volume may be returned.

There is a certain charm about the ancient law of market overt, uncomfortable though it may be for deprived owners. By this legal rule, all goods sold at a market established by law — and that includes most auction houses and recognised open markets — become the property of the buyer and cannot be recovered, even though it can be proved that the items have been lost or stolen. This law does not apply to shops and markets not legally constituted, though the curious anomaly exists that shops within the strict boundaries of the City of London are covered if they are selling the type of goods in which they normally deal.

Another exception to the market overt law could only be found in a country which, I believe, still cherishes on its statute book a regulation that all pocket-handkerchieves shall be round. By a case tried in the reign of Elizabeth I, for the market overt rule to apply the sale must not take place at night. In a fairly recent case some stolen goods were bought in the Caledonian Market at 7 a.m., before the sun had risen. The owner recovered his property, the magistrate relying on this august precedent.

Buyers are sometimes worried by the presence in books offered for sale of ownership labels of libraries and learned institutions. Unless these indications of ownership are recent, the collector rarely need feel disturbed. The volumes may well have been surplus or discarded copies. If they disappeared from their original homes by less legal means a long time ago, it is very difficult for the institution concerned to establish the fact, especially when adequate records have not been maintained. In the case of rare books, libraries have been known to buy back quite happily from antiquarian booksellers.

In the auction world, sales tend to have a rather different atmosphere from that of more general types. The book auctioneer is usually quieter and less expansive than his brothers-in-arms selling tumble-down cottages, souped-up cars or herds of Friesian cows. He will sell the greatest treasures with a surprising lack of emotion and, often, equally surprising speed. Some collectors are timid of intruding into the circle of hard-faced and tight-lipped professional buyers, all of them commanding unlimited resources, all of them experts with an encyclopaedic knowledge of points, editions, issues and the like. The fears are groundless. Many of them are human, and have wives, children and pet goldfish. Their bank balances, if one can credit their doleful stories, are often smaller than those of collectors; and, more important, the general bookseller sometimes cannot match the knowledge of the specialist collector in his own field. Nevertheless, the auction room is a dangerous place for the novice, who will be well advised to take a friendly bookseller into his confidence and ask him to check the books and do the bidding. This he will normally be glad to do for a modest fee if he is not himself especially interested in the books in question and is not carrying a conflicting commission.

Alternatively, the collector can consult the auctioneer and leave a fixed bid 'on the book'. By this means he will not be led into temptation and wild excesses in the heat of the moment. Even the oldest hands have been known to cast discretion aside at the sight of a smirk on the face of a rival.

What of the infamous 'ring', outlawed by Act of Parliament in 1927 but never, to my knowledge, successfully brought to trial?[1] This is the system by which any two or more people, usually dealers, agree beforehand not to bid against each other and, by thus eliminating much of the competition, get goods much more cheaply. At a subsequent private auction, 'knock out' or settlement, held in the nearest hostelry or a

---

1 Since writing the above there has at last been a prosecution — and a successful one.

convenient car, someone pays a more realistic price, and the difference is divided between members of the ring. It has been asserted that the practice, at least in London, has dwindled to microscopic proportions since the 1927 Act. This is to put one's head in the sand. Knock outs need not be held in seedy back rooms. They can be as effective in the bosom of an exclusive club or expensive hotel. So far as the provincial rooms go it is still a thriving industry. But the collector should not be too easily intimidated. The dealer has to make a profit. The collector, usually, has not and can therefore afford to go that much higher. If he knows his books and his financial limit he can never be taken for a ride by a group of dealers.

It is as well, before buying at auction, to know the terms under which the dealer is operating. Following the fashion of the major metropolitan auction houses, many of the provincial rooms now impose a 10% buyer's premium on the purchase price, and the Government demands, at the time of writing, 15% Value Added Tax on that premium. This can make a good deal of difference to the eventual price paid. Thus, on a book nominally knocked down for £100, the buyer is going to pay £110 + £1.50. This may be all very well for one item, but he is going to feel the draught if he buys twenty lots. On the other hand, some auctioneers still charge only the hammer price, with no commission and, therefore, no VAT. In the mysterious world of Government economics, no one objects to this diversity of practice.

If you have a special interest in some lot, do not hesitate to ask the auctioneers for guidance as to what they expect it to make. They may publish, or display, price guides, but these are likely to be pure guesstimates. A much more reliable guide is the bidding that has already come in and is 'on the book'. With its aid, and without breaching confidentiality, the auctioneer will be able to tell you with some accuracy whether you will need to think in terms of £50-£500.

From time to time collectors sell books, when they wish to buy a particular treasure, when they have acquired a better quality example to replace a poor one, or when they are plain hard up. If this happens to you, and you decide that the saleroom is the place for them, be certain to put a suitable protective reserve on them beforehand. This is one effective way of dealing with any machinations of the ring.

The auction room is not much loved by booksellers (unless they are selling their own books *sub rosa*), who hate to see so many fine books coming under the hammer instead of privately and less expensively into their emporia. I have met booksellers who tell me that they frequently buy books from people who have attended sales and give them a handsome profit. If the auctioneer has known his business, such stories require a very large pinch of salt. Some members of the trade, encouraged by their

An enviable prize for the auctioneer. Part of a country house library awaiting the cataloguer.

professional associations, display an advertisement in their shops discouraging the public from sending books to auction when they are likely to do much better at the hands of a beneficent and altruistic trade. From the growth of auction houses and specialist sales, I deduce that this optimistic plea has not been greatly regarded. As one commentator put it succinctly:

> The gist of the ad. is "Why go to auction?" when Mr. X is "prepared to pay as much by private treaty...By dealing directly owners can therefore realise more." But what of the rare book (and this is surely what auctions are all about) which attracts private and institutional commissions and drive the price far beyond expectations? What dealer would have offered outright the $4,500 paid at Parke Bernet for a copy of the first edition of *The Wind in the Willows...* or £4,500, (including premium) for the awful copy of Blaeu's *England and Wales* at Sotheby's last summer?

I recall that a well-known antiquarian bookseller, who has been particularly vociferous in this matter, telephoned me before a sale at a country house with a very good library, to enquire whether the auction house with which I was then associated would sell him all the books beforehand. He said that both the vendor and the auctioneers would do better that way. I seem to remember that, at the actual sale, he managed to buy one lot, after a struggle.

My final contribution to this dispute is, if auction rooms are, from the vendor's point of view, such unprofitable places, why do so many second-hand and antiquarian booksellers themselves enter, or try to enter, their books for sale?

A comparatively recent arrival on the auction scene in this country has been the postal auction. Practices vary but most have certain features in common. The bookseller or dealer issues a catalogue describing his wares and setting on each item a reserve which he considers a fair current market value. Customers are then invited to submit an offer by a stated date, a bidding form often being included. At noon, or some other specified time on the auction day, all bids are scrutinised and, as at an ordinary auction, the top bid wins.

There are, however, one or two important differences. The most scrupulous of the postal auctioneers consider it unethical to alter their estimate of prices after the catalogue has been circulated. The ordinary auctioneer will alter his estimate, and some recommend prospective buyers to contact the firm near the date of sale to see if the figure has changed substantially. This seems to me unexceptionable. If a customer 'phones to ask for guidance on his bid, it is not much good telling him that the published estimate or price guide of, say, £100 still holds good when the auctioneer knows very well that he has already received postal bids of £175, £190 and £200 — a situation by no means uncommon.

The other vital difference is that, when a bidder at an ordinary auction has had a lot knocked down to him, there is no retreat. Assuming that the goods are as described, they are legally his at the fall of the hammer. With the postal auctioneer, there is often a proviso that a customer can return goods within forty-eight hours of receipt. While methods of operation differ, the basic principles in postal auctions are the same. I do not doubt that the best of them are entirely fair in their protection of buyers' interests. There are undoubtedly bad apples, and proper care must be exercised.

For myself, this disembodied and remote form of auction loses all the warmth and excitement of conflict on the actual floor of the room, or perhaps the marquee grass at a country house, though in these less leisurely days we have lost for good the sort of occasion described by

George Clulow in Derbyshire, in 1881:

> It was summer time...the country at its best. The sale was announced for noon, but it was an hour late before the auctioneer put in an appearance, and the first operation in which he took part, and in which he invited my assistance, was to make a hearty meal of bread and cheese and beer.

Such behaviour is a little out of line with the auctioneer William Cooper's admonition in 1676:

> The Gentlemen will be pleased to come at the hour appointed...Many have confessed they have lost the opportunity for buying for themselves and their friends by coming or sending too late.

If, despite all warnings to the contrary, you become an auction addict, take heart from yet another auctioneer, Richard Davis of Oxford, whose 1686 catalogue promised: ''It shall be managed with all fairness and (if possible) to a general satisfaction.''

Another recent phenomenon of some importance has been the spread of the book fair, when twenty, thirty, fifty or more second-hand and antiquarian booksellers come together to set out their wares under a single roof in some centre of population. There were, of course, book fairs of great antiquity and importance, especially on the Continent. In this country there was a great sale of books in the sixteenth century at a fair held in the North Hundred of Oxford, and similar events took place at St. Giles, Oxford, and at Stourbridge. But matters have now become more extensively organised and 'fairs' (indoors) very much more frequent. In 1980 book fairs were held in London, St. Albans, Oxford, Exeter, Loughborough, Chester, Bath, Harrogate, Perth, Bury St. Edmunds, Kendal, Tunbridge Wells, Salisbury, Droitwich, Manchester, Glasgow, Plymouth, Hove, Sherborne, Stirling, Cardiff, Cambridge, Ilkely, Truro, Aberdeen, King's Lynn, Norwich, Torbay, Tiverton, Stratford, Canterbury, York, Inverness, Edinburgh, Gerrards Cross, St. Andrew's, Bristol, Nottingham, Solihull, and other places of which I have lost count. In a number of localities there were fairs more than once. The number of exhibitors ranged from twenty to over one hundred, the average probably being thirty to forty.

I am not sure who benefits most from these occasions, but suspect it is the refreshment areas in the many hostelries in which they are staged. Reactions to them are varied and often surprisingly frank, even from the professionals. To cull a few:

> One might be excused for thinking that a superhuman

effort had been made to discourage the general public from attending.

> . . . supremely beneficial to the book-trade.

> I bought three books at this fair — a definite record.

> The man in the street was conspicuously absent. . . many exhibitors reported that ninety per cent of their turnover was with the trade.

> If you regard a fair as an opportunity for the trade to get together, strike a few bargains, exchange a few books, and repair to the bar, then this fair was surely a success.

This is a book of practicalities, with some unashamed preferences and even a few prejudices. Perhaps I have been unfortunate in my choices; but I must admit I find myself faintly allergic to book fairs. I dislike seeing booksellers away from the fascinating milieu of their own book shops, stately or nondescript, elegant or shabby. An extraordinary amount of bonhomie exists between the stall holders, but too little of this is extended to the general public, who are too often greeted by faintly gloomy figures who, the fraternising temporarily suspended, are slumped desultorily in chairs despairingly reading their own books. There is too much horse-trading before the amateurs are admitted, and certainly collectors need not look for anything in the nature of a bargain.

But who am I to challenge these festivals organised so effectively (usually) by the Antiquarian Booksellers' Association and the Provincial Booksellers' Fairs Association? At the first PBFA Fair in 1972, held at the Eden Hotel, South Kensington, there were eight participating exhibitors. Now, each month, there are about a hundred. Add to these, fairs in America, Canada, Australia and most of the known globe, and it is amazing that booksellers are ever at home. I do not doubt that there will be one at North Cape before long.

****

Appendix I

The Roman Notation of Numerals

Fewer and fewer people seem to be familiar and fluent with the Roman notation, and since this was often employed on the title-pages (and in other places, including the colophon) of early books, and is still used occasionally by publishers and presses, it will perhaps be useful to set it out for those who are not confident in its translation. The system was in general use in central Europe for up to 1,500 years.

There are only seven numerals to be mastered:

M = 1000 D = 500 C = 100 L = 50 X = 10 V = 5 I (or i) = 1

The generally accepted rules are equally simple:

(1) I and C may be repeated, but not more than three times.
(2) A numeral placed after one of greater value means addition, e.g. XI = 10 + 1 = 11; CCCX = 100 + 100 + 100 + 10 = 310.
(3) A numeral placed before one of greater value means subtraction, e.g. IX = 10 – 1 = 9; XL = 50 – 10 = 40.

Variations may occasionally be met with (probably because the printer was apt to get as confused as the reader[1]), but they should not be over difficult to interpret and the good sense of the rules still holds. As the *British Encyclopaedia,* with a rare flash of wry humour, remarks: "In the days when one of the ways of writing 7,291ft. was MMMMMMMCCLXXXXI pedes, it was convenient to reduce the length of the written number."

One other thing to look out for is a curious form of M. Instead of the usual classic clean-cut lines you may find it written CIↃ and half of it, i.e. IↃ for D. It is taken from the Greek letter *phi.* On a staircase in the Ashmolean Museum, Oxford, you may read CIↃIↃCCCXLV (1845) and on a sixteenth century Dutch commemorative medal CIↃ.IↃ.XCII, which reads as 1592.

As a further aid, here is a complete century set out, from which I hope any date can be identified in that, or any other, hundred years:

---

1 As already noted in the chapter on Provincial Presses, in the first Oxford printing the printer set the dates as 1468 instead of 1478.

216

1600	=	MDC	1634	=	MDCXXXIV
1601	=	MDCI	1635	=	MDCXXXV
1602	=	MDCII	1636	=	MDCXXXVI
1603	=	MDCIII	1637	=	MDCXXXVII
1604	=	MDCIV	1638	=	MDCXXXVIII
1605	=	MDCV	1639	=	MDCXXXIX
1606	=	MDCVI	1640	=	MDCXL
1607	=	MDCVII	1641	=	MDCXLI
1608	=	MDCVIII	1642	=	MDCXLII
1609	=	MDCIX	1643	=	MDCXLIII
1610	=	MDCX	1644	=	MDCXLIV
1611	=	MDCXI	1645	=	MDCXLV
1612	=	MDCXII	1646	=	MDCXLVI
1613	=	MDCXIII	1647	=	MDCXLVII
1614	=	MDCXIV	1648	=	MDCXLVIII
1615	=	MDCXV	1649	=	MDCXLIX
1616	=	MDCXVI	1650	=	MDCL
1617	=	MDCXVII	1651	=	MDCLI
1618	=	MDCXVIII	1652	=	MDCLII
1619	=	MDCXIX	1653	=	MDCLIII
1620	=	MDCXX	1654	=	MDCLIV
1621	=	MDCXXI	1655	=	MDCLV
1622	=	MDCXXII	1656	=	MDCLVI
1623	=	MDCXXIII	1657	=	MDCLVII
1624	=	MDCXXIV	1658	=	MDCLVIII
1625	=	MDCXXV	1659	=	MDCLIX
1626	=	MDCXXVI	1660	=	MDCLX
1627	=	MDCXXVII	1661	=	MDCLXI
1628	=	MDCXXVIII	1662	=	MDCLXII
1629	=	MDCXXIX	1663	=	MDCLXIII
1630	=	MDCXXX	1664	=	MDCLXIV
1631	=	MDCXXXI	1665	=	MDCLXV
1632	=	MDCXXXII	1666	=	MDCLXVI
1633	=	MDCXXXIII	1667	=	MDCLXVII

1668	=	MDCLXVIII
1669	=	MDCLXIX
1670	=	MDCLXX
1671	=	MDCLXXI
1672	=	MDCLXXII
1673	=	MDCLXXIII
1674	=	MDCLXXIV
1675	=	MDCLXXV
1676	=	MDCLXXVI
1677	=	MDCLXXVII
1678	=	MDCLXXVIII
1679	=	MDCLXXIX
1680	=	MDCLXXX
1681	=	MDCLXXXI
1682	=	MDCLXXXII
1683	=	MDCLXXXIII
1684	=	MDCLXXXIV
1685	=	MDCLXXXV
1686	=	MDCLXXXVI
1687	=	MDCLXXXVII
1688	=	MDCLXXXVIII
1689	=	MDCLXXXIX
1690	=	MDCXC
1691	=	MDCXCI
1692	=	MDCXCII
1693	=	MDCXCIII
1694	=	MDCXCIV
1695	=	MDCXCV
1696	=	MDCXCVI
1697	=	MDCXCVII
1698	=	MDCXCVIII
1699	=	MDCXCIX
1700	=	MDCC

Note: the general rule most likely to be broken is that concerning the repetition of I and C, which may often be found in sequences of four, e.g. MDCIIII (1604). Another point to be observed is that sometimes numerals occur in upper and lower case numerals, e.g. MDCCLxxviii (1778).

Other examples can be seen in the following:

From the first edition of Caxton's *The Dictes and sayengis of the philosophres:*

Here endeth the book named the dictes or sayengis of the philosphres enprynted by me william Caxton at Westmestre the yere of our lord M.CCCC.Lxxvii. (1477.)

From the colophon of the first book printed in Hamburg, Voragine's *Laudes Beate Marie Virginis:*

Per me Joannē & Thomā borchard. Anno dñi M.cccc.xci.
[1491.]

Note the abbreviations, of a type frequently to be found. They are normally indicated by a short stroke or double curve above the shortened word or name. Here 'Joannes', 'Thomas' and 'domini' have been so abbreviated.

From an early Naples printing:

Impressum   Neapoli...M.D.XX.XV.Decemb.Leone.x. Ponti. [1520 15 December in the Pontificate of Leo X.]

From the title-page of Doctor Johnson's *London: A Poem:*

LONDON
Printed for R. Doddesley, at Tully's Head in Pall-Mall

MDCCXXXVIII [1738.]

From the title-page of *The Life and Strange Surprizing Adventures of Robinson Crusoe, of York, Mariner:*

LONDON
Printed for W. TAYLOR at the Ship in Pater-Noster-Row.   MDCCXIX. [1719.]

From the title-page of Sawyer and Darton's *English Books.*

PUBLISHED IN THE CITY OF WESTMINSTER,
MCMXXVII [1927.]

✽✽✽✽✽✽✽✽✽✽✽✽✽✽✽✽✽

Appendix II

Old and New Style

Some readers may recall hearing, during their schooldays, of people at some period in history shouting out 'Give us back our eleven days'; but they can rarely remember the circumstances and, since they collect neither books nor documents, have never encountered the problems it can raise.

The collector of autograph material, and occasionally of books, will come across such datings as:

$$\text{February 3 } 164\frac{8}{9}$$

Unless this peculiarity is understood, it is possible to be a whole year out in ascribing a date. Since we are concerned with results rather than causes, it is unnecessary to go into details of Julian and Gregorian styles, astronomical calculations of bisextiles, three sextiles retrenched and the like; but simply say that by 1751 the 'Old Style' used in this country was 11 days out, in common with Sweden and Russia. Lord Chesterfield expressed himself pithily as usual by saying that "it was very dishonourable for England to remain in such a gross and avowed error, especially in such company." With the astronomer George Parker, second Earl of Macclesfield, and James Bradley, Astronomer Royal, Chesterfield drew up a scheme to correct the absurdity and a Bill passed both Houses of Parliament.

Under the existing practice, what might be termed the historical year began on 1 January; whereas the legal year began on 25 March; so that, on exactly the same day, a parson writing in his country rectory might date a letter '5 January 1659' while a lawyer in London, not having reached the end of his legal year, would put '5 January 1658'.

By the new Act the year 1752 was to begin on 1 January and the 3 September was to be called 14 September, thus causing the election cry 'Give us back our eleven days', the ordinary populace, understandably enough, thinking an unscrupulous Government had knocked nearly a fortnight off its mortal span.

For a period the device was commonly used of writing the date as in the example given above, covering both systems. It is easy to interpret if it is remembered that it is always the lower placed figure that gives the date now used in our calendar. If a document stated that Charles I was executed on 30 January 164$\frac{8}{9}$, you would be correct in deducing that, by modern reckoning, the king handed over his Order of the Garter to Bishop Juxon and said "Remember" in 1649.

❋❋❋❋❋❋❋❋❋❋❋❋❋❋❋❋❋

Appendix III

A Shelf of Bookmen

BIBLIOCLAST — A destroyer of books.

BIBLIOGNOST — One having a deep knowledge of, and insight into, books.

BIBLIOGRAPHER — One skilled in matters of book history, format, editions, printing, etc.; also one who compiles a systematic list of an author's works, or one relating to a specific limited subject.

BIBLIOKLEPT — A stealer of books.

BIBLIOLATER — One beset with excessive worship of books; more particularly, one with an undue reliance on the letter of the Bible.

BIBLIOMANCER — One who tells fortunes by books.

BIBLIOMANE (BIBLIOMANIAC) — One with a mania for collecting and owning books.

BIBLIOPEGIST — One having knowledge, or special love of, bindings.

BIBLIOPHILE — A book lover.

BIBLIOPHOBE — A book hater.

BIBLIOPOLE — A bookseller.

BIBLIOTAPH — A concealer or hider of books.

BIBLIOTHECARY — A keeper of books, a librarian.

MONOBIBLIOPHILIST — A lover of one book.

POLYBIBLIOPHILIST — A lover of many books.

❋❋❋❋❋❋❋❋❋❋❋❋❋❋❋❋❋

Appendix IV

The Antiquarian Booksellers' Association (International)

Directory of Members, 1983

The Association, whose headquarters are at Book House, 45 East Hill, London, SW18 2QZ, was founded in 1906. Some firms have been members since its inception. In the words of the Association ''some firms have shops or offices in towns or cities, others work by post and catalogue from houses in the country; a few are large corporations, but most are family businesses, or with sole proprietors. Some have general stocks, some are specialists, but all share a love of fine and rare books...Books for sale should be found clearly priced, and if any are found to be faulty or imperfect (which is unlikely), they will be taken back without demur.''

Members are elected only after at least five years' experience in the trade and upon strong recommendation of other members who are prepared to vouch for their knowledge and standards of ethics. While booksellers with wide knowledge and impeccable standards exist outside the Association, its badge on windows and notepaper offers a useful guarantee to the collector.

In the listing the specialisations of members are indicated at the end of each entry.

ABINGTON BOOKS
29 Church Lane
Little Abington, Cambridge
CB1 6BQ
(01 267) 2701
Oriental Rugs and Classical Tapestries, Hand-made Oriental Textiles

AFRICANA ANTIQUARIANS
Penlan, Crowborough Hill
Crowborough, Sussex, TN6 2EA
Crowborough (089 26) 2454
Africana

ALLEN & CO. LTD., J.A.
(The Horseman's Bookshop)
1 Lower Grosvenor Place
Buckingham Palace Road
London, SW1W 0EL
(01 834) 5606/7
Equine and Equestrian publications (all languages)

ALLSOP, DUNCAN M.
26 Smith Street, Warwick
CV34 4HS
(0926) 493266
Warwickshire

ANGLEBOOKS LTD.
2 Cecil Court
Charing Cross Road
London WC2
(01 836) 2922
*Angling, English Local History and
Topography, Fine General Books*

APPLETON, TONY
The Old School
Buckland Dinham, Frome
Somerset, BA11 2QR
Frome (0373) 62929
*Printing History, Books about Books,
Private Presses, Fine Modern Bindings,
Papermaking*

ATTIC (SEVENOAKS) LTD.,
THE
(J. & R. Brydon)
The Village House, Brasted
Westerham, Kent, TN16 1HU
Westerham (51) 63507
*Travel, Art, Topography and General
Antiquarian*

BAIN LTD., JAMES, EST. 1816
(Rodney & Sonia Drake)
The Merlin Gallery, High Street
Petworth, West Sussex
GU28 0AU
Petworth (0798) 42235
*English Literature, Bibliography, Modern
Illustrators, Maps and Prints, Sussex
Topography*

BARNARD, THOMAS
11 Windsor Street, Uxbridge
Middlesex
Uxbridge (89) 32751

BARON, H.
136 Chatsworth Road
London, NW2 5QU
(01 459) 2035
*Music (printed and manuscript), Musical
Literature, Autograph Letters*

BARRIES BOOKSHOP
4 Montpellier Walk, Cheltenham
Gloucestershire, GL50 1SD
Cheltenham (0242) 515813
Voyages and Travel

BAYNTON-WILLIAMS
14 Sheen Common Drive
Richmond, Surrey, TW10 5BN
(01 876) 6614
*Old Maps, Prints, Atlases, Illustrated
Books*

BAYNTUN, George
(H. & C. Bayntun-Coward)
Manvers Street, Bath
Avon, BA1 1JW
Bath (0225) 66000
*Fine Bindings, First and Fine Editions of
English Literature and General*

BEACH, D.M.
52 High Street, Salisbury
Wiltshire, SP1 2PG
Salisbury (0722) 3801
*Colour Plate Books, Atlases, Topography,
Bindings, Children's Books*

BEELEIGH ABBEY BOOKS
(W. & G. Foyle Ltd.)
Beeleigh Abbey, Maldon, Essex
Maldon (Essex) (0621) 56308
*English Literature 1500-1800, Coloured
Plate Books, Voyages and Travel, Fine
Bindings*

BELL, BOOK & RADMALL LTD.
4 Cecil Court
London, WC2N 4HE
(01 240) 2161 & (01 836) 5888
Modern First Editions

BICKERSTETH, DAVID
38 Fulbrooke Road
Cambridge, CB3 9EE
Cambridge (0223) 352291
English Literature, Science and Medicine

BISSET LTD., JAMES G.
12/14 Upperkirkgate, Aberdeen
AB9 1BG
Aberdeen (0224) 644528

BLACKWELL'S RARE BOOKS
(B.H. Blackwell Ltd.)
Fyfield Manor, Fyfield, Abingdon
Oxfordshire
OX13 5LR
Frilford Heath (0865) 390692/3
Telex: 83118
Art, Literature, Private Presses, Travel,
General Antiquarian
Large stocks of Academic and General
Secondhand at Blackwells, Broad
Street, Oxford (0865) 249111

BLOCK, ANDREW
20 Barter Street, London
WC1 2AH
(01 405) 9660
Music-halls, Conjuring, Gordon Craig,
Circus

BONDY, LOUIS W.
16 Little Russell Street
London, WC1A 2HN
(01 405) 2733
Miniature Books, Caricature, Children's
Books, Illustrated Books 16th to 20th
centuries

BOOK HOUSE, THE
37 Frederick Street
Loughborough
Leicestershire, LE11 3BH
Loughborough (0509) 261421
Industrial and Transport History

BOOKROOM, THE
(Edward Searle)
13a Eligius Street
Cambridge, CB2 1HS
Cambridge (0223) 69694
Good General Stock in most subjects

BOOKS & THINGS
(Martin Steenson)
Dolphin Arcade
157 Portobello Road
London W11
(01 370) 5593
Children's and Illustrated, Decorative Art,
Modern First Editions, Original Art

BOOKSHOP BLACKHEATH
LTD., THE
74 Tranquil Vale
London, SE3 0BN
(02 852) 4786
Local History, London, General
Topography

BOW WINDOWS BOOKSHOP
128 High Street, Lewes
East Sussex, BN7 1XL
Lewes (079 16) 2839
Natural History, Travel, Topography,
Literature, Medicine and Science

BOYLE, ANDREW
(BOOKSELLER) LTD.,
21 Friar Street
Worcester, WR1 2NA
Worcester (0905) 23893
Juveniles, Education, Literature,
Biography, Old Novels, History,
Topography

BOYLE & CO., JOHN
40 Drayton Gardens
London, SW10 9SA
(01 373) 8247
Telex 298983 RPAMAN
Political Economy, Printing and the Mind
of Man first editions, Science and
Medicine, English Literature

BREMAN LTD., PAUL
1 Rosslyn Hill
London, NW3 5UL
(01 435) 7730
Architecture (Military, Garden, Bridge),
Perspective Books, Related Prints

BROADHURST & CO. LTD., C.K.
5-7 Market Street, Southport
Merseyside, PR8 1HD
Southport (0704) 32064 & 34110
Natural History, Rare Books, First
Editions, Bibliography, General Literature

BURDEN LTD., CLIVE A.
46 Talbot Road, Rickmansworth
Hertfordshire, WD3 1HE
Rickmansworth (87) 78097 & 72383
Atlases, Maps, Prints, Coloured Plate
Books, Americana

BURKE, J.
6 Woodberry Down
London, N4 2TG
(01 800) 5161

BURTON-GARBETT, A.
35 The Green, Morden
Surrey, SM4 4HJ
(01 540) 2367
Latin America, Mexico, and the Caribbean

BYGONE BOOKS
(Geoffrey Armstrong)
Axmas Cottage, Faygate Lane
Rusper, West Sussex
RH12 4RF
Rusper (029 384) 256
English Literature, History, Travel,
Military, Sporting

CAMPBELL, FIONA
158 Lambeth Road
London, SE1 7DF
(01 928) 1633
Travel, Italy

CASTLE BOOKSHOP, THE
(A.B. Doncaster)
37 North Hill, Colchester
Essex, CO1 1QR
Colchester (0206) 77520
Archaeology, History, Folklore, English
Literature, Topography (Great Britain)

CAVENDISH RARE BOOKS
(Barbara Grigor-Taylor)
2/4 Princes Arcade, Piccadilly
London, SW1Y 6DS
(01 734) 3840
Travel and Topography, Maritime,
Mountaineering, Sets and Bindings

CHAPEL COURT BOOKSHOP
(Louise E. Ross)
Shutta Road, East Looe
Cornwall, PL13 1BJ
Looe (05036) 3700
Cornish Literature and Topography,
Illustrated Books, Fine Bird Books,
English County Maps and Atlases

CHAPMAN LTD., G. KEN
2 Ross Road, London, SE25 6SF
(01 653) 4469
Science-Fiction, Weird and Fantastic
Fiction, Mystery and Detective Fiction

CHECKER BOOKS
2 Checker Walk, Abingdon
Oxon., OX14 3JB
Abingdon (0235) 28172
Bowls, Bowling Clubs, Berkshire —
Topography, History, Archaeology

CHELSEA RARE BOOKS
313 King's Road
London, SW3 5EP
(01 351) 0950
English Literature (17th-20th Centuries),
Illustrated Books, Travel and Topography,
Art and Architecture

CLARKE, JANET
3 Woodside Cottages, Freshford
Bath, Avon, BA3 6EJ
Limpley Stoke (022 122) 3186
Gastronomy, Cookery, Wine

CLARKE-HALL LTD., J.
7 Bride Court
London, EC4Y 8DU
(01 353) 4116
Johnsoniana, First Editions, Illustrated
Books
also at
22 Bride Lane, London
EC4Y 8DU
(01 353) 5483
19th Century Maps and Prints only

COMMIN'S BOOKSHOP
(Peter Kennedy)
100 Old Christchurch Road
Bournemouth, Dorset
BH1 1LR
Bournemouth (0202) 27504
General Antiquarian and Secondhand,
Maps and Prints, Natural History and
Gardening, English Literature and
History, Archaeology

CONNOISSEUR, THE
(Makram Irani)
11 Fordham Court, De Vere
Gardens
London W8
(01 937) 0127
*Antique Maps, Prints, Manuscripts,
Topography of the Middle East*

COOK, R.L.
Belmont House, Little Horton
Devizes, Wiltshire, SN10 3LJ
Cannings (Wilts.) (0380) 86214
Rare and Fine Books

COOMBES, A.J.
24 Horsham Road, Dorking
Surrey, RH4 2JA
Dorking (0306) 880736
British Topography and Local History

COX, CHARLES
Two Bells, Chawleigh
Chulmleigh, Devon, EX18 7HA
Chulmleigh (0769) 80582
English Literature 1780-1914

COX, CLAUDE
The White House, Kelsale
Saxmundham, Suffolk, IP17 2PQ
Saxmundham (0728) 2786
*Literature, History, Education
Fine Printing, Natural History*

CRAVEN BOOKS
3 Newmarket Street
Skipton-in-Craven
Yorkshire, BD23 2JE
Skipton (0756) 2677
Northern Topography, Maps and Prints

CROWE, PETER R.
75 Upper St. Giles' Street
Norwich, Norfolk, NR2 1AB
Norwich (0603) 24800
Norfolk Topography, Maps and Prints

CROWE, THOMAS
77 Upper St. Giles' Street
Norwich, Norfolk, NR2 1AB
Norwich (0603) 21962
*Voyages and Travel, English Literature,
Natural History*

D.L. BOOKS
(Mr. & Mrs. T.E. Fisher)
'Whiteways', 28 Lowfield Road
Haywards Heath, West Sussex
RH16 4DW
Haywards Heath (0444) 59455

DALWOOD, PETER
44 Causewayhead, Penzance
Cornwall, TR18 2SS
Penzance (0736) 3702
English Literature and History

DAVID, G.
3 & 16 St. Edwards Passage
Cambridge, CB2 3PJ
Cambridge (0223) 354619
*General Antiquarian, Secondhand,
Remainders*

DAY, H.V.
The Old Roman Catholic Church,
25 High West Street
Dorchester, Dorset, DT1 1UW
Dorchester (0305) 64904
*Antiquarian Books, Maps, Prints and
Watercolours*

DEIGHTON, BELL & CO.
13 Trinity Street
Cambridge, CB2 1TD
Cambridge (0223) 353939
*English Literature, Private Presses, British
Topography, Travel, Illustrated Books*

DELGROSSO, JOSEPH
(Bibliopola)
The Antique Market
13-25 Church Street
Marylebone, London NW8
(01 723) 0429
*Antiquarian and Illustrated Books, Private
Presses and Children's*

DE LOTZ, PETER GEORGE
20 Downside Crescent
Hampstead, London, NW3 2AP
(01 794) 5709
*Military, Naval, Aviation, General War
Studies*

DEMETZY BOOKS
113 Portobello Road, London W11
Correspondence only to:
Manor House, Ducklington
Oxfordshire, OX8 7UX
Witney (0993) 2209
*Antiquarian Cookery Books, Miniature
Books, Architecture, Fine Bindings,
Dickens First Editions*

DILLON'S UNIVERSITY
BOOKSHOP
Antiquarian and Secondhand
Department
1 Malet Street, London
WC1E 7JB
(01 636) 1577

DOLPHIN BOOK CO. LTD.
(John L. Gili)
58 Hurst Lane, Cumnor
Oxford, OX2 9PR
Oxford (0865) 862175
Spanish and Spanish America

DOUWMA, ROBERT
PRINTS & MAPS LTD.
4 Henrietta Street
The Piazza, Covent Garden
London, WC2E 8QU
(01 836) 0771
*Prints and Maps, Atlases, Illustrated
Books*

DRURY (RARE BOOKS) LTD.,
JOHN
72 Culver Street East
Colchester, Essex, CO1 1LP
Colchester (0206) 46755
*Economics, Numismatics, Social History,
Philosophy, Politics*

DUCK, WILLIAM
The Glebe House, Brightling
East Sussex, TN32 5HE
Brightling (042 482) 295
*Art, Architecture, Civil Engineering,
Technology, Transport*

DUPONT ET FILS, MME J.
68 Lincoln Road, East Finchley
London N2 9DL
(01 883) 7852
*Travel and Topography of Europe, Malta,
Madeira, Gibraltar, Near East, Middle
East, Views, Maps, Decorative Prints,
Flowers, Sporting etc.*

DUVAL, K.D.
Frenich, Foss, Pitlochry
Perthshire, Scotland, PH16 5NG
Tummel Bridge (088 24) 215
Philosophy, Economics, Modern Bindings

EATON (BOOKSELLERS) LTD.,
PETER
80 Holland Park Avenue
London, W11 3RE and
Lilies, Weedon, Aylesbury, Bucks.
(01 727) 5211 and Whitchurch
(0296 641) 393
General Antiquarian

EMERALD ISLE BOOKS
539 Antrim Road, Belfast
BT15 3BU
Belfast (0232) 771798
*Ireland, Theology, Travel, Scotland,
Antiquarian*

EXETER RARE BOOKS
(Roy Parry)
Guildhall Shopping Centre
Exeter, Devon, EX4 3HG
Exeter (0392) 36021
Devonshire Topography

EXPORT BOOK CO.
(W. Halewood)
340 Garstang Road, Fulwood
Preston, Lancashire, PR2 4RY
Preston (Lancs.) (0772) 862347
Botanical, Maps and Atlases, Travel

FAUPEL, W.J.
3 Halsford Lane, East Grinstead
Sussex, RH19 1NY
East Grinstead (0342) 27043
Americana

FERROW, DAVID
77 Howard Street South
Great Yarmouth, Norfolk
NR30 1LN
Great Yarmouth (0493) 3800
(Private (0493) 62247)
Antiquarian Books on all Subjects,
Speciality Local Topography, Maps and
Prints

FIFTEENTH CENTURY
BOOKSHOP
(Eric Blundell)
99 High Street, Lewes
Sussex, BN7 1XH
Lewes (07916) 4160
General Antiquarian and
Secondhand

FISHER & SPERR (J.R. Sperr)
46 Highgate High Street
Highgate, London, N6 5JB
(01 340) 7244
Colour Plate Books, London, Antiquarian,
Fine Books on all Subjects

FLETCHER, H.M.
27 Cecil Court
London, WC2N 4EZ
(01 836) 2865
Old and Rare Books

FLOREY, C.P. (MRS.)
18 Whitethorn Gardens
Addiscombe Road, Croydon
Surrey, CR0 7LL
(01 654) 4724
Art, Children's Books, Illustrated Books,
Topography

FORSTER, W.
83a Stamford Hill
London, N16 5TP
(01 800) 3919
Bibliography, Bookbinding, Palaeography,
Typography, Sale Catalogues

FOYLE LTD., W. & G.
(Miss Christina Foyle)
119/125 Charing Cross Road
London, WC2 0EH
(01 437) 5660
General Antiquarian and Secondhand

FRANCES BOOKS
(Mr. M.J. & Mrs. M.F. Lee)
3 Crescent Road, Worthing
West Sussex, BN11 1RL
Worthing (0903) 31169
Natural History, Topography, Travel,
Fine Bindings

FRANKLIN, COLIN &
CHARLOTTE
Home Farm, Culham
Oxfordshire, OX14 4NA
Abingdon (0235) 22544
Fine and Rare Printing, Manuscripts,
Illustrated Books, Bindings

FRIZZELL, ALEX. M.
Castlelaw, West Linton
Peeblesshire, Scotland, EH46 7EA
West Linton (0968) 60450
Scottish Books, Typography, Antiquarian

FROGNAL RARE BOOKS
(Edith Finer)
18 Cecil Court
Charing Cross Road
London, WC2N 4HE
(01 240) 2815
Law , Economics, Legal History,
Banking, Currency, Parliamentary and
General History

GALLOWAY & PORTER LTD.
30 Sidney Street
Cambridge, CB2 3HS
Cambridge (0223) 67876
Fine and Rare, Classics, Topography, all
Academic Subjects

GENDT, A.L. van
The Lodge, Sandy Lane
Old Lakenham, Norwich, NR1 2NR
Norwich (0603) 26913
(Business by appointment only)
Bibliography, Incunabula, Manuscripts,
Public Sales, Typography

GEORGE'S SONS LTD.,
WILLIAM
89 Park Street, Bristol, BS1 5PW
Bristol (0272) 276602
Arts, English Literature, History,
Bibliography, Travel and Topography

GIBBONS, DEREK
c/o The Gallery, 8 King's Parade
Cambridge, CB2 1SJ
Cambridge (0223) 312913 & 68169
*Children's and Illustrated Books of all
Ages, also General Antiquarian*

GIBB'S BOOKSHOP
(Robert Gibb)
83 Mosley Street, Manchester 2
Manchester (061 236) 7179

GILBERT, H.M.
(B.L. & R.C. Gilbert)
19 The Square
Winchester, Hampshire
Winchester (0962) 52832

GLENDALE, M. & R.
58 Davies Street, London W1
(01 629) 2851
Juveniles, Illustrated Books, Feminism

GODFREY LTD., THOMAS C.
21 Stonegate, York, YO1 2AP
York (0904) 24531
*Literature, Local History, Archaeology,
History*

GOLDSCHEIDER, GABY
29 Temple Road, Windsor
Berkshire
Windsor (95) 61517
*General, Arthur Conan Doyle &
Children's Books*

GOLDSCHMIDT & CO. LTD., E.P.
(Prop. J.L. Vellekoop)
64 Drayton Gardens
London, SW10 9SB
(01 373) 2266
*Architecture, Early Science, Gastronomy,
Illustrated Books*

GOUGH BOOKS, SIMON
3 Fish Hill, Holt, Norfolk
Holt (026 371) 2650 and 2761
*Natural History, East Anglia, Fine
Bindings and Sets, Modern First Editions,
Books on the Household*

GRANGE BOOKSHOP
(William Blair)
186 Causewayside
Edinburgh, EH9 1PN
Edinburgh (031 667) 2759
Scottish and Fine Books on Most Subjects

GRANT, JOHN
9 & 13C Dundas Street
Edinburgh, EH3 6QG
Edinburgh (031 556) 9698
*Fine Bindings, 18th and 19th Century
English Literature, Scottish Standard Sets*

GREER, ROBIN
30 Sloane Court West
London, SW3 4TB
(01 730) 7392
Children's Illustrated, and Travel

GREGORY, GEORGE
(H.H. Bayntun-Coward)
Manvers Street, Bath
BA1 1JW
Bath (0225) 66055
*General Stock, Engraved Portraits and
Views*

GRESHAM BOOKS
(James & Maggie Hine)
The Old Swan, Akeman Street
Tring, Hertfordshire, HP23 6AN
Tring (044 282) 3976
*Fine Arts, Architecture, Embroidery and
Textiles, Natural History*

GRINKE, PAUL
(ALSO WAVENEY BOOKS)
Sustead Old Hall, Sustead,
Norfolk, NR11 8RV
Matlaske (026 377) 247
*English and Continental Books Before
1850, Art, Architecture and Bibliography*

GUILDHALL BOOKSHOP, THE
(A.F. Wallis Ltd.)
25 York Street, Twickenham
Middlesex *and* The Guildhall
Bookshop (Warehouse), Rear of 8
Victoria Road, Surbiton, Surrey
(01 892) 0331 and (warehouse) (01
390) 2552
*Literature, The Sciences, The Humanities,
The Arts, Old and Rare*

GURNEY LTD., R.D.
23 Campden Street
London, W8 7EP
(01 727) 6644
Early Medicine, Science and Technology

HAAS, OTTO
(A. & M. Rosenthal)
49 Belsize Park Gardens
London, NW3 4JL
(01 722) 1488 (by appointment only)
*Music Manuscripts, Early Printed Music,
Autograph Letters*

HALEWOOD & SONS
37 Friargate, Preston
Lancashire, PR1 2AT
Preston (Lancs.) (0772) 52603
*Voyages and Travel, Africana, Americana,
Australasia, etc.*

HALL, ANTHONY C.
30 Staines Road, Twickenham
Middlesex, TW2 5AH
(01 898) 2638
*Russia and Eastern Europe, Middle East,
Africa, Asia, Social History*

HALL'S BOOKSHOP
20 Chapel Place
Tunbridge Wells, Kent
TN1 1YQ
Tunbridge Wells (0892) 27842

HANNAS, T. & L.
33 Farnaby Road, Bromley
Kent, BR1 4BL
(01 460) 5702
*English Literature before 1850,
Scandinavica*

HAN-SHAN TANG LTD.
(Christer von der Burg)
717 Fulham Road
London, SW6 5UL
(01 731) 2447
*Travels and Arts and Cultures of China,
Japan, Korea*

HARVEY'S BOOKSHOP LTD.
(V. Hulme)
37 Chartwell Drive, Wigston
Leicester, LE8 2FL
Leicester (0533) 881334
*19th and 20th Century Literature, General
Antiquarian*

HEAD, JOHN & JUDITH
The Barn Book Supply
88 Crane Street, Salisbury
Wiltshire, SP1 2QD
Salisbury (0722) 27767
*Angling, Shooting, Horse, Falconry and
Natural History*

HEATH, A.R.
179 Whiteladies Road, Bristol 8
Bristol (0272) 311183
*Rare Books, Pamphlets and Manuscripts
16th-19th Centuries*

HERALDRY TODAY
(Mrs. R. Pinches)
10 Beauchamp Place
London SW3
(01 584) 1656
(open Monday, Tuesday,
Wednesday 9.30 to 5.30) *and*
Parliament Piece, Ramsbury
Nr. Marlborough, Wiltshire
Marlborough (0672) 20617
(open Monday to Friday 9.30 to
5.00, weekends by appointment)
*Heraldry, Genealogy, Peerage,
Topography, Biography*

HILL LTD., G. HEYWOOD
10 Curzon Street, London W1
(01 629) 0647
*Fine Illustrated Books, Victoriana,
Natural History, Children's Books*

HODGKINS & CO. LTD., IAN
Mount Vernon, Butterow
Rodborough, Stroud
Gloucestershire, GL5 2LP
Stroud (045 36) 4270
*Pre-Raphaelites & Associates, 19th
Century Illustrated Books, Literary Women
of 19th Century*

HOFMANN & FREEMAN
(ANTIQUARIAN BOOK-
SELLERS) LTD.
8 High Street, Otford, Sevenoaks
Kent, TN14 5PQ
Otford (095 92) 2430
By appointment only
English Literature, 17th-19th Centuries
Also, general secondhand stock and
Kent books at The Darenth
Bookshop, same address, open
Thursday-Saturday

HOGG, KEITH
82 High Street, Tenterden
Kent, TN30 6JJ
Tenterden (058 06) 2050
By appointment only
*Printing History, Typography,
Bibliography, Book Trade and Publishing*

HOLLETT & SON, R.F.G
6 Finkle Street, Sedbergh
Cumbria, LA10 5AG
Sedburgh (0587) 20298 & 20286
*Natural History, Travel & Topography,
Fine Arts*

HOLLEYMAN & TREACHER LTD.
21a & 22 Duke Street, Brighton
Sussex, BN1 1AH
Brighton (0273) 28007
Archaeology, Fine Arts, Music, Sussex

HOPPEN, STEPHANIE
The Studio, 17 Walton Street
London SW3
(01 589) 3678
*Voyages, Atlases, Maps, Fine and Early
Illustrated Books, Food and Wine*

HOSKING, MICHAEL
(THE GOLDEN HIND
BOOKSHOP)
85 Beach Street, Deal
Kent, CT14 6JB
Deal (030 45) 5086
Modern First Editions

HOWES BOOKSHOP
(Raymond Kilgarriff)
Trinity Hall, Braybrooke Terrace
Hastings, East Sussex
TN34 1HQ
Hastings (0424) 423437
*Antiquarian and Scholarly Books on the
Humanities*

HUBBARD'S BOOKSHOP,
DOGGIE
(Clifford L.B. Hubbard, FIAL)
Ffynnon Cadno, Ponterwyd,
Aberystwyth
Ceredigion, Wales
Aberystwyth (0970) 85224
Rare Books on Dogs

HUGHES RARE BOOKS, SPIKE
Leithen Bank, Leithen Road
Innerleithen, Peeblesshire
Scotland, EH44 6HY
Innerleighten (0896) 830019
*General Antiquarian, Scottish Books,
English Literature, History, Illustrated*

HUGHES & SMEETH LTD.
26 St. Thomas Street, Lymington,
Hants.
Lymington (0590) 76324
*Topography, Travel, Natural History,
Maps and Prints*

HÜNARSDORFF, RICHARD VON
P.O. Box 582, London SW10
(01 373) 3899
*Continental Books in Early and Rare
Editions, History of Medicine and Science,
Latin Americana, Military Science,
Linguistics*

HUNNINGS, P.J.M.
Penn Barn, By the Pond, Elm Road
Penn, Bucks.
Penn (049 481) 5691
*19th Century Illustrated, Leather
Bindings, Art Reference, Antiquarian
Maps and Prints, Cricket*

HUSTWICK, IAN
13 Rodwell Court
Walton-on-Thames, Surrey
Walton-on-Thames (98) 25612
Small general stock

JACKSON, IRENE M., MISS
27 Norma Road, Waterloo
Liverpool, L22 0NS
Liverpool (051 928) 6847
Postal business only

JAMES, DEREK W.
Corner Croft
33 Old Lodge Lane
Purley, Surrey
(01 660) 5072
Aviation, Military, Travel

JOSEPH, E.
1 Vere Street (Third Floor)
London, W1M 9HQ
(01 493) 8353/4/5
*Standard Sets in Binding or Original
Cloth, Colour Plates and Natural History,
Modern Illustrated Books, Press Books,
Victorian and early 20th Century
Watercolour Paintings*

JUBILEE BOOKS LTD.
18 High Street, Burford
Oxfordshire OX8 4QE
Burford (099 382) 2209
Literature, History, Theology

K BOOKS
Waplington Hall, Allerthorpe
York, YO4 4RS
Pocklington (075 92) 2142
*Travel, Classics, Natural History, Early
Printing and Fine Books on most Subjects*

KATANKA BOOKS, MICHAEL
PO Box 39, Stanmore
Middlesex, HA7 3XN
(Postal business only)
*Political Ephemera, Labour History,
Modern First Editions*

KEEN, A. & S.
19 Pier Street, Ventnor, Isle of
Wight
Ventnor (0983) 853706
English Literature, Out of Print Fiction

KERR, EWEN
1 & 2 New Road, Kendal
Cumbria, LA9 4AY
Kendal (0539) 20659

KERR, NORMAN
c/o Priory House, Priest Lane,
Cartmel
Grange-over-Sands
Cumbria, LA11 6PX
Cartmel (044 854) 247
*Railways, Naval, Maritime, Motoring,
Aircraft, Natural History*

KEW BOOKS
(J.P. Chancellor)
14 Hillsleigh Road
London, W8 7JG
(01 229) 3043
*Botany and Gardening, Natural History,
Music, Private Presses*

KING, CLIFFORD E.
2 St. John's Lodge, Harley Road
London, NW3 3BY
(01 722) 8067
*Old and Rare Books, Early Italian
Printing, Topography, Literature, Science*

KOHLER, C.C.
12 Horsham Road, Dorking
Surrey, RH4 2JL
Dorking (0306) 81532
*Assembling of Special Collections, English
Literature, George Gissing*

KOKORO
(Brian and Colin Page)
36 Duke Street, Brighton
Sussex, BN1 1AG
Brighton (0273) 25954
*Natural History, Topography, Illustrated
Books, Japanese Block Printed Books,
Japanese Colour Prints*

KORN, M.E.
51 Lady Margaret Road
Kentish Town
London, NW5 2NH
(01 267) 2936 & 5035
*Darwinism, Natural History, Science and
Medicine, General Antiquarian Literature*

KRUML, RICHARD
47 Albemarle Street
London, W1X 3FB
(01 629) 3017
*Fine Japanese Prints and Illustrated Books
and Literature pertaining to the collecting
of these*

LAING (BOOKRANGER)
(James W.B. Laing)
14 Hepburn Gardens, St. Andrews
Fife, Scotland
St. Andrews (0334) 75066
Literature, First Editions, Art,
Antiquarian

LAWSON & CO., E.M.
(W.J. & K.M. Lawson)
Kingsholm, East Hagbourne
near Didcot, Oxfordshire
OX11 9LN
Didcot (0235) 812033
17th & 18th Century English Literature,
Early Science and Medicine, Economics,
Voyages and Travels

LAYWOOD, ANTHONY W.
Knipton, Grantham
Lincolnshire, NG32 1RF
Grantham (0476) 870224
English Books on most Subjects before
1850, British Topography, Bibliography

LLOYD'S BOOKSHOP
(Jane Morrison)
27 High Street, Wingham
Canterbury, Kent, CT3 1AW
Wingham (022 772) 774
Children's Books, Music

LLOYD-ROBERTS, TOM
Old Court House, Caerwys
Mold, Clwyd, CH7 5BB
Caerwys (0352) 720276
Topography, Travel, History, Literature,
Wales

LYLE, JOHN, BOOKSELLER
(Lyle & Davidson Ltd.)
Harpford, Sidmouth
Devon, EX10 0NH
Sidmouth (0395) 68294
Cookery, Wine, Surrealism

LYON, H.D.
18 Selwood Terrace
London, SW7 3QG
(01 373) 2709
Bindings, Architecture and Art, French,
Italian and Irish Books

MACNAUGHTON, DAVID
16 Gosford Place
Edinburgh, EH6 4BJ
Edinburgh (031) 554 7318
Literature, Scottish Topography, History

MCNAUGHTAN'S BOOKSHOP
(Elizabeth Strong)
3a Haddington Place
Edinburgh, EH7 4AE
(031 556) 5897
Fine Art, Illustrated Books, Early
Children's Books, Literature, Travel

MACNUTT LTD., RICHARD
29 Mount Sion, Tunbridge Wells,
Kent, TN1 1TZ
Tunbridge Wells (0892) 25049
(Visitors by appointment only)
Music, Theatre, Dance, Autographs,
Ephemera

MAGGS BROS. LTD.
50 Berkeley Square
London, W1X 6EL
(01 499) 2007 and (01 499) 2051
Travel and Military, Early Printing and
Bindings, Autographs & Manuscripts,
Bibliography, Western & Oriental
Miniatures

MAGNA GALLERY
(Brian Kentish)
41 High Street
Oxford, OX1 4AP
(0865) 245805
Atlases and Maps, Prints, Oxfordshire
Topography

MAP HOUSE OF LONDON, THE
54 Beauchamp Place, Knightsbridge
London, SW3 1NY
(01 589) 4325 and 01 589 9821
Antiquarian Maps and Engravings,
Antique Atlases, Mounting and Framing

MARKS LIMITED, BARRIE
5 Princes Avenue, Muswell Hill
London, N10 3LS
(01 883) 1593
Illustrated, Private Press, Colour Plate,
Colour Printing, Modern Firsts

MARLBOROUGH RARE BOOKS LTD.
(M.C. Brand)
35 Old Bond Street
London, W1X 4PT
(01 493) 6993
Finely Printed and Illustrated Books, Art,
Architecture and Bibliography, Natural
History

MARRIN & SONS, G. & D.I.
149 Sandgate Road, Folkestone
Kent, CT20 2DA
Folkestone (0303) 53016
Kent, Topography, Travel, Natural
History, Industry

MARSDEN, FRANCIS
c/o 140-142 King's Road
Chelsea, London, SW3 4VX
(01 735) 8570
British Art and Architecture,
Topographical Engravings by British
Artists

MARSHALL BRUCE
24 River Street, Ayr
Ayrshire, KA8 0AX
(Day) Ayr (0292) 84505
(Evening) Craigie (056 386) 274
Natural History, Travel, Atlases,
Illustrated Books

MATHEWS, ALISTER
"Fremington"
58 West Overcliff Drive
Bournemouth
Dorset, BH4 8AB
Bournemouth (0202) 761547
Old Master Drawings, English
Watercolours, Drawings by Book-
Illustrators

MENDEZ, CHRISTOPHER
51 Lexington Street
London, W1R 4HL
(01 734) 2385
Old Master Prints

MEYNELL'S BOOKSHOP
(Offord & Meynell Ltd.)
11 The Hornet, Chichester
West Sussex, PO19 4JL
Chichester (0243) 82018
Topography, Natural History, Illustrated
Books, Naval, Aviation

MOON, MICHAEL
41-42 Roper Street
Whitehaven, Cumbria
Whitehaven (0946) 62936
Cumbriana

MONK BRETTON BOOKS
107 New Bond Street
London, W1Y 9AA
(01 629) 7084
Private Press and Finely Printed Books,
Modern Illustrated Books

MOORE, ERIC T.
24 Bridge Street, Hitchin
Hertfordshire, SG5 2DF
Hitchin (0462) 50497
General

MOORE, PETER
P.O. Box 66, (200a Perne Road)
Cambridge, CB1 3PD
Cambridge (0223) 211846
(Office only)
Australasia and the Pacific

MORTEN (BOOKSELLERS)
LTD., E. J.
2, 4, 6, 8, 9 Warburton Street
Didsbury, Manchester, M20 0RA
Manchester (061) 445 7629
MORTEN'S BOOKSHOPS LTD.
50, 52, 54 Chestergate, Macclesfield
Cheshire
Macclesfield (0625) 23679
Illustrated Books, Local History, Standard
Sets, Rare Books, English Literature

MORTON-SMITH, I. & M.
Maysleigh, Milland, Liphook
Hants., GU30 7JN
Milland (042876) 396
Music, Calligraphy, Anglo-Saxon Printing
Types, General Antiquarian Books

MOSDELL FINE BOOKS, G.W.
Hillside, St. Issey
Nr. Wadebridge, Cornwall
Rumford (08414) 666

MURRAY HILL (RARE BOOKS)
LTD., PETER
(Martin Hamlyn)
35 North Hill, Highgate
London, N6 4BS
(01 340) 6959
*17th, 18th and Early 19th Century
English Literature*

MYERS (AUTOGRAPHS) LTD.,
WINIFRED A.
Suite 52, 91 St. Martin's Lane
London WC2
(01 836) 1940
*Autograph Letters, Manuscripts, Inscribed
Books*

NOTT BOOKSELLER, MIKE
(M.J. Nott)
17 Cathedral Yard
Exeter, Devon, EX1 1HB
Exeter (0392) 35086

ORSKEY, MARTIN
Little Gains House, Elmsted
Ashford, Kent, TN2 5JU
Elmsted (023 375) 204
*Travel, Photography, Trade Catalogues,
Early Printed Ephemera*

O'SHEA GALLERY, RAYMOND
6 Ellis Street, Off Sloane Street
Belgravia, London, SW1 9AL
(01 730) 0081/2
*Old Maps, Prints, Atlases, Illustrated
Books and Cartographical Curiosities*

OTWAY, RODNEY & SUSAN
Dutch Barton Cottage
Church Street, Bradford-on-Avon
Wiltshire, BA15 1LN
Bradford-on-Avon (022 16) 3885
*English Literature 17th-19th Centuries,
Fine Bindings, General Books*

OXLEY, LAURENCE
THE STUDIO BOOKSHOP
17 Broad Street, Alresford
Winchester, Hampshire
SO24 9AW
Alresford (096 273) 2188
*India, Far East, General Stock incl. Maps
and Prints*

PAGE & CO. LTD., K.N.W.
8 Barclay Terrace
Edinburgh, EH10 4HP
Edinburgh (031 228) 1815
Scottish, Bindings

PAIN, JEAN
34 Trinity Street
Cambridge, CB2 1TB
Cambridge (0223) 358279
*English Literature, Fine Bindings, Prints,
Maps, General Books*

PARIKIAN, DIANA
The Old Rectory, Waterstock
Oxfordshire, OX9 1JR
Ickford (084 47) 603
*Mythology, Iconography and Emblemata,
Continental Books before 1800*

PETERSFIELD BOOKSHOP, THE
16a Chapel Street, Petersfield
Hampshire, GU32 3DS
Petersfield (0730) 63438
Sport, Topography, Travel

PHELPS, MICHAEL
19 Chelverton Road, Putney
London, SW15
(01 785) 6766
*History of Medicine, Science and
Technology*

PICCADILLY RARE BOOKS
LTD. (Paul Minet)
30 Sackville Street
London, W1X 1DB
(01 437) 2135
*Biography, History, Travel, Large General
Stock*

PICKERING & CHATTO LTD.
17 Pall Mall
London, SW1Y 5NB
(01 930) 2515
*Economics, English Literature, Medicine
and Science, Travel, Autographs and
Manuscripts*

PLEASURES OF PAST TIMES
(David Drummond)
11 Cecil Court
Charing Cross Road
London, WC2N 4EZ
(01 836) 1142
Juvenilia, Ephemera, Entertainment incl.
Theatre and Allied Arts

POLLAK, DR. P.M.
29 Droridge, Dartington, Totnes
South Devon, TQ9 6JQ
Totnes (0803) 862543
Science, Medicine, Natural History,
Technology

POTTER LTD., JONATHAN
1 Grafton Street
London, W1X 3LB
(01 491) 3520
Atlases, Maps, Travel Books, Books on
History of Cartography

PROBSTHAIN, ARTHUR
41 Great Russell Street
London, WC1B 3PH
(01 636) 1096
Oriental History and Culture, Oriental
Art, Oriental Languages and Literature,
Africana

QUARITCH LTD., BERNARD
5-8 Lower John Street
Golden Square
London, W1R 4AU
(01 734) 2983 Telex London 8955509
Early Printed Books and Manuscripts

QUEVEDO (J.F.T. Rodgers)
25 Cecil Court
London, WC2N 4EZ
(01 836) 9132
Rare Books before 1830, Spanish Books

RADFORD, P.J.
Sheffield Park, near Uckfield
Sussex
Danehill (0825) 790531
Early Maps and Prints

REEVES BOOKSELLER LTD.,
WILLIAM
1A Norbury Crescent
London, SW16 4JR
(01 764) 2108
Music and Books about Music

REMINGTON, REG & PHILIP
Suite 33, 26 Charing Cross Road
London WC2H 0HY
(01 836) 9771
and 14 Cecil Court
Charing Cross Road
London WC2
Voyages, Travels, Natural History, Maps
and Prints

ROBERTS, J.T.
43 Triangle West, Clifton
Bristol (0272) 28568
Local and West Country Topography,
Natural History, Literature, Prints

ROGOYSKI, ALEXANDER
22 Staveley Road, Chiswick
London, W4 3ES
(01 994) 5884
Continental Books (before 1800)

ROSENBERG & CO. LTD., C.G.
92 Great Russell Street
London, WC1B 3PU
(01 636) 0639
Fine and Applied Arts, Archaeology

ROSENTHAL LTD., A.
9-10 Broad Street
Oxford, OX1 3AP
Oxford (0865) 43093
Continental Literature, Early Printed
Books, Autograph Letters and
Manuscripts, Judaica

ROTA LTD., BERTRAM
30 & 31 Long Acre
London, WC2E 9LT
(01 836) 0723
Modern First Editions, Private Press
Books, Literary Manuscripts and
Autographs, English Literature, History

ROTHWELL AND DUNWORTH
15 Paul Street, Taunton, Somerset
Taunton (0823) 82476
Cricket, Natural History, Literature,
Classics
and at
Rolworth, Melton House, High Street
Dulverton, Somerset
Dulverton (0398) 23169
Specialising in Field Sports

SANDERS OF OXFORD LTD.
104 High Street
Oxford, OX1 4BW
Oxford (0865) 242590
Oxford Books, Prints and Maps, English
Literature, Life and Thought, Fine and
Applied Arts, Literary Manuscripts

SAWERS, ROBERT G.
PO Box 40a, London W1A 4QA
(01 409) 0863
Japan, China, General Oriental, Japanese
Prints and Paintings

SAWYER, CHAS J.
1 Grafton Street
Old Bond Street, London W1
(01 493) 3810
Fine Bindings, English Literature, Private
Press Books, Churchilliana, and Africana

SCOTT BOOKSELLER,
GRAHAM K.
68-69 St. John's Street
Bury St. Edmunds
Suffolk, IP33 1SJ
Bury St. Edmunds (0284) 3933
History, Biography, Military and Naval
History, Architecture, Penguin Books

SCHUSTER, THOMAS E.
9 Gillingham Street
London, SW1V 1HN
(01 828) 7963
Topography, Natural History, Colour
Plate Books, Atlases and Maps

SHAW'S BOOKSHOP LTD.
11 Police Street, off King Street
Manchester, M2 7LQ
(061) 834 7587
Antiquarian and Secondhand (all Subjects),
Maps, and Prints

SHOTTON, J.
89 Elvet Bridge
Durham City, DH1 3AG
(0385) 64597
General Antiquarian and Secondhand

SIDDLEY & HAMMOND LTD.
(Miss Kay Hammond)
19 Clarendon Street
Cambridge, CB1 1JU
Cambridge (0223) 350325
Theatre, Literature, Modern Firsts and
Private Presses, Illustrated Books

SMITH & SON (GLASGOW)
LTD., JOHN
57 St. Vincent Street
Glasgow, G2 5TB
(041) 221 7472
General Antiquarian, Scottish Literature,
Prints and Maps

SMITH, RAYMOND
30 South Street, Eastbourne
Sussex, BN21 4XB
Eastbourne (0323) 34128
English and Foreign Literature, The Arts,
Theology, Railways

SMITH, STANLEY
& FAWKES, KEITH, BOOKSHOP
1-3 Flask Walk, Hampstead Village
London NW3 1HJ
(01 435) 0614
Antiquarian, Art, History, Literature,
Illustrated

SMITH (BOOKSELLERS) LTD.,
WILLIAM
35-39 London Street
Reading, Berkshire
(0734) 595555

SOTHERAN LTD., HENRY
2, 3, 4 & 5 Sackville Street
Piccadilly, London, W1X 2DP
(01 734) 1150 & 0308
English Literature, Natural History,
Finely Bound Books and Sets, Old and
Rare Books, Antique Maps and Prints

SPAIGHT, R.H.S.
5 Kelvin Court
Marlborough Road, Richmond
Surrey, TW10 6JS
(01 940) 7820
(Postal business only)
Military Books (Out of Print)

SPELMAN, KEN
70 Micklegate, York, YO1 1LF
York (0904) 24414
*History of Art, English Literature,
Yorkshire Topography*

STEEDMAN, ROBERT D.
9 Grey Street
Newcastle upon Tyne, NE1 6EE
Newcastle upon Tyne (0632) 326561
*Fine and Rare Books, English Literature,
Natural History, Voyages and Travel*

STERLING BOOKS
(David Nisbet)
Green Lodge, 11 Cecil Road
Weston-Super-Mare
Avon, BS23 2NG
Weston-Super-Mare (0934) 25056
*Travel, Topography, Fine Bindings,
General Antiquarian Literature*

STEVENS & BROWN LTD., B.F.
(Adrian Burkett)
Ardon House, Godalming
Surrey, GU7 1HA
Godalming (048 68) 4391

STEVENS, ERIC & JOAN
74 Fortune Green Road
London, NW6 1DS
(01 435) 7545
Literature, Art, First Editions, Feminism

STEVENS, SON & STILES, HENRY
4 Upper Church Lane
Farnham, Surrey, GU9 7PW
Farnham (0252) 715416
*Americana, Canadiana, The West Indies
and Polar Regions*

STOREY, HAROLD T.
(Norman T. Storey)
3 Cecil Court
Charing Cross Road
London, WC2N 4EZ
(01 836) 3777
*Bindings, General Literature, Illustrated
Books, Travel*

SULLIVAN, JAMES C. &
THE HON. MRS. JENNIFER
11 Westbourne Grove
Lincoln, Lincolnshire
Lincoln (0522) 42310
(Business by appointment)
*Scholarly Books 16th-20th Century, Fine
Printing and Binding, Typography*

TARA BOOKS LTD.
(Peter & Elizabeth Watson)
South End House, 17 Church Lane
Lymington, Hampshire, SO4 9RA
Lymington (0590) 76848
*Social and Economic History, Costume
and Fashion, Feminism, Travel and
Philosophy*

THEATRE BOOKSHOP
(Ryman Atkinson)
26 New Road, Brighton
East Sussex, BN1 1UG
Brighton (0273) 681405
*19th and 20th Century English Literature,
Modern First Editions, Performing Arts,
Art, Illustrated Books*

THIN, JAMES
54 South Bridge, Edinburgh
Edinburgh (031) 536 6743

THOMAS BOOKSELLER
ALAN G.
c/o National Westminster Bank
300 King's Road
London, SW3 5UJ
(01 352) 5130
*Incunabula, Manuscripts, Literature,
Early Theology, Bibles*

THORNTON AND SON, J.
11 Broad Street
Oxford, OX1 3AR
Oxford (0865) 42939
Classics, Oriental, History, Philosophy,
Theology

THORP, THOMAS
9 George Street
St. Albans, Herts.
(0727) 65576
English Literature, Early English Law,
Natural History, Old and Rare Books,
Angling

TITLES (Gillian & Ralph Stone)
The Old Post Bookshop
Shipton-under-Wychwood
Oxfordshire, OX7 6BP
Shipton-under-Wychwood (0993)
831156
Environment, especially Agriculture, Local
Topography, the Arts

TRAVIS & EMERY
(Valerie Emery)
17 Cecil Court
London, WC2N 4EZ
(01 240) 2129
Music, Books on Music, Ballet, Opera
and Costume

TRAYLEN, CHARLES W.
Castle House, 49/50 Quarry Street
Guildford, Surrey, GU1 3UA
Guildford (0483) 72424
English Literature, Incunabula, Fine
Bindings, Travel and Illustrated Books

TREVERS, STRATFORD
The Long Room, 45 High Street
Broadway, Worcestershire, WR12
7DP
Broadway (0386) 853668
General Antiquarian, Prints, Maps

UPDIKE (RARE BOOKS), JOHN
7 St. Bernard's Row
Edinburgh, EH4 1HW
Edinburgh (031) 332 1650
Fine Books of 19th and 20th Centuries,
First Editions, Illustrated and Private
Press Books

VAUGHAN, ROBERT
20 Chapel Street
Stratford-upon-Avon
Warwickshire, CV37 6EP
Stratford-upon-Avon (0789) 5312
First and Fine Editions of English
Literature, Shakespeareana, Theatre and
Allied Arts

WALEY, ANTONY
14 High Street, Reigate
Surrey, RH2 9AY
Reigate (07372) 40020
Illustrated Books, Private Press Books,
Folio Society

WALFORD (BOOKSELLERS), G.W.
186 Upper Street, Islington
London, N1 1RH
(01 226) 5682
A prior telephone call is advisable
Natural History, Illustrated Topography
and Travels, Social History, Science

WALLIS, DEREK & GLENDA
6 Chapel Row, Queen Square
Bath, Avon, BA1 1HN
Bath (0225) 24677
Early Children's Books, Illustrated Books,
Folklore, Canadiana

WARRACK & PERKINS
Rectory Farm House
Church Enstone
Oxford, OX7 4NN
Enstone (060 872) 572
Illustrated Books (1880-1920), Prints and
Drawings

WATERFIELD LTD., ROBIN
36 Park End Street
Oxford, OX1 1HJ
Oxford (0865) 721809
17th and 18th Century English Books,
20th Century Literature, Autograph and
Association Material, Scholarly Books in
the Humanities

WAY, R.E. & G.B.
Brettons, Burrough Green
Newmarket, Suffolk
Stetchworth (063 876) 217
*Hunting, Horses, Racing, and Field
Sports*

WEATHERHEAD'S BOOKSHOP
LTD
58 Kingsbury, Aylesbury
Buckinghamshire, HP20 2JG
Aylesbury (0296) 23153 & 24985
Buckinghamshire, Large General Stock

WEINER, GRAHAM
78 Rosebery Road
London, N10 2LA
(01 883) 8424
Science, Technology, Medicine

WEINREB ARCHITECTURAL
BOOKS LTD., B.
93 Great Russell Street
London, WC1B 3QL
(01 636) 4895
Architecture and Civil Engineering

WESTLEGATE BOOKSHOP
(Charles Cubitt)
10 All Saints Green
Norwich, Norfolk
Norwich (0603) 22569
*Norfolk, Natural History, General
Antiquarian*

WESTWOOD, MARK
Little Mill, Glasbury
via Hereford, HR3 5LG
Powys
Glasbury (04974) 436
*Wales, Science and Technology, Medicine,
Aeronautica*

WHELDON & WESLEY LTD.
Lytton Lodge, Codicote
Hitchin, Hertfordshire, SG4 8TE
Stevenage (0438) 820370
Natural History

WHITEHART, F.E.
40 Priestfield Road, Forest Hill
London, SE23 2RS
(01 699) 3225
*Medicine, Science, Technology,
Bibliography*

WHITESON LTD., EDNA
343 Bowes Road, London N11
(01 361) 1105 and (01 449) 8860
*Modern First Editions, Signed and
Presentation Material, Topography and
Travel, Early Maps and Prints*

WILLIAMS, CHRISTOPHER
23 St. Leonard's Road
Bournemouth, Dorset, BH8 8QL
Bournemouth (0202) 519683
*The Arts, Bibliography, Topography,
Cookery and Wine*

WILSON, ALAN
37 Bluecoat Chambers
School Lane
Liverpool, L1 3BX
Liverpool (051 708) 0204 & (051 722)
7134
*Aviation, Topography of North West
England*

WILSON, (AUTOGRAPHS)
LTD., JOHN
50 Acre End Street, Eynsham,
Oxford
Oxford (0865) 880883
*Autograph Letters, Historical Documents,
Manuscripts*

WORDS ETCETERA
(Julian Nangle)
327 Fulham Road
London, SW10 9QL
(01 352) 3186
*Modern First Editions, Modern Literary
Autograph Material, Literary and Art
Periodicals*

ZWEMMER LTD., A.
24 Litchfield Street
London, WC2H 9NJ
(01 836) 4710
Fine and Applied Arts, Architecture

****

Glossary

(The great majority of these terms, which are here supplied for easy reference, are explained more fully in the book. A few others have been added.)

ADDENDA (singular Addendum) — Matter added, usually not enough to form a supplement. It will normally have been printed separately after the rest of the text has been set.

a.e.g. — Standard abbreviation for 'all edges gilt', i.e. all three book edges have been cut smooth and gilded. Very occasionally in England, and more commonly in France, gilt is applied 'on the rough'.

ALL PUBLISHED — Applied to a series or number of volumes not completed as was originally intended.

ANTIQUE — In the book world, a modern binding, more often than not in calf, dressed up in an earlier style.

ARMORIAL — A binding carrying the achievement of arms or crest of its owner, past or present, in gilt or blind (q.v.). Schools and other institutions often use such devices on gift or prize bindings.

AS ISSUED — Term employed to describe a publication in precisely its original condition, especially when it is a little off the beaten track; e.g. 'in wrappers, as issued'.

ASSOCIATION COPY — Book which has close links with a person or event, through an inscription, ownership signature, annotations, etc.

AUTOGRAPH — As a noun, and in common parlance, the signature of some notability; as an adjective, e.g. in 'autograph manuscript', material, preferably signed, in the hand of the person involved.

BASTARD TITLE — Another term for half-title.

BATTLEDORE — The original battledore was a short-handled bat or racket, roughly like a hand mirror in shape, used for knocking a shuttlecock about. The name was transferred to the simple school primers of much the same shape and carrying the alphabet, etc., that followed the hornbook (q.v.). There is little doubt that the young did, in fact, use them as bats for despatching paper balls and similar missiles. Later still, in the nineteenth century, publishers continued to use the name for the folding reading cards, now without a handle.

BIFOLIUM — A double leaf.

BLACK LETTER — Script or fount of type with the thick angular forms of early printing, often known as Gothic.

BLIND — Applied to the decorative impressions made on book covers, etc. without gold or colouring.

BOARDS — In a special sense, the paper-backed boards used for novels, etc., over the period c.1780-1840; in another, literal, sense, for the thin oak and beech, leather or vellum-covered, used for binding early books; in a third, general, sense, for any book in hard covers, whether clothed in paper, cloth, buckram, etc.

BOOK — Apart from its everyday meaning, one of the separate sections of a work contained in one volume and listed as such by the author on the title-page or in the list of contents. See Volume.

BOOK FORM — Used of a book whose contents have previously appeared in a periodical (e.g. as a serial) or in monthly parts.

BOOKPLATE — Decorative large label, often specially designed, stuck inside a book with the owner's name and, often, such distinguishing features as his coat of arms or other personal allusion.

BOOK TICKET — A smaller form of the bookplate, usually with just the owner's name.

BOUND — Strictly speaking, applied to a book held together as an entity by sewing the sections on to horizontal cords, the ends of which are attached to the boards: all this as distinct from a cased book, where binding and printed sections are made separately.

BREAKER — Either a book destined to be taken apart for the sake of its plates or the individual who does the despoiling. Hence, Breaking Copy.

BROADSHEET OR BROADSIDE — Large sheet printed on one side only.

BROWNING — Patchy discoloration on book pages caused by damp, the passage of time, etc. See also Foxing.

BUCKRAM — Strong book covering material of linen, cotton, etc., stiffened with size or glue.

CALF — Commonest bookbinding leather, polished and smooth, capable of taking almost any colour. If the inside of the skin is used outside and left unpolished it is 'reversed or 'rough' calf.

CALLED FOR — Commonly used expression when establishing the completeness or otherwise of a book; e.g. 'with the 52 plates as called for', 'without the half-title called for by X' (who presumably has written the standard bibliography).

CAOUTCHOUC BINDING — Binding in which a rubber solution is substituted for sewing to hold the leaves together in the binding; invented by Thomas Hancock, c.1838.

CASED — Said of book whose printed sections and binding are made up separately, usually in quantity, and brought together by machinery. See Bound, above, for the opposing method.

CATCHWORD — Word printed in the bottom right hand corner of a page, underneath the last line of text, coinciding with the first word at the top of the next page. Now largely discontinued, they were originally intended as a guide to the binder in assembling the book.

CHAIN LINES — The widely spaced lines, normally vertical, visible when paper is held up to the light, resulting from the wire mesh in the bottom of the papermaker's tray holding the pulp.

CHAPBOOK — Small, crudely illustrated popular booklet of fiction, romance, history, educational character, etc., carried by chapmen and pedlars.

CLOTH — Common book-covering material, usually of treated calico of various textures and thicknesses, used by binders from the mid-1820s.

COLLATE — To perform any one of several operations: (1) compare one book with another, using the same edition and impression; (2) check any copy of a book for the completeness of its text, plates, etc., not necessarily with reference to any other copy; (3) describe a book in precise bibliographical terms, giving every detail of its make-up; (4) put the sections of a book in order in the binding process.

COLOPHON — Note at the conclusion of a book, especially an early example, giving such particulars as name of printer, place of printing, date of completion, etc. It is often accompanied by a printer's particular device or trade mark.

CORRIGENDA (singular Corringendum) — Correction of mistake, usually not spotted until the book was printed and inserted on a special leaf or slip of paper.

CROPPED — Applied to book margins over-heavily trimmed by the binder's knife, often with disastrous results to marginal notes, catchwords, running titles, etc.

CRUSHED — Morocco leather that has been so pressed or ironed that the characteristic grain has almost disappeared before polishing. Other leathers can also be treated in this way.

CUM LICENTIA — 'By licence' or 'with permission' granted by a secular or ecclesiastical body.

CUT — As a noun, the old term for an engraving or simple illustration, especially a woodcut. As an adjective, applied to book edges, meaning trimmed, though it is little used compared with its opposite, uncut (q.v.).

DENTELLES — Lacy patterns on the outer edges of bindings. They may also be used on the inside, where they are usually called inside dentelles.

DEVICE — Trade mark used by printers and publishers on the title or at the colophon, a custom begun in the fifteenth century and still in vogue today. Early devices consisted of shields, crosses, elaborate initials, etc.

DIAPER — Pattern of tiny diamonds, lozenges or squares used on bookbindings or as the background to pictures in illuminated manuscripts.

DICED — Having a pattern akin to diapering, consisting of small cubes or squares.

DISBOUND — Applied to pamphlets, booklets, etc., taken out of bound collections. It should be distinguished from unbound (q.v.), which may mean that the publication in question was issued without covers.

DISTRIBUTED — Said of type when it is broken up and returned to the printer's case after the completion of an edition.

DIVINITY CALF — Leather of a disagreeable purplish hue (often accompanied by equally unpleasant bevelled boards and red edges), popular with nineteenth century binders for devotional and theological works.

DOCUMENT — Used somewhat loosely in the autograph letter and manuscript world, but properly to be reserved for official and legal papers prepared by a clerk or scribe but often signed by some notability.

DOUBLURE — Inside lining or paste-down of a book cover made of leather or material, e.g. watered silk, instead of the usual paper.

DROP. INITIAL — Initial capital letter, normally at the beginning of a chapter, ranging at the foot over three or four lines.

DROP TITLE (Dropped-head title) — Title, in the absence of a title-page, placed at the head of the first page of text in pamphlets, etc.

DUST JACKET — Protective cover on modern books to safeguard the binding. Though the earliest known example dates from the 1830s, only recently have they received much attention from artists and collectors.

The debate continues as to whether the latter should regard them as an essential part of the book or whether they may be discarded. See also Wrappers.

DUST WRAPPERS — Common term, though preferably to be avoided, for the decorated paper cover wrapped round a book to protect the cloth or other binding material. 'Dust jacket' or simply 'jacket' avoids any confusion with Wrappers (q.v.). The dust jacket, unlike the true wrapper, is not part of the essential book, though some collectors value it and pay for its presence.

EARLY PRINTED — Formerly applied almost exclusively to books printed before 1500, but now more liberally interpreted to mean up to 1600 or, because of the influence of the Short-Title Catalogue (see p.30) up to 1640.

EDITION — All copies of a book printed from one setting of type.

EDITION DE LUXE — An edition which, at least in the opinion of the publishers, is to be admired for its appearance and format.

ENDPAPERS — The double leaves used by the binder at the beginning and end of a book, the outer leaf (paste-down) being fixed to the insides of the cover, the other being 'free' and thus forming first and last leaves.

EPHEMERA — Wide general term covering printed trifles not originally destined to endure but whose survival now makes them collectable.

ERRATA (singular Erratum) — Errors of fact or printing discovered after a book has been printed and noted in the preliminaries, on a separate pasted in leaf or slip.

ETRUSCAN — Style of calf binding ornamented with motifs and patterns from Etruscan and other classical pottery.

EX-LIBRARY — Having formerly been in a lending or cirulating library which has left its mark with a large label, or the remains of it, on the cover or inside it.

EX-LIBRIS — Common term for a Bookplate (q.v.).

EXTENDED — Used of works enlarged by additional illustrations and sometimes needing to be rebound or enlarged to several volumes. See Grangerised.

EXTRA-ILLUSTRATED — Having additional portraits, etc., inserted, but not necessarily on a large scale, as in a grangerised work.

FACTOTUM — Word deriving from the Latin, meaning 'I do all the work'; hence, a general handyman employed on all sorts of duties; and, in books, a printer's ornament with a centre space in which any letter can be inserted, e.g. at the beginning of a chapter. A factotum title is one that can be used for a series of volumes, with a space left for certain details to be filled in later, often by hand.

FIRST PUBLISHED EDITION — Means that there has already been a printed edition, but one for private and restricted circulation, not for sale to the general public.

FLEURON — Small flower-like decoration used by printers and binders.

FLY-LEAF — Sometimes used of the free front endpaper but, properly speaking, a blank additional to, and following, this free endpaper.

FLY TITLE — A second half-title sometimes found in nineteenth and twentieth century books; an extra, usually very elaborate title, e.g. of a pictorial or engraved nature; or a divisional title for every distinct section of a book.

FOLIATION — The numbering of leaves only on the front or recto, which preceded pagination or numbering of pages.

FOLIO — Half a sheet of any standard size of paper; a book of this format; one leaf of a printed book or manuscript numbered only on the front.

'FOLLOW THE FLAG' — The title given to the controversy arising when a book is first published outside the author's own country. Should this rank as the true 'first' or the edition that subsequently appears in the home country?

FORE-EDGE — The edge of a book opposite the back and furthest from it.

FORE-EDGE PAINTING — Any painting on the fore-edge, but especially the concealed type obtained by clamping tight the fanned leaves, painting a scene on the narrow edges thus displayed, releasing the leaves to their normal position, then gilding. The picture will then remain invisible till the leaves are fanned out again.

FOREL(L) — An inferior parchment, thin and off-white or yellowish in colour.

FORMAT — The size and shape of a book; more precisely, the number of times the original sheet has been folded, resulting in a folio, quarto, octavo, etc.

FOXING — Brownish-yellow spots, varying in intensity, caused by damp and chemical action in poor paper.

FRANKED — Said of an envelope that carries the signature of, for instance, a peer or member of parliament, giving it free passage through the post. The system was at its height in the nineteenth century.

FREE ENDPAPER — The half of the double leaf, used by the binder at the beginning and end of the book, that is not pasted down to the inside of the cover but remains 'free'.

FRONTISPIECE — The illustration facing the title-page of a book.

GATHERING — A single group of leaves formed by folding a sheet to the required size for the intended book.

GAUFFERED (Gauffred, Goffered) — Book edges decorated by impressing heated tools, normally before gilding.

GLOSS — An explanation or commentary, varying in length from a few words to complete paragraphs, inserted in the margin or text, to clarify or amplify a difficult passage. In the case of early manuscripts it can be written several hundreds of years later and will therefore be in an entirely different hand.

GOTHIC — General term for (1) black letter type faces (see Black Letter); (2) a style of handwriting of angular form and thick vertical strokes typical of northern Europe from the twelfth century.

GRAIN — Pattern on leather, either natural or artificially produced with the aid of engraved metal plates.

GRANGERISED — Extra-illustrated on a fairly large scale with the addition of portraits, plans, facsimiles, etc., sometimes laid down on interleaves or inlaid, sometimes merely tipped-in at the edges.

GUARDED — Used to describe a leaf or illustration which is pasted by its inner edge to a specially provided stub.

GUTTA-PERCHA BINDING — See Caoutchouc.

HALF BOUND — Having the back and corners bound in one material (e.g. half calf or half morocco) and the sides in another.

HALF CALF (morocco, vellum, etc.) — Having the spine and outer corners covered with leather, vellum, etc., the rest of the sides being of cloth or paper-covered boards, often marbled.

HALF-TITLE — Leaf before the main title-page, usually giving only the title (sometimes shortened) without other details except, perhaps, the volume number.

HEAD — The top of the book.

HEADBAND — The decorative band at the top of the spine.

HEAD MARGIN — The margin above the first line of text.

HEAD-PIECE — A decoration or vignette above the beginning of a chapter, etc.

HINGE — The meeting place (front or back) between the binding and the body of the book, making a small valley which is one of the weakest parts of the job. The word is often reserved for the inside, keeping 'joint' for the outside, but there is no fixed rule.

HISTORIATIONS — In manuscripts, the initials and capitals which carry pictures of people, animals, etc. as part of the story. The term can also be applied to margins decorated in this way rather than with formal designs.

HOLOGRAPH — Term (noun or adjective) usually reserved for literary manuscripts and meaning one entirely in the hand of the author.

HORNBOOKS — Devices for teaching the young the alphabet, the Lord's Prayer, etc., the earliest examples, dating from the fifteenth and sixteenth centuries, being strips of thin oak covered with paper and protected by transparent cattle horn. There are many fakes about. Andrew Tuer's *History of the Horn Book* (1896) contains a number of imitation hornbooks. See Battledores.

ILLUMINATED — Decorated in gold, silver and colours in various combinations, with or without historiations (q.v.). The term is properly applied to manuscripts coloured by hand but has been borrowed for printing books produced in imitation of them.

IMPENSIS — Latin for 'at the cost/expense of'; found on the title-page or at the colophon of a number of early printed works, with the name of the person who had financed the publication, followed, usually, by the name of the printer.

IMPRESSION — The number of copies of an edition printed at one time; e.g. a first impression of 5,000 copies, followed by a second impression of 1,000 copies, both from the same type and, therefore both belonging to the same edition.

IMPRIMATUR — 'Let it be printed'; that is, a permission to print the work found in many early books, the publication of which had to be sactioned by Church or State. It still occurs in many works written under the aegis of the Roman Catholic Church.

IN TEXT — Applied to illustrations set within the printed text rather than used as separate plates.

INCIPIT — Latin for 'it begins'. Many early books and manuscripts had no title-page, the relevant information being given in the opening words of the text, beginning 'hic incipit' (here begins). This introduction, often printed in a distinguishing colour, is familiarly known as 'the incipit'.

INCUNABULUM (plural Incunabula) — A book printed before 1500.

INITIA — 'Beginnings'. An alternative name for the 'incipit' (q.v.).

INLAY — An insertion of coloured leather into the main skin of a binding. In the text, the margins of a plate can be enlarged or renewed by inlaying it into a larger leaf.

INSCRIBED — Applied to a book when it has been autographed by the author.

ISSUE — Part of an edition, corrections or some rearrangement having been made when some copies have already been published; so that a book may be described as the 'second issue of the first edition'.

ITALIAN HAND — The beautiful style of writing, sometimes known as Roman or humanistic, which developed during the Italian Renaissance, coming into England before 1483, and taught to all Henry VIII's children, thus setting a fashion among the educated classes.

ITALIC — Type face designed about the year 1500 by Francesco Griffo for the famous printer Aldus Manutius (1450-1515) at Venice, the first book printed in it being a Virgil of 1501.

JACKET — See Dustwrappers; Wrappers.

JAPANESE VELLUM (Japon) — Not a vellum at all, but a thickish cream-coloured, glossy-surfaced paper beloved by publishers of editions de luxe.

LABEL — Spine strip, usually of morocco, carrying the title and author's name (and volume number if necessary). If not of leather usually specified as 'paper label', etc. The leather type is often known as a lettering-piece.

LABEL TITLE — Name sometimes given to the first sort of title-page in early books, giving on an otherwise blank prefatory leaf the title and author without any other detail.

LAID DOWN — Mounted on a stronger (and sometimes on a different coloured) paper, especially for book illustrations. If there is a distinction to be made between 'laid down' and 'mounted' it is that the former usually means firmly stuck and the latter more lightly attached.

LAID PAPER — Paper showing parallel sets of chain lines and wire lines from the mould in which it was made; or bestowed on it by a modern machine in imitation.

LEAF — The double-sided unit in the make-up of a book, the front side being one page and the reverse another page. A leaf should never loosely be called a page.

LETTERING-PIECE — See Label.

LEVANT — High quality fairly coarse-grained morocco much favoured for elegant bookbinding.

LICENCE LEAF — A permission to print, often, but not invariably, on a separate leaf. See Imprimatur.

LIMITED EDITION — An edition limited to a stated number of copies, which may be large or small, the natural tendency being for greater value to be attached to the small. With certain less reputable publishers the stated low number should not be too much relied on.

LIMP — Term used to describe a binding, leather, vellum or cloth, not backed by boards.

LOOSE — Applied to books whose leaves are wholly or partly detached from the binding.

MANUSCRIPT — Something written by hand, usually something of a literary and fairly lengthy nature. More loosely, it can mean an author's typewritten draft.

MARBLED — Used to describe paper covers or endpapers decorated by floating colours transferred from the surface of a gum solution. They can also be applied to the edges of the book.

MINIATURE BOOKS — A special category whose smallness, as a curiosity, is often their only noteworthy feature. Though there are no fixed dimensions, something in the neighbourhood of 5cm by 4cm or less might be expected.

MINIATURES — Originally very small painted scenes, etc. in illuminated manuscripts, but a term now customarily embracing even the large whole-page pictures.

MISBOUND — Having some leaves or plates bound out of the correct order — a fault fairly common in earlier books but not, unless the errors are gross, generally reckoned much of a defect. Plates especially have a habit of wandering from their predestined places and should not lightly be pronounced missing.

MOROCCO — Bookbinding leather made from goatskin, rightly esteemed for its elegant appearance, durability and suitability for taking any colour. If the binder has been fairly lavish in his decorative use of gold, a book so bound would be described as morocco gilt.

MOTTLED — Used to describe a calf binding treated with acid or dyes to produce an irregular pattern. See Sprinkled.

MOUNTED — See Laid Down.

MULL — Coarse muslin glued to the back of the book during bookbinding.

N.D. (n.d.) — Abbreviation for 'no date', frequently appearing in catalogues when a date of printing is not specifically given. It may, however, be known, in which case the date will normally be given in square brackets.

NEW STYLE — The reformed method of dating adopted by England and the American Colonies in 1752; the Gregorian, as opposed to the Julian, calendar.

NIGER — A soft and flexible type of morocco with no very marked grain, originating from West Africa.

NIHIL OBSTAT — 'Nothing stands in the way'. The go-ahead for publication from a religious body. See Imprimatur.

OBLONG FOLIO — A folio volume whose horizontal measurement is greater than its height.

OBVERSE — See Recto.

OCTAVO — Format resulting from folding the original sheet three times to give eight leaves and sixteen pages.

OFFSET — Unpremeditated transfer of ink from an illustration or section of print to the opposite page.

OFF THE WALL — Used to describe a bid which some auctioneers pluck out of thin air in order to encourage higher bidding from the 'room'.

OLD STYLE — The Julian calendar, in use before the reform of 1752. See New Style.

ONLY — Interpolated in the description of an incomplete book; e.g. '25 plates (only)', meaning there should properly be more.

ON THE BOOK — Auctioneers' term for bids that have come in by post and telephone, etc., and are already entered on the sale leaves before the public auction begin.

ON THE ROUGH — On the edges of a book which have not been trimmed and cut smooth.

OPENED — See Unopened.

OPENING — The left and right hand pages of an opened book.

OUT OF SERIES — Term used to describe an unnumbered book in an edition which is otherwise limited and numbered. There are often a few extra copies printed as a contingency measure.

PAGE — Either side of a leaf.

PAGINATION — The consecutive numbering of pages. 'Separately paginated' would apply, e.g., to a two-volume work, each of which begins with the numeral 1 or other low number.

PALAEOGRAPHY — The study and deciphering of ancient manuscripts and inscriptions.

PAPIER MACHE — Tough material compounded of paper pulp and liquid adhesive, hardened and capable of shaping and moulding, as with a number of nineteenth century book covers.

PARCHMENT — Material for writing or book covers made from the degreased inner piece of the split skin of a sheep. In early times vellum and parchment seem to have been synonymous, but nowadays parchment appears to be reserved for an inferior skin.

PARTS — Term for the instalments — weekly, fortnightly or monthly — in which many popular works, especially in the nineteenth century, were first published.

PASTE-DOWN — That part of the endpaper, at either end of the book, which is stuck down to the inside of the cover. See Free Endpaper.

PICTORIAL — Description applied to book covers, and sometimes to endpapers, which incorporate figures, animals, scenes, etc., in their designs. On the covers they will normally be gilt or blind (q.v.).

PIRATED — Published without the author's and original publisher's authority (and consequently without payment).

PLATE — A whole page illustration printed separately from the text and usually on glossier paper.

PLATE MARK — The rectangular indentation made on the leaf by the edge of the metal plate impressed on it when engravings are used.

POINT — Any eccentricity or particular feature of a book, usually of a minor nature, which marks off one edition, impression or issue from another, thus helping to establish priority.

PRELIMS — Abbreviation for preliminaries, the pages of a book preceding the main text.

PRESS BOOKS — Umbrella term covering books issued by private presses and those which, though commercially motivated, specialise in printing of a high standard.

PRIVATE PRESS — A press whose owner prints what he chooses (whether or not he sells to the public), not what a publisher directs him to.

PRIVATELY PRINTED — Term usually implying that the book, etc., was not brought out at the expense of a publisher but was financed privately; and was circulated only among a limited circle, not offered for sale to the general public.

PRIVILEGE LEAF — Leaf recording that the publisher or printer has been licensed to print a book or a particular category of books, e.g. prayer books, law books, music.

PROTECTED — Word sometimes used of plates faced with tissue, either loose or tipped-in, to prevent foxing of the illustration or off-setting on to the opposite page.

PROVENANCE — The previous history and pedigree of a book, indicating its successive owners and movements.

QUARTER CALF (Morocco, vellum, etc.) — A book whose spine is covered with leather, vellum, parchment, etc., but not the outer corners. See Half Calf.

QUARTO — Format produced by folding a sheet twice at right angles, producing sections of four leaves and eight pages.

RAISED BANDS — The horizontal cords onto which the gathered sections of a bound book are sewn.

REBACKED — Having the spine recovered, preferably in a style and material approximating to the old.

RECTO — The front (or obverse) of a leaf, on the right hand side of an opened book and bearing an odd page number.

REGISTER — The list of signatures (q.v.) which appears at the end of many early printed books as a guide to the binder in putting the gatherings together.

REVERSE — See verso.

RING — Any group of two or more people in the auction room who agree not to bid against each other, with the intention of holding a private auction afterwards and dividing the difference in the price eventually paid between the participating members.

ROAN — A cheap kind of soft, poor-wearing sheepskin used in binding as an indifferent substitute for morocco.

ROLLS — Binders' tools with an engraved design round the edge of a wheel producing a repeated pattern when rolled along leather.

ROMAN — Adjective describing our familiar letter forms, first used in Roman manuscripts, characterised by their rounded upright shapes as distinct from the heavier Gothic and sloping italic.

RUBBED — Used to describe a binding not necessarily weak but showing signs of external wear.

RUBRICATED — Having initial capitals for paragraphs, etc., painted in red by the rubricator.

RULED IN RED (Red-ruled) — having borders (often double) and underlinings on the title-page ruled in red, a common feature of some kinds of book in the seventeenth century. The ruling, usually by hand, may be continued throughout the book.

RUNNING HEAD (Running title) — Line of type above the text consisting of the repeated title of the book or chapter.

RUSSIA — Reddish-brown hide imported from Muscovy c.1700 and often impregnated with fragrant oil. As a binding it is often diced (q.v.).

SCRIM — See Mull.

SCRIPTORIUM — The part of a monastery where manuscripts were written and copied, presided over by the monk known as the armarius or armarian. In ancient Rome the armarium was a bookcase, the term later being applied to the monastic library.

SECRETARY HAND — The cursive hand in general use in England before the Italian style gradually took over from c.1550.

SHEET — The printer's unit; the large piece of paper which, when folded, gives a gathering of folio, quarto, octavo size, etc.

SIGNATURES — The letters (in alphabetical sequence) and numbers in the bottom margins of books, at the beginning of each gathering and sometimes more frequently, to guide the printer in putting them together in the right order.

SIGNED BINDING — Bookbindings carrying the binder's name stamped, often so unostentatiously as to need a search, along one of the inside edges of the front or back cover, occasionally at the foot of the spine or along the hard fore-edge of the board.

SILKED — Said of the fragile leaf of a book or a disintegrating document which has been faced on both sides with a special very thin transparent fabric.

SINGLE SHEET — Occasional name for a Broadside (q.v.).

SLIP CASE — Open-sided box to show the spine of the book, often designed to match the binding.

SOLANDER CASE — Protective case for a book, maps or prints, which will normally open up, with at least one side lying flat.

SPINE — The back or backstrip of a book, visible when it stands in company on the bookshelf.

SPINE LABELS — Strips of leather or paper stuck to the backs of books, carrying the title and name of author.

SPRINKLED — Speckled by acid; used to describe a way of patterning calf binding with a regular speckled surface. See Mottled.

STATE — Synonymous with 'condition' when applied to degrees of wear, and used with 'fine', 'sound', 'clean' etc.; or applied to titles, illustrations, etc., which may have been issued in more than one form, when such adjectives as 'first', 'second', 'original' etc., would be relevant.

STATIONERS — The early name for booksellers, printers and binders. The Stationers' Company, to regulate the various branches of the trade, was established in 1557.

TAIL — The bottom edge or lower part of a book or page, hence 'tailband', 'tail-piece', etc. See Head.

TALL — Used to describe the copy of a book whose top and bottom margins are more generous than those of the bulk of the copies from the same printing.

t.e.g. — Common abbreviation for 'top edges gilt'.

THREE-DECKER — A book published in three volumes, a term applied almost exclusively to nineteenth century fiction.

THREE-QUARTER CALF (morocco, vellum, etc.) — Akin to half calf (q.v.), but with the back and outside corners having wider leather.

TIPPED-IN — Lightly glued or pasted in at the inside edge.

TISSUED — Having the plates protected by tissue paper.

T.L.S. — Abbreviation for Typed Letter Signed. The somewhat pretentious Authorial Typed Letter Signed means that the author has not only signed but has also laboured at the typewriter himself, or at least has corrected the typescript.

TREE CALF — Polished calf with a pattern resembling some combination of trunk, boughs, grain, etc., produced by chemical reaction before polishing.

TURKEY — Goatskin for binding, originally from Turkey.

UNBOUND — Never having had covers. The term is sometimes used, improperly, as synonymous with Disbound (q.v.).

UNCUT — Said of a book whose edges have not been trimmed off by the binder's knife or guillotine. The term should never be confused with Unopened (q.v.).

UNIFORM — Applied to books (as in sets) set in the same type, bound in the same style and perhaps jacketed. Many popular writers eventually have their works produced in a uniform edition.

UNOPENED — Said of a book whose folded pages need opening up with a paper knife before it can be read.

UNTOUCHED — Applied to an early manuscript whose capitals have not been filled by the scribe, even though their place has been indicated.

VARIANT — Term used, especially when there is some doubt of priority of issue, of a copy of a book which displays some dissimilarity in title, illustration or text from the rest of the edition.

VELLUM — Skin of a calf (and, more recently, of a number of other animals) degreased and specially prepared for the purposes of writing or printing.

VERSO — The reverse side, or back, of a leaf, as opposed to the recto or front. The verso will always lie on the left hand of an opened book and will carry an even number in the pagination.

VIGNETTE — Small picture or design used on a title-page, or at the head or tail of a chapter or section of a book.

VOLUME — Often used as synonymous with Book (but see that entry); any bound book with its own title-page; one of a set, e.g. Volume I, 'four volumes in two', etc.

w.a.f. — The most common warning sign to collectors. The abbreviation for 'with all faults', signifying that the buyer has no redress if imperfections, even of a major nature, are discovered after purchase.

WATERED SILK — Material sometimes used for doublures (q.v.), showing a watery or wavy pattern.

WATERMARK — Papermaker's design or trade mark incorporated in the wire mesh of the mould in which the pulp settles, and visible when the paper is held up to the light. A smaller mark, often consisting of the maker's initials and occurring on the opposite half of the sheet, is known as the countermark.

WIRE LINES — The close-set lines visible in laid paper, as distinct from the chain lines (q.v.) which run at right angles to them and are much more widely spaced. Characteristic of hand-made paper, they can also be imitated by machines.

WOVE PAPER — Paper, first used for the printing of books c.1757, showing an even fine mesh pattern uncrossed by chain and wire lines.

WRAPPERS — Paper covers of a book, plain, printed or decorated, as with marbling. They must be completely distinguished from dust wrappers or dust jackets (q.v.)., which are extraneous and not a true part of the book.

YELLOW-BACK — General term for the cheap editions, more often than not in a yellowish binding, evolved in the nineteenth century, for sale on station bookstalls, etc.

❉❉❉❉❉❉❉❉❉❉❉❉❉❉❉

A Questionary
or Quodlibet

A test, for the amusement of initiates, the chastening of *arrivistes* and the condescension of experts. The possible score is 200, on the system provided with the solutions (which no self-respecting bibliophile could in good conscience consult before attempting the questions). Covert visits to the reference shelf are defensible.

1 If, on your retirement, a grateful managing director offered you a complete set of the first editions of either 'Bozzie', 'Boz' or 'Bosie', which would you choose on financial grounds?

2 Which writer do you associate with each of the following residences?
   1 The Villa Rose
   2 The Villa Rubein
   3 The House with the Green Shutters
   4 The House of Pomegranates
   5 The Small House at Allington
   6 The Mill on the Floss
   7 The Castle of Otranto
   8 The House of Fame
   9 Castle Rackrent
   10 The House of the Wolfings

3 Writers have often, since the late nineteenth century, used a quotation from an earlier work as a book title, e.g. Ethel M. Dell in 1912 wrote the novel *The Way of an Eagle* from the verse in the *Book of Proverbs* which lists 'the way of an eagle in the air' as one of the mysteries of creation. Track down each of the following titles to the original that inspired it:
   1 Thomas Hardy, *Far from the Madding Crowd*
   2 A.S.M. Hutchinson, *If Winter Comes*
   3 Baroness Orczy, *I Will Repay*
   4 Helen Mather, *Comin' thro' the Rye*
   5 Robert Browning, *Childe Roland to the Dark Tower came*
   6 Aldous Huxley, *Eyeless in Gaza*
   7 A.R. Waugh, *Myself when Young*
   8 Bishop Trevor Huddleston, *Naught for Your Comfort*
   9 Rhoda Broughton, *Not Wisely but Too Well*
   10 Henryk Sienkiewicz, *Quo Vadis?* (Whither Goest Thou?)

4 Working from the beginning to the end of a book, put the following in

258

their normal correct order: index, front inside dentelles, half-title, first drophead title, colophon, frontispiece, second divisional title, paper labels, back free endpaper, title.

5 A catalogue offers you a Shakespeare First Folio, described as being superior to the other four Folios since it was the only one overseen by the playwright himself. It has some defects, however. One leaf (pp.158/159) is torn, the frontispiece portrait by Lely is missing, and the colophon, at the end of the Comedies, is defaced. Why should you query the accuracy of the cataloguing before investing your life's savings?

6 Subtract DV from MDCCCCLXXXII and say why the resulting date is important in the history of English literature.

7 Of the following famous English writers:
    1 One was a dwarf
    2 One was pitted by smallpox and had one eye lower than the other
    3 One had a twice-broken nose
    4 One had a face like a horse
    5 One was excessively short-sighted
    6 One employed a servant to comb out his dirty hair
    7 One had eyes of different colours
    8 One invariably lived and worked in squalor
    9 One was so ugly that he had an 'ingrained conviction' that no woman would accept him
  10 One, according to a self-description, was like a frisky Yorkshire cow, with "the majesty of an overloaded hay-wagon"
Can you identify them?

8 You are a Thomas Hardy collector and are much in need of a first edition of one of his rarest books, *Desperate Remedies*. You receive an offer of a copy from a bookseller claiming to be a Hardy specialist, his report reading: "Hardy, Thomas. Desperate Remedies. 2 vols. 4to original cloth, Bradbury Evans, 1871. Author's christian name on title spelt without the 'h'. His first published work." Why should you find another specialist?

9 The following list of writers can be divided into five pairs who are acquainted with each other. Can you sort them out?

The Ettrick Shepherd	The Great Cham
Dapper Jemmy	The Wizard of the North
The Bard of Twickenham	Guilelmus Russaeus
Desiderius Roterodamus	The English Atticus
The Lady of Christ's	Huig van Groot

10   Which famous book, compiled over a period of twenty-five years in America but produced in England, was sold at Sotheby's for £600 in 1922 and, in the same rooms forty-seven years later, for £90,000 — at that time the highest price ever paid for a printed book? What was the original price, £25, £174, £95 or £300? Which king failed to pay for his copy? What prominent naturalised English financier with a foreign title returned his copy, saying he would not give more than £5 for it?

11   "Kemys, Lawrence. A Relation of the Second Voyage to Guiana...32mo contemporary English binding of brown morocco, Thomas Dawson 1596. Full-page arms on recto of title. S.T.C. (1920 edit.) 26143." Can you spot five errors in this catalogue description?

12   As a bookman or woman, which five are most likely to be of interest to you from ICE, RSA, ILP, ABMR, RCP, BPC, ABA, OSB, ABC, BMC, and what exactly do they stand for?

13   Can you explain the difference between 'juveniles' and 'juvenilia'; 'unbound' and 'disbound'; a 'bound copy' and a 'binding copy'; an 'armorial' and an 'armarius'; 'conjugate leaves' and 'singletons'?

14   Give the more familiar names, to English readers, of:
    1 J. Korzeniowski
    2 Ellis Bell
    3 Dikran Kouyoumdjian
    4 John Sinjohn
    5 Bjarme Brynjolf
    6 Walter Ramal
    7 Silas Tomkyn Comberback
    8 Corno di Bassetto
    9 Mary Ann Evans
    10 Mrs. Max Mallowan

15   Work the following sum: John Buchan's steps + Lawrence's pillars of wisdom + Jerome's men in a boat + Shakespeare's gentlemen of Verona + Hardy's people on a tower + Meredith's conquerors + Dana's years before the mast + Thackeray's Georges + Tusser's points of good husbandry. Subtract the total from Verne's leagues under the sea.

16   Who is the odd man out from The Swan of Lichfield, A.L.O.E., Ouida, George Sand, Fiona McLeod and Acton Bell?

17   You find in a shop a dusty official document apparently emanating from Tudor times. It is signed 'Elizabeth I' at the bottom right hand corner and in the opening lines the Queen is described as Queen of Great Britain, France and Ireland, Defender of the Faith. The document is

concerned with the repair of ships after the Spanish Armada and is dated in the 29th year of her reign. On what grounds would you dismiss it as not authentic?

18 The names of Henry E. Huntingdon (1850-1927), Henry Clay Folger (1857-1930), John Pierpont Morgan (1837-1913), Sir Thomas Bodley (1545-1613) and John Rylands (1801-1888) are all associated with the foundation of great libraries of surpassing interest to scholars and book-collectors. Where would you travel to see each of them? In each case, give a significant fact about the origin or nature of the collection.

19 Winchester, Lambeth, Bedford, Sherborne, Lindisfarne. What is the common factor? Only in one case would a journey to the place be justified to see the original. Which? Can you give three other present locations?

20 As a collector of books and/or autograph letters and documents, which of these common abbreviations is of significance to you: t.e.g.; w.a.f.; n.p.; d.s.; c.; cont.; hf.; pp.; cl.; facs.?

Solutions overleaf.

❊❊❊❊❊❊❊❊❊❊❊❊❊❊❊❊

Solutions

1 You should unquestionably opt for 'Boz' (Charles Dickens), rather than 'Bozzie' (James Boswell) or 'Bosie' (Lord Alfred Douglas, Oscar Wilde's friend), because of the number of his works, many of them of considerable value in first edition form. Although Boswell's *Life of Johnson* is one of the most celebrated books in the language, it could well cost less than *Pickwick* in the original 20/19 parts in fine condition. (It is, incidentally, little known that, because of its derivation from the nickname of one of the author's younger brothers, 'Boz' should be pronounced to rhyme with 'nose'.)
(10 marks — 2 for each of the nicknames you knew, 2 for the right choice, and 2 for having an adequate reason.)

2 All are book titles, the various properties having been put on the market by:

1 A.E.W. Mason (The Villa Rose)
2 John Galsworthy (The Villa Rubein)
3 George Douglas, pseud. G. Douglas Brown (The House with the Green Shutters)
4 Oscar Wilde (The House of Pomegranates)
5 Anthony Trollope (The Small House at Allington)
6 George Eliot (The Mill on the Floss)
7 Horace Walpole (The Castle of Otranto)
8 Geoffrey Chaucer (The House of Fame)
9 Maria Edgeworth (Castle Rackrent)
10 William Morris (The House of the Wolfings).

(10 marks — 1 for each correct attribution.)

3
1 *Far from the Madding Crowd* — Gray's 'Elegy in a Country Churchyard'
2 *If Winter Comes* — Shelley's 'Ode to the West Wind'
3 *I Will Repay* — The Bible, *Epistle of Paul to the Romans*
4 *Comin' thro' the Rye* — Robert Burns, who took it from an old song, 'The Bob-tailed Lass'
5 *Childe Roland to the Dark Tower came* — Shakespeare's *King Lear*
6 *Eyeless in Gaza* — John Milton's 'Samson Agonistes'
7 *Myself when Young* — Edward Fitzgerald's 'Omar Khayyam'
8 *Naught for Your Comfort* — G.K. Chesterton's 'Ballad of the White Horse'
9 *Not Wisely but Too Well* — Shakespeare's *Othello*

10 *Quo Vadis?* — *St. John,* V (Vulgate)
(10 marks — 1 for each.)

4 In any normal book: (1) paper labels (2) front inside dentelles (3) half-title (4) frontispiece (5) title (6) first drophead title (7) second divisional title (8) colophon (9) index (10) back free endpaper.
(10 marks — 1 for each answer in the correct slot.)

5 A Comedy of Errors, in fact. (1) There were not another four Folios — only three; (2) the playright died in 1616 and the First Folio was not published till 1623, so he could not have overseen it; (3) there could not be a leaf, pp.158/159, since these would be the left and right hand pages of an opening — two leaves being involved; (4) the portrait was by Martin Droueshout, not Lely; (5) the colophon comes after the Tragedies, not the Comedies.
(10 marks — 2 for each error spotted. Subtract one for any error you imagined but which did not exist.)

6 1982 – 505 = 1477 — the date of the publication of William Caxton's *The Dictes or Sayengis of the Philosophres,* the first book printed in England.
(10 marks — 2 for a correct sum, 2 for mentioning Caxton, 2 for knowing it was the date of his first book in England and 4 — well deserved — for the title.)

7   1 Alexander Pope was about four feet six inches and hump-backed
        2 Ben Jonson was "punched full of eylet-holes like the cover of a warming pan"
        3 Thackeray, who broke his nose, first, in a school fight and, second, in a fall from a donkey
        4 George Eliot — according to Frederick Locker-Lampson
        5 Charlotte Brontë who, when a book was given her, "dropped her head over it until her nose nearly touched it"
        6 Samuel Pepys, whose head was foul with stale powder and, probably, things more mobile
        7 Charles Lamb, with one eye hazel, the other speckled with grey, "mingled as we see red spots in the bloodstone"
        8 William Blake, of whom his wife said "Mr. Blake's skin don't dirt"
        9 Edward Lear, who backed up his plainness by a style of dress that could "only be called careless by courtesy"
        10 Mary Russell Mitford.
(10 marks — 1 for each identification.)

8 Following Doctor Johnson's example, you should fell him with the nearest folio. *Desperate Remedies* was in three volumes, not two; it was an

octavo, not a quarto; the publisher was Tinsley, not Bradbury Evans; the book was published anonymously, so Hardy's name did not appear on the title; and it was not his first published work.

(10 marks — 2 for each error spotted. Subtract 1 for any error you invented.)

9   The pairs who knew each other were:

> The Ettrick Shepherd and The Wizard of the North (James Hogg and Sir Walter Scott)
>
> Dapper Jemmy and The Great Cham (James Boswell and Doctor Johnson)
>
> The Bard of Twickenham and The English Atticus (Alexander Pope and Joseph Addison)
>
> Desiderius Roterodamus and Guilelmus Russaeus (Erasmus and Sir Thomas More)
>
> The Lady of Christ's and Huig van Groot (Milton and Hugo Grotius)

(10 marks — ½ for each pseudonym or name you identified, 1 for each pair correctly coupled.)

10   John James Audubon's *The Birds of America* (1827-38); original price for the eighty-seven parts in England was £174; George IV failed to pay up; Lord Rothschild returned his set.

(10 marks — 2 for the author, 2 for the title, 2 for each of the other three questions.)

11   (1) A format of 32mo — approx. 4¾ ins. by 3ins. — is hardly likely for an important travel book; (2) contemporary brown morocco would be a near miracle since morocco did not come into use in England till the next century; (3) the arms must be on the verso (back) of the title. If they were on the recto they would obliterate the title; (4) S.T.C. (Short-Title Catalogue) was not published till 1926; (5) since the Catalogue starts with the number 1 and runs alphabetically, a 'K' book could not possibly have such a high number, which is, in fact, the last number of the 'Z' entries in the 1946 edition.

(10 marks — 2 for each error spotted. Deduct 1 for any mistake you invented.)

12   Unless you can establish devious literary links with, e.g. The Royal College of Physicians and The Order of St. Benedict, your choices should be ABMR (Antiquarian Book Monthly Review), BPC (Book Prices Current), ABA (Antiquarian Booksellers' Association), ABC (American Book-Prices Current) and BMC (British Museum Catalogue).

(10 marks — 2 for each.)

13   'Juveniles' is an accepted jargon word for children's books, especially

early examples, 'juvenilia' are the very early writings of an author; 'unbound' is properly applied to a work which never had covers, 'disbound' to something which has been deliberately taken out of a composite volume containing a number of pamphlets, etc.; strictly speaking, a 'bound' book (as opposed to a 'cased' book) is one where binding and printed text are an entity, and a 'binding copy' is one whose covers are in such a disreputable state that only rebinding will make it acceptable; an 'armorial' is a book whose covers carry a crest or coat of arms, an 'armarius' or 'armarian' was the monk in charge of the monastery library and, often, the scriptorium; 'conjugate leaves' are pairs that, traced through a book's make-up, form a single piece of paper, the rest are 'singletons'.

(10 marks — 1 for each correct definition.)

14   1 Joseph Conrad
     2 Emily Brontë
     3 Michael Arlen
     4 John Galsworthy
     5 Henrik Ibsen
     6 Walter de la Mare
     7 Samuel Taylor Coleridge (the pseudonym is one he adopted when he enlisted in the 15th Dragoons)
     8 G. Bernard Shaw (when writing his music criticisms in *The Star*)
     9 George Eliot
     10 Agatha Christie

(10 marks — 1 for each.)

15   The sum is $39 + 7 + 3 + 2 + 2 + 1 + 2 + 4 + 500 = 560$. $20,000 - 560 = 19,440$.

(10 marks for the whole sum. If your addition and subtraction failed, 1 mark for each correct number in a title.)

16   The odd 'man' out is, literally, Fiona McLeod, otherwise William Sharp (1856-1906), biographer, poet and novelist. The others are Anna Seward (The Swan of Lichfield), Charlotte M. Tucker (A.L.O.E. = A Lady of England), Louise de la Ramée (Ouida), Armandine Lucile Aurore Dupin, Baroness Dudevant (George Sand), and Anne Brontë (Acton Bell).

(10 marks — 4 for the correct answer and 1 for each of the six pseudonyms you recognised.)

17   Five reasons for blowing the dust all over the proprietor: (1) The 'number' of a monarch is never given and, in any case, a ruler is never labelled 'first', until there has been a second; (2) on an official document

the Queen would have signed at the head, usually top left, not at the bottom; (3) Elizabeth was never Queen of Great Britain, but of England, though the other titles are correct; (4) the 29th year of her reign (which ran from 17 November 1586 – 16th November 1587) was before the Spanish Armada.

(10 marks — 2 for each error, and a bonus of 2 if you knew that the Armada was fought in 1588.)

18   The Huntingdon Library is at San Marino, Pasadena, California. Henry Huntingdon formed his collection in less than twenty years by buying a number of important libraries *en bloc*. The special building containing it now holds over five million autograph letters, historical documents and manuscripts; over five thousand incunabula; a Gutenberg Bible; every Shakespeare quarto except one in the first edition; twenty-five Caxtons; twenty thousand English first editions; and a vast collection of rare Americana.

The Folger collection, bequeathed to the nation, is housed in a special building in Washington, D.C. Folger spent forty years amassing a library of twenty thousand volumes of Shakespeariana and Elizabethan literature, including no less than fifty First Folios.

The John Pierpont Morgan library is in New York in a building designed on the model of an Italian Renaissance palace. The chief treasures are not only princely volumes but a superb collection of illuminated manuscripts. Conspicuous are a Gutenberg Bible on vellum, a Mainz Psalter of 1459, a ninth century Gospels in a jewelled binding, the tenth century 'Golden Gospels' on purple vellum which had belonged to Henry VIII, the only complete copy of Caxton's printing of Malory's *Morte D'Arthur,* and the autograph MSS. of *A Christmas Carol* and 'Endymion'. As well there are 2,275 incunabula, including sixty Caxtons.

Sir Thomas Bodley, on his retirement from public life and diplomatic employments, determined to "set up his staff at the library door in Oxford." The result was the great Bodleian Library, whose creation from the old University Library was financed by Bodley, 1598-1602, when it was opened with a stock of some two thousand volumes, solicited from the wealthy and learned and purchased abroad by Bodley's agents. In 1610 he made an arrangement with the Stationers' Company to receive a copy of every book printed by its members. This was the forerunner of the present requirement for so-called 'statutory copies' to be supplied free of charge, on demand, to a number of university and national libraries. The Bodleian now contains more than 1,500,000 books and manuscripts.

The Rylands Library was founded in Manchester by Mrs. John Rylands in memory of her husband (1801-88), the Lancashire merchant who spent large sums in printing religious works for free distribution in England and on the Continent. The magnificent nucleus of the library (opened in 1900) was the great Spencer collection at Althorp, purchased by Mrs. Rylands for £250,000. George John, 2nd Earl Spencer (1758-1834) had the finest private collection in Europe, with an unrivalled assembly of incunabula, including fifty-six Caxtons, fourteen block books (i.e. printed from wooden blocks with the text and illustrations cut by hand and now of excessive rarity) and all four of the great Mainz Bibles and Psalters by Gutenberg and Fust and Schoeffer.

(10 marks — 1 for each of the locations and an additional mark in each case for any essential fact about the library or its founder, whether or not given above.)

19 All are famous medieval manuscripts, named from their place of origin, except the Bedford, which is a fifteenth century Parisian Missal commissioned by John, Duke of Bedford (1389-1435), when Regent of France. The Lambeth Bible was, however, probably written at Canterbury.

The Winchester Bible is still in the Cathedral Library; the Lambeth Bible was destroyed at Metz in World War II. Two leaves survive at Avesnes; the Bedford Missal or Book of Hours is in the British Museum, where it has been since 1852; the Sherborne Missal is in Alnwick Castle, Northumberland; The Lindisfarne Gospels are in the British Museum.

(10 marks — 2 for the common factor, 2 for knowing that the Winchester Bible is still at Winchester, 2 each for three other locations.)

20 All are of significance, the abbreviations standing for: t.e.g., top edges gilt; w.a.f., with all faults; n.p., no place (or occasionally printer/publisher); d.s., document signed; c., circa or about, referring to a date; cont., contemporary; hf., half, as in half calf, half morocco, etc.; pp., pages; cl., cloth; facs., facsimile.

(10 marks — 1 for each.)

RATING

    200 Incredible (and highly irritating)
180-199 Meriting profound obeisances
150-179 Highly creditable
100-149 Like most of us
  75-99 Faint but pursuing
Less than 75 Don't be discouraged; you're in very good company

In case the title of the test (A Questionary or Quodlibet) perplexed you, it can loosely be translated as 'A quiz, or what you will'.

****

Index

(The reader is also referred to the Glossary for a number of terms that are not included below.)

Bernard (or Barnard), Mrs. Elizabeth, 117-118

Bewick, Thomas, engraver, 64, 77, 125-126, 176

Bibles, 113, 117, 119, 134-143, 146; Authorised Version, 137, 141, 143; Baskerville, 141; Baskett's, 140-141; Becke's, 138; Bishops', 139; Breeches, 134, 136-137; Bug, 138; Christian Soldier's Penny, 140; Coverdale's, 137-138; Doves Press, 86, 90, 93, 141; Geneva, 136-137; Goose, 139; Great, 139; Gutenberg, 137; Lambeth, 267; Luther's, 134; Matthew, 138; Mazarin, 137; Nonesuch, 92, 141; Revised Version, 141; Souldier's Pocket, 140; Treacle, 138; Vinegar, 141; Whig, 139; Wicked, 139-140; Wife-beater, 138; Winchester, 267; Wycliffe's, 136

Biblioclast, 160

Bibliographies, 27

Bibliomaniac, 13, 29-30

Bickham, George, *The Universal Penman* (1743), 71

Bidding at auctions, 210

Bifolium, 196

Binders, Francis Bedford, 61, 158 Thomas James Cobden-Sanderson, 61-62; Douglas Cockerell, 61; Edwards of Halifax family, 53-54; Charles Hering, 61; John Henry Mason, 86; Samuel Mearne, 53; William Nott, 53; Roger Payne, 53; Claude de Picques, 52; R.B., 59-60; Robert Riviere, 61; Francis Sangorski and George Sutcliffe, 61; Joseph Zaehnsdorf, 61

Bindings, armorial, 59; boards, 50, 164-165; calf (half, quarter, diced, tree, etc.), 54-56; caoutchouc, 50, 243; cathedral, 142; cloth, 56-58; decorated, 58-59; Etruscan, 53; forel, 52; gutta-percha, 50; morocco, (half, quarter, etc.), 54-57; papier-mâché, 50; parchment, 53; roan, 254; russia, 53; vellum, 53; Victorian, 59; wrappers, 56

Bishop, William W., bibliographer, *Checklist of American Copies of Short-Title Catalogue Books,* 28

Black-letter, 168, 242

Black-letter ballad, 168

Blades, William, bibliographer, 24, 100

Blake, William, 177

Blind decoration, 59, 242

Blount, Charles, 36

Blunden, Edmund, 117, 121

Blunt, Wilfrid, 31

Boards, 242 (*see* also Bindings)

Bodleian Library, 89, 116, 266

Bodley, Sir Thomas, 266

Bohn, Henry G., bookseller and publisher, (*see* Lowndes, William Thomas)

Bonaparte, Prince Lucien, 143

Book, definitions of, 15

'Book' (as opposed to 'volume'), 149-151

Book Auction Records, 27-28

Bookbinding, 47-63

Book cases and shelves, 161

Book-collectors, 13, 27, 30

Book of Common Prayer, 116, 141

Book dressings, 161, 164

Book Fairs, 214-215

Bookmen, types of, 220

Bookplates (Ex Libris), 174-178

Book sizes, 20, 22

Books of Homilies, 116, 118

'Bound' books, 50, 242

'Boz' (*see* Dickens, Charles)

Bradbury, Henry, 82; *Nature-Printing: its Origin and Objects* (1856), 82; *The Ferns of Great Britain and Ireland* (1855), 82; *Nature-printed British Sea-Weeds* (1859), 82

Bradford, 128

'Breaker', 151, 154-155

Brecknock, 128

Bridge, Sir John Frederick, musician, 117, 122-123

Bridgwater, 128

Briquet, Charles Moise, bibliographer, *Les Filigranes* (1906), etc., 24

Laid down, 249

Laid paper, 22-24, 250

Laing, John (*see* Halkett, Samuel and Laing, John)

Lamb, Charles, 41, 160, 182; *Essays of Elia* (1823), 36; *Last Essays of Elia,* 108

Lanolin, 161

Lawrence, Thomas Edward (Lawrence of Arabia), *Seven Pillars of Wisdom* (1926 and 1935 edits.), 105

Lear, Edward, *Book of Nonsense* (1846), 50

Lecky, Halton Stirling, *The King's Ships* (1913-14), 151

Lee, Brian North, *British Bookplates* (1979), 176

Legatt, John, printer, 125

Le Prince, Jean-Baptiste, 78

Lewes, 131

Libraries, Alnwick Castle, 267; Althorp, 13, 267; Bibliotheque Nationale, 53; Bodleian, 116, 266; British, 28, 61, 267; Chichester Cathedral, 116; Folger, 261, 266; Huntingdon, 261, 266; Middle Hill, 29; Pierpont Morgan, 261, 266; Rylands, 261, 266-267; Winchester Cathedral, 267

Licence leaf, 35, 250

Limited editions, 250

Lincoln, 131

Lindisfarne Gospels, 261, 267

Lithography, 71-72, 76

Locker family, 200

Locker, Edward Hawke, *Views in Spain* (1824), 201

Locker, Captain William, 200-201

Locker-Lampson, Frederick, 73, 158, 201-202; *London Lyrics* (1857), 202; *Lyra Elegentiarum* (1867), 202; *Patchwork* (1879), 202; *London Rhymes* (1882), 202; *My Confidences* (1896), 202

Longman, House of, publishers, 50, 56, 71, 102

Louis V's daughters, 52

Loutherbourg, Philip James, artist, 74

Lowndes, William Thomas, bibliographer, 41; *Bibliographer's Manual of English Literature* (1834, revised Henry Bohn 1858-64), 29, 85, 101, 103

Ludlow, 131

Lytton, Edward George Earle Lytton Bulwer-, first Baron Lytton, 121; *Eugene Aram* (1832), 121; *The Last Days of Pompeii* (1834), 121; *The Caxtons* (1849), 121; *The Last of the Barons* (1843), 121

Lytton, Edward Robert Bulwer, first Earl of Lytton, *Lucile* (1860), 117, 121

Macaulay, Thomas Babington, first Baron, 112

Machiavelli, Niccolo, 197

McKerrow, Ronald B., bibliographer, *Introduction to Bibliography for Literary Students,* 25, 99, 190

Macmillan, House of, publishers, 107

Magazines and periodicals, 181-182

Maidstone, 131

Mainz Psalter, 43

Malory, Sir Thomas, *Morte D'Arthur,* 183

Malton, 131

Malton, Thomas (the younger), architectural draughtsman, *A Picturesque Tour through the Cities of London and Westminster* (1792-1801), 74, 77

Manuscript, 186-187, 250

Manutius, Aldus (*see* Aldus Manutius)

Marbling, 32-33, 250

Market overt, 209-210

Marryat, Captain Frederick, *Pacha of Many Tales* (1835), 59; *Mr. Midshipman Easy* (1836), 18-19, 57

Mary I, 125

Mary, Queen of Scots, 52

'Mary Rose', 48

Masefield, John, 196

Mason, John Henry, binder (*see* Binders)

Mearne, Samuel, binder (*see* Binders)

Medici Society, 91

Mendel, Vera, printer, 92

'Meredith, Owen' (*see* Lytton, Edward Robert Bulwer)

❋❋❋❋❋❋❋❋❋❋❋❋❋❋❋❋❋❋❋